LIVING *the* WORD

**Scripture Reflections and Commentaries
for Sundays and Holy Days**

**Dianne Bergant, C.S.A., and
Rev. James A. Wallace, C.Ss.R**

NOVEMBER 27, 2011 THROUGH NOVEMBER 25, 2012   YEAR B

LIVING *the* WORD

Scripture Reflections and Commentaries
for Sundays and Holy Days

Vol. 27 November 27, 2011–November 25, 2012

Published annually

Individual copy: $14.95
(2-9 copies: $10.95 per copy;
10-24 copies: $9.95 per copy;
25-99 copies: $8.95 per copy;
100 or more copies: $6.95 per copy)

Editor: Alan J. Hommerding
Copy and Production Editor: Marcia T. Lucey
Typesetter: Tejal Patel
Cover Design: Jane Pitz and Tejal Patel
Director of Publications: Mary Beth Kunde-Anderson

In accordance with c. 827, with the material having been found free from any doctrinal or moral error, permission to publish is granted on July 6, 2011, by the Very Reverend John F. Canary, Vicar General of the Archdiocese of Chicago.

Our liturgy presumes that those who gather for Eucharist, as members of the Body of Christ, are already familiar with the word that they hear proclaimed every Sunday. *Living the Word* is designed to assist individuals, homilists, catechumens, candidates, discussion groups, religious education classes, and similar gatherings to deepen that familiarity with the Sunday scriptures.

Inside this book you will find the readings for each Sunday, holy day, and major celebration from November 2011 through November 2012, Year B of the liturgical cycle. Each day's readings are preceded by a brief passage intended to suggest a focus or approach to consider while reading these particular scriptures. The readings are followed by a commentary that provides a context for understanding them, making use of biblical scholarship and the Church's longstanding traditions. Then a reflection is offered that expands upon the initial focus and incorporates the fuller understanding from the commentary section. The discussion questions and suggestions for responses that follow are provided as helps to move from reflection to action, since the word of God always invites us to respond not only with our hearts but with our hands and lives as well.

When reflecting on the scriptures in a group setting or individually, it is best to do so in the context of prayer. Users of this book are encouraged to create an atmosphere that will foster prayerful reflection: in a quiet space, perhaps with lit candle and simple seasonal decoration (incense or soft music may also be appropriate), begin with a prayer and reading of the scriptures aloud for that day, even if you are alone. In a group, encourage members to focus on one word or idea that especially strikes them. Continue with each reading the same way, perhaps taking time to share these ideas with one another.

After you spend some quiet time with the readings, ask yourself how they have changed you, enlightened you, moved you. Move on to the commentary, reflection, and response. Allow the discussion questions to shape your conversation, and try the "response" on for size. Will you rise to its challenge? Does it give you an idea of something to try in your own life? Share your ideas with someone else, even if you have been preparing alone.

Once you have spent a suitable time in reflection or discussion, you may wish to make a prayerful response to the readings by means of a song or a blessing of someone or something. Pray spontaneously as you think about the texts' meaning for you, or invite people in the group to offer prayers informally.

Finally, challenge yourself, or each other in your group, to take action this week based on your understanding of the readings. You may propose your own prayer for help to undertake this mission or simply stand in a circle and pray the Lord's Prayer. If you are in a group, offer one another a sign of peace before departing. If alone, surprise someone with a sign of peace, either in person, by making a phone call, or offering a simple prayer.

As you repeat this pattern over time, your prayerful reflection can deepen your appreciation of God's word and enable you to live it more fully every day.

Table of Contents

Prayers Before Reading Scripture

Lord Jesus,
we give you praise.
Speak to us as we read your word,
and send your Spirit into our hearts.
Guide us today and each day in your service,
for you are our way, our truth, our life.

Lord Jesus, we love you:
keep us in your love for ever and ever. *Amen!*

or

Blessed are you, Lord God,
king of all creation:
you have taught us by your word.
Open our hearts to your Spirit,
and lead us on the paths of Christ your Son.

All praise and glory be yours for ever. *Amen!*

or

Lord, open our hearts:
let your Spirit speak to us
as we read your word. *Amen!*

or

Lord Jesus,
to whom shall we go?
You have the words of eternal life.

Speak, Lord,
your servants are listening:
here we are, Lord,
ready to do your will. *Amen!*

Prayers After Reading Scripture

Blessed are you, Lord God,
maker of heaven and earth,
ruler of the universe:
you have sent your Holy Spirit
to teach your truth to your holy people.
We praise you for letting us read your word today.

Grant that we may continue to think and pray
over the words we have read,
and to share your thoughts with others
throughout this day.

Loving God, we praise you
and thank you in Jesus' name. *Amen!*

or

God of all graciousness, we thank you
for speaking to us today
through your holy word. *Amen!*

We often think of the combined seasons of Advent and Christmas as a time to reflect on promise and fulfillment. Actually, the readings for this period provide a much richer view of the meaning and spirituality of the seasons. Advent itself offers three perspectives. The first readings trace a dialogue of lamentation and comfort between the people and God. Looking at the readings in this way, we see Advent as a time of our lamentation and crying out for life, and of God's response. Taken together, the second readings form a kind of epistle of their own. The first three point to the coming of the Lord, not as a helpless child, but as a glorious herald of the dawning of the reign of God. The reading for the Fourth Sunday praises God for having brought all things to conclusion. The Gospel readings of the first three Sundays of Advent alert us to the coming of the Lord, but it is only the final Advent Gospel passage that refers specifically to his birth.

The Advent readings prepare us for more than the celebration of Christmas. They acknowledge that there is much in life that causes us to cry out in complaint or lament. They also assure us that God hears our cries and responds with compassion. In fact, God has promised that there will be a time in the future when this compassion will embrace us fully. It is the fulfillment of this promise that turns our gaze to the future. It is from that future that Christ establishes the reign of God, making that glorious future a reality in our present. Christmas, then, marks the dawning of that future. It announces that God has indeed come into our midst. The manner in which God comes, as a vulnerable child, alerts us to the character of God's reign. It will not be one of power and conquest, but of tenderness and compassion.

The Gospels read during the Christmas season sketch events surrounding the birth and childhood of Jesus, but the first and second readings do not. They provide insight into those events. The Mass during the Night at Christmas contains a word of emancipation. The child who is born heralds a profound reversal. Something cosmic has happened. In the midst of the darkness, the light that emanates from this child reveals God's intention to enlighten the ends of the earth. The other first readings unpack the richness of the transformation that this birth brings about. All of the second readings are meditations on salvation, which is the way this transformation enters into our lives.

The readings show that the Advent/Christmas period initiates us into the plan of God, a plan that transforms our present needy existence into the glorious future of God.

November 27, 2011

FIRST SUNDAY OF ADVENT

Today's Focus: Ye Watchers and Ye Holy Ones

Advent begins with an urgent call to keep an eye on the future as we deal with the present. World events, personal difficulties, and our moral failures can overwhelm us. By watching for the Lord, we remain a people of hope and trust that the Lord who comes can save us.

FIRST READING
Isaiah 63: 16b–17, 19b; 64:2–7a

You, LORD, are our father,
   our redeemer you are named forever.
Why do you let us wander, O LORD, from your ways,
   and harden our hearts so that we fear you not?
Return for the sake of your servants,
   the tribes of your heritage.
Oh, that you would rend the heavens and come down,
   with the mountains quaking before you,
while you wrought awesome deeds we could not hope for,
   such as they had not heard of from of old.
No ear has ever heard, no eye ever seen, any God but you
   doing such deeds for those who wait for him.
Would that you might meet us doing right,
   that we were mindful of you in our ways!
Behold, you are angry, and we are sinful;
   all of us have become like unclean people,
   all our good deeds are like polluted rags;
we have all withered like leaves,
   and our guilt carries us away like the wind.
There is none who calls upon your name,
   who rouses himself to cling to you;
for you have hidden your face from us
   and have delivered us up to our guilt.
Yet, O LORD, you are our father;
   we are the clay and you the potter:
   we are all the work of your hands.

PSALM RESPONSE
Psalm 80:4

Lord, make us turn to you; let us see your face and we shall be saved.

SECOND READING *1 Corinthians* *1:3–9*	Brothers and sisters: Grace to you and peace from God our Father and the Lord Jesus Christ. I give thanks to my God always on your account for the grace of God bestowed on you in Christ Jesus, that in him you were enriched in every way, with all discourse and all knowledge, as the testimony to Christ was confirmed among you, so that you are not lacking in any spiritual gift as you wait for the revelation of our Lord Jesus Christ. He will keep you firm to the end, irreproachable on the day of our Lord Jesus Christ. God is faithful, and by him you were called to fellowship with his Son, Jesus Christ our Lord.
GOSPEL *Mark 13: 33–37*	Jesus said to his disciples: "Be watchful! Be alert! You do not know when the time will come. It is like a man traveling abroad. He leaves home and places his servants in charge, each with his own work, and orders the gatekeeper to be on the watch. Watch, therefore; you do not know when the lord of the house is coming, whether in the evening, or at midnight, or at cockcrow, or in the morning. May he not come suddenly and find you sleeping. What I say to you, I say to all: 'Watch!' "

❖ Understanding the Word

The first reading consists of a communal lament and a prayer that recounts events in the history of Israel. The people are in a desperate situation, unable to help themselves, in need of someone who can rescue them from their plight. They feel abandoned even by their ancestors, and so they cry out to God. Attention then shifts from their distress to the mighty works of God. Those who seemed to be the least deserving of divine kindness hope that God, who worked wonders in the past, will work wonders now on their behalf.

Paul is grateful for blessings granted in the past to the Corinthians. He reminds them that these blessings came from God through Christ. This may indicate that the Corinthians have developed a certain smugness about their abilities. Paul then moves to the point of the passage, namely, the community's waiting for the revelation of the Lord. The Christians are living in the "time between." Christ has already been born, died, and raised from the dead. They now live in anticipation of his return. At issue are the manner of their lifestyle and the character of their commitment during this "time between."

A thrice-repeated command—"Watch!"—surrounds a parable that emphasizes the need to be ready at all times, because Christians do not know when the Lord will return. The Greek word for "time" (*kairos*) refers to a special time, a decisive moment, more than mere chronological or sequential time (*chronos*). The short parable brings this point home. Like the servants in the parable, the Christians are instructed to be prepared at all times. The coming of the householder will be sudden and unscheduled, a *kairos* moment. Life between the times will go on as usual. There are responsibilities that must be carried out. However, life must still be lived with the realization that this is a time of vigilance. "Watch!"

✥ Reflecting on the Word

Are you a watcher? Some are people watchers. I remember a former teacher of mine saying how he liked to sit by the window in a restaurant or, if the day was nice, on a park bench, and just watch people go by. It served as a reminder of God's infinite imagination in creating us. Or, perhaps you are a clock-watcher, checking your watch frequently, even searching to find a clock whenever you enter an unfamiliar place. Clock-watchers tend to be on time and are especially appreciated when running meetings.

Advent calls us to be watchers, but neither of clocks nor of people merely passing by. We are called to be watchers for the Lord's return. Now this might not seem as interesting as watching people, or as practical as watching the clock, or even as likely to get results, but its importance is on a deeper level. We are called to take seriously Jesus' promise that he will return and that we are to live now in light of that return, that is, to live in the light this promise offers us for our lives.

As we watch for the Lord's return in glory, we might catch glimpses of him more frequently here and now because he returns more often than we might suspect, but we miss it because we are not watching for it. So when we hear Jesus commanding his disciples, "Be watchful! Be alert!" this holds for us today—and tomorrow.

✥ Consider/Discuss

- Are you a watcher? Of what?
- In your watching, have you had any experiences of *kairos* time, those moments of grace when you felt the presence of God, of Christ, of the Holy Spirit?
- Can you become more watchful and grow into a deeper confidence that the Lord will return?

✥ Responding to the Word

Make us a watchful people, Lord, living in such a way that we keep one eye watching for your return, while we meet the challenges of the present. Let us not grow discouraged or fearful that you will not return. Help us recognize how you come even now in your word and in the sacraments. Amen.

December 4, 2011

SECOND SUNDAY OF ADVENT

Today's Focus: Roadwork in Progress

Preparing for Christmas is one way we remind ourselves that we are always in a state of preparing to celebrate the coming of Jesus Christ. Opening up a roadway for the Lord to come into our lives is a never-ending process. The heart can be resistant to expansion.

FIRST READING
Isaiah 40:1–5, 9–11

Comfort, give comfort to my people,
    says your God.
Speak tenderly to Jerusalem, and proclaim to her
    that her service is at an end,
    her guilt is expiated;
indeed, she has received from the hand of the Lord
    double for all her sins.

A voice cries out:
In the desert prepare the way of the Lord!
    Make straight in the wasteland a highway for our God!
Every valley shall be filled in,
    every mountain and hill shall be made low;
the rugged land shall be made a plain,
    the rough country, a broad valley.
Then the glory of the Lord shall be revealed,
    and all people shall see it together;
    for the mouth of the Lord has spoken.

Go up onto a high mountain,
    Zion, herald of glad tidings;
cry out at the top of your voice,
    Jerusalem, herald of good news!
Fear not to cry out
    and say to the cities of Judah:
    Here is your God!
Here comes with power
    the Lord God,
    who rules by his strong arm;
here is his reward with him,
    his recompense before him.
Like a shepherd he feeds his flock;
    in his arms he gathers the lambs,
carrying them in his bosom,
    and leading the ewes with care.

PSALM RESPONSE
Psalm 85:8

Lord, let us see your kindness, and grant us your salvation.

SECOND READING
2 Peter 3:8–14

Do not ignore this one fact, beloved, that with the Lord one day is like a thousand years and a thousand years like one day. The Lord does not delay his promise, as some regard "delay," but he is patient with you, not wishing that any should perish but that all should come to repentance. But the day of the Lord will come like a thief, and then the heavens will pass away with a mighty roar and the elements will be dissolved by fire, and the earth and everything done on it will be found out.

Since everything is to be dissolved in this way, what sort of persons ought you to be, conducting yourselves in holiness and devotion, waiting for and hastening the coming of the day of God, because of which the heavens will be dissolved in flames and the elements melted by fire. But according to his promise we await new heavens and a new earth in which righteousness dwells. Therefore, beloved, since you await these things, be eager to be found without spot or blemish before him, at peace.

GOSPEL
Mark 1:1–8

The beginning of the gospel of Jesus Christ the Son of God. As it is written in Isaiah the prophet:
Behold, I am sending my messenger ahead of you;
    he will prepare your way.
A voice of one crying out in the desert:
    "Prepare the way of the Lord,
    make straight his paths."
John the Baptist appeared in the desert proclaiming a baptism of repentance for the forgiveness of sins. People of the whole Judean countryside and all the inhabitants of Jerusalem were going out to him and were being baptized by him in the Jordan River as they acknowledged their sins. John was clothed in camel's hair, with a leather belt around his waist. He fed on locusts and wild honey. And this is what he proclaimed: "One mightier than I is coming after me. I am not worthy to stoop and loosen the thongs of his sandals. I have baptized you with water; he will baptize you with the Holy Spirit."

✥ Understanding the Word

The second major section of Isaiah tells the people to prepare for the coming of their God by removing any obstacle that might prevent God's approach or obstruct the view of God's glory that onlookers might enjoy. A second directive is given to people living within the broken and desolate city of Jerusalem. They too are to be heralds of good news, announcing that the mighty, victorious God is coming to them. In both cases, the people are directed to act out their release even before they have tangible evidence of it, suggesting that future events are being accomplished in the present. The people's faith in this prophetic word is itself the strongest evidence of their deliverance.

The author of Second Peter insists that despite the long delay, the Day of the Lord will indeed come. Its timing, like that of a thief in the night, is unpredictable. Therefore, the Christians should not grow weary of waiting, nor should they become careless. As God has been patient in the face of their sinfulness, so they must be patient in the face of God's apparent delay. The author of the letter then employs apocalyptic imagery to describe the dissolution of everything, both the heavens and the earth. Finally, behavior that suits one who stands in anticipation of the salvation that is to come is addressed briefly but succinctly.

Mark's Gospel points to the new beginning of God's manifestation to all. He interweaves the words of the prophets Malachi (3:1, 23) and Isaiah (40:3; cf. Exodus 23:20). By using these two references to identify John the Baptist, he identifies the prophetic authority of the man whose austere life and exacting message may have appeared too demanding to be accepted by some. John got the attention of the crowds, but he quickly deflected it from himself, pointing instead to Jesus, the long-awaited one. John's appearance, his message, and his baptism all announced that the reign of God was about to appear.

❖ Reflecting on the Word

I remember hearing about a little boy coming home from church and being asked what the preacher had spoken about. The church used the King James Version of the scriptures and the preacher had spent some time on the reading from Isaiah we heard today. But that translation began: "Comfort ye, comfort ye, my people, saith your God." In response to his parents' inquiry, the child said, "It was just lovely. The priest told us how God is saying, 'Come to tea, come to tea, my people.' "

While Isaiah's message today is certainly comforting, with God telling the prophet to speak tenderly and tell an exiled people that all is forgiven, that the punishment for sin has run its course, these words are not the equivalent of an invitation to a relaxing cup of tea. Now as then, they serve as an invitation to get to work, to remove any obstacle that prevents God from coming into our hearts. This means that we have to get our hearts into shape, and our voices have to become willing to announce that God lives and comes with power to save.

John the Baptist remains a model for us today. He spoke out boldly, calling people to prepare a way for the Lord, which was a call to conversion and inner transformation. We are to take in this same message, first as listeners, then as heralds ourselves, witnessing to family, friends, and any who will listen that Jesus desires to come more fully into our lives.

- Do you accept God's commission to work at preparing a way for the Lord?
- What does it mean today to be a herald, a proclaimer of the gospel?

✢ *Responding to the Word*

Loving God, you come to us with compassion, mercy, and forgiveness, but at times we set up barriers that prevent your entry into our hearts. Teach us how to prepare a way for you so you have access into our lives. May Jesus, who is the way, show us the way. Amen.

December 8, 2011

IMMACULATE CONCEPTION OF THE BLESSED VIRGIN MARY

Today's Focus: God's Passionate Love for Us

How do we explain the gift of salvation given to us in Jesus Christ? What explains God creating humankind? Even more, what prompted God to recreate humankind in Christ, when such disarray had been—and continues to be—made of creation?

FIRST READING
Genesis 3:9–15, 20

After the man, Adam, had eaten of the tree, the LORD God called to the man and asked him, "Where are you?" He answered, "I heard you in the garden; but I was afraid, because I was naked, so I hid myself." Then he asked, "Who told you that you were naked? You have eaten, then, from the tree of which I had forbidden you to eat!" The man replied, "The woman whom you put here with me—she gave me fruit from the tree, and so I ate it." The Lord God then asked the woman, "Why did you do such a thing?" The woman answered, "The serpent tricked me into it, so I ate it."

Then the LORD God said to the serpent:
    "Because you have done this, you shall be banned
        from all the animals
        and from all the wild creatures;
    on your belly shall you crawl,
        and dirt shall you eat
        all the days of your life.
    I will put enmity between you and the woman,
        and between your offspring and hers;
    he will strike at your head,
        while you strike at his heel."
The man called his wife Eve, because she became the mother of all the living.

PSALM RESPONSE
Psalm 98:1a

Sing to the Lord a new song, for he has done marvelous deeds.

SECOND READING
Ephesians 1:3–6, 11–12

Brothers and sisters: Blessed be the God and Father of our Lord Jesus Christ, who has blessed us in Christ with every spiritual blessing in the heavens, as he chose us in him, before the foundation of the world, to be holy and without blemish before him. In love he destined us for adoption to himself through Jesus Christ, in accord with the favor of his will, for the praise of the glory of his grace that he granted us in the beloved.

In him we were also chosen, destined in accord with the purpose of the One who accomplishes all things according to the intention of his will, so that we might exist for the praise of his glory, we who first hoped in Christ.

why

GOSPEL
Luke 1:26–38

The angel Gabriel was sent from God to a town of Galilee called Nazareth, to a virgin betrothed to a man named Joseph, of the house of David, and the virgin's name was Mary. And coming to her, he said, "Hail, full of grace! The Lord is with you." But she was greatly troubled at what was said and pondered what sort of greeting this might be. Then the angel said to her, "Do not be afraid, Mary, for you have found favor with God. Behold, you will conceive in your womb and bear a son, and you shall name him Jesus. He will be great and will be called Son of the Most High, and the Lord God will give him the throne of David his father, and he will rule over the house of Jacob forever, and of his kingdom there will be no end." But Mary said to the angel, "How can this be, since I have no relations with a man?" And the angel said to her in reply, "The Holy Spirit will come upon you, and the power of the Most High will overshadow you. Therefore the child to be born will be called holy, the Son of God. And behold, Elizabeth, your relative, has also conceived a son in her old age, and this is the sixth month for her who was called barren; for nothing will be impossible for God." Mary said, "Behold, I am the handmaid of the Lord. May it be done to me according to your word." Then the angel departed from her.

❖❖ *Understanding the Word*

The first reading is a story meant to explain the antagonism among human beings as well as the struggle they experience against evil. The story is set in primeval time in order to show that such antagonism and struggle are universal and perennial. This is a story about sin and its consequences. Contrary to artistic representations of Mary as the Immaculate Conception, it is the woman's offspring, not the woman herself, who will be in constant conflict with the offspring of the serpent. According to this story, human beings might have to struggle with evil, but they will not be conquered by it.

Paul insists that believers were not chosen because they were holy and blameless, but that they might be holy and blameless. In other words, salvation is the cause of and not the reward for righteousness. We do not earn it, it is given to us. Furthermore, it is through Christ, the only real Son of God, that others can become God's adopted children. The reading begins and ends with praise of God. Regardless of when believers may be called, they are called to praise God's glory. Adoption, redemption, and forgiveness of sin are the primary reasons for praising God's glory.

Reading the account of the promise of the conception of Jesus on the feast of the conception of Mary has led to great confusion. However, the Gospel story is explicitly about Mary, not Jesus. She has been chosen to be the mother of God. As the first reading reminds us, all human beings struggle with sin and its consequences. At issue is not the question of a virgin being a mother, but of a vulnerable human being bearing the Son of God. This feast assures us that Mary was "full of grace," God's "favored one." We were chosen and made holy after Christ's resurrection; she was chosen and made holy in anticipation of it. God's plan for the whole world is now being accomplished.

✦ Reflecting on the Word

A stained glass window in the Redemptorist house chapel in Washington, D.C. offers visitors an image of the Annunciation. Mary looks like a beautiful princess, wearing a white gown embroidered with gold stars, shrouded in a dark blue cloak. Her blond hair falls around her face, her eyes are cast down in humility, and her arms folded across her breast. She is in a sunlit room with multicolored coverings on various pieces of furniture, a lily by her side. An open book of the scriptures is behind her. Most striking is the handsome angel hovering above her, hair wreathed with flowers, and wrapped in enough cloth to drape several large windows. Above them, a dove.

For years I confess I found it all a little silly. After all, wasn't Mary an illiterate peasant woman, living in a small town? Her appearance, clothing, and household furnishings would have been quite simple. But one day, the look in the angel's eyes caught my attention as it never had before. I realized what the artist was trying to communicate. Gabriel, whose name means "God is strong," was looking so lovingly and protectively at her that I found myself thinking of those words in the Song of Songs that speak of a love "stronger than death," one that "deep waters cannot quench, nor floods sweep away." As Gabriel stands in for God in this scene, so Mary does for us. Today's feast celebrates God's saving love waiting again and again to become incarnate in all human flesh.

✦ Consider/Discuss

- Consider God's gift of grace to you, given at your baptism into Christ. You are chosen to be holy, destined for glory, as Ephesians reminds us.

- Does this feast separate Mary from us or bring her closer?

✦ Responding to the Word

Creator God, your grace touched Mary from the moment of her conception, making her worthy to be the mother of your Son. May your grace work with our freedom so that we might bear your Son in our lives and be holy, all to the praise and glory of your name. Amen.

December 11, 2011

THIRD SUNDAY OF ADVENT

Today's Focus: Rejoice Always

Paul's words to the Thessalonians signal today's message: "Rejoice always." How is this possible? Because the God of peace can "make you perfectly holy" and "preserved blameless" for the day when Christ comes again. We cannot do this, but God can. "The one who calls you is faithful, and he will accomplish it."

FIRST READING
Isaiah 61:1–2a, 10–11

The spirit of the Lord GOD is upon me,
　because the LORD has anointed me;
he has sent me to bring glad tidings to the poor,
　to heal the brokenhearted,
to proclaim liberty to the captives
　and release to the prisoners,
to announce a year of favor from the LORD
　and a day of vindication by our God.

I rejoice heartily in the LORD,
　in my God is the joy of my soul;
for he has clothed me with a robe of salvation
　and wrapped me in a mantle of justice,
like a bridegroom adorned with a diadem,
　like a bride bedecked with her jewels.
As the earth brings forth its plants,
　and a garden makes its growth spring up,
so will the Lord GOD make justice and praise
　spring up before all the nations.

PSALM RESPONSE
Isaiah 61:10b

My soul rejoices in my God.

SECOND READING
1 Thessalonians 5:16–24

Brothers and sisters: Rejoice always. Pray without ceasing. In all circumstances give thanks, for this is the will of God for you in Christ Jesus. Do not quench the Spirit. Do not despise prophetic utterances. Test everything; retain what is good. Refrain from every kind of evil.

May the God of peace make you perfectly holy and may you entirely, spirit, soul, and body, be preserved blameless for the coming of our Lord Jesus Christ. The one who calls you is faithful, and he will also accomplish it.

GOSPEL
John 1:6–8,
19–28

A man named John was sent from God. He came for testimony, to testify to the light, so that all might believe through him. He was not the light, but came to testify to the light.

And this is the testimony of John. When the Jews from Jerusalem sent priests and Levites to him to ask him, "Who are you?" he admitted and did not deny it, but admitted, "I am not the Christ."

So they asked him, "What are you then? Are you Elijah?" And he said, "I am not." "Are you the Prophet?" He answered, "No." So they said to him, "Who are you, so we can give an answer to those who sent us? What do you have to say for yourself?" He said:
"I am *the voice of one crying out in the desert,*
make straight the way of the Lord,
as Isaiah the prophet said."
Some Pharisees were also sent. They asked him, "Why then do you baptize if you are not the Christ or Elijah or the Prophet?" John answered them, "I baptize with water; but there is one among you whom you do not recognize, the one who is coming after me, whose sandal strap I am not worthy to untie." This happened in Bethany across the Jordan, where John was baptizing.

❖ Understanding the Word

The anointing of the prophet mentioned in the first reading may be a figure of speech, but the duties that accompany it are very real and explicitly social. They include healing and comforting. The primary duty is prophetic proclamation. The good news promises the coming of the "year of the Lord," a time when the poor will be the beneficiaries of the blessings of God. This will be a time when the oppressive economic and political systems will have to contend with the vengeance of God. The reading begins with a promise of salvation and ends with a prayer of thanksgiving for the salvation granted.

The Letter to the Thessalonians includes exhortation, encouragement, and blessing. Paul does not overlook the realities of suffering in life, nor does he advocate a false sense of happiness. The joy he urges is the joy that comes from knowing that in Christ's resurrection, even death itself has been overcome. This should be the source of their thanksgiving. He admonishes the Christians to discern the spirits active within the community. He prays that God will bring to completion their holiness in every aspect: spirit, soul, and body. He ends on a note of confidence, assuring them of God's faithfulness to the promises of salvation made to them.

The first verses of the Gospel reading clarify the identity of John the Baptist in relation to the light that is to come into the world. John is not the light, but is to bear testimony to the light. He is the voice that proclaims that the light is soon to come. The second section contains his own testimony regarding his relationship with Jesus, the man who was to come after him. John refuses to be identified with any messianic figure. He is not the messiah. His role is preparatory; he explains this when the officials question his reasons for baptizing. John is content to be the witness and the herald, nothing more.

Certain watchwords are associated with each season of the church year, almost becoming a motto. Advent's is "Wake up." It then leads to other words like "Watch," "Wait," and "Witness." But every Third Sunday of Advent, we anticipate the coming Christmas season, whose key word is "Rejoice." This Sunday was traditionally called *Gaudete* ("Rejoice") Sunday. Priests continue to wear rose-colored vestments today, signaling joy.

Joy is not only for Christmastime and the occasional Sunday. I remember as an altar boy, before Vatican II, Mass began with the "prayers at the foot of the altar." The priest would begin: "I will go up to the altar of God." The server responded: "To God who gives joy to my youth," or as some translations had it, "To God, my exceeding joy."

It was a reminder that God is the source of all joy and that joy is one of the great gifts of God, one of the fruits of the Holy Spirit. St. Paul reminds us that "the fruit of the Spirit is love, joy, peace, patience, kindness, generosity, faithfulness, gentleness, self-control" (see Galatians 5:22). Now there is a good list for Christmas giving. Tell your loved ones your Christmas gift this year will be to pray throughout the coming year that the Spirit will bring them one of these gifts.

John's gift to the people who came out into the wilderness was to call them to prepare for the Lord, to give them a sense of heightened anticipation that the One coming to them would fill them with joy.

❖ Consider/Discuss

- How do you think of joy? Is it the same as happiness?
- Do you recognize that the Spirit who dwells in us is the giver of joy?
- Have you asked for this gift?

❖ *Responding to the Word*

Dear God, source and giver of joy, open my heart to receive your joy. As the Advent season continues, help me to live in a spirit of anticipation and watchfulness for how Christ continues to come into the world, a spirit of joy rooted in the awareness that you are faithful to your children. Amen.

December 18, 2011

FOURTH SUNDAY OF ADVENT

Today's Focus: The Best Dwelling Place

In the Old Testament God's desire to dwell among the Chosen People took many forms: a burning bush, a pillar of cloud by day and of fire by night, the tent of Mt. Sinai, the Ark of the Covenant, the temple built by Solomon, and the second temple built after the Exile. Then along came Mary.

FIRST READING
2 Samuel 7:1–5, 8b–12, 14a, 16

When King David was settled in his palace, and the Lord had given him rest from his enemies on every side, he said to Nathan the prophet, "Here I am living in a house of cedar, while the ark of God dwells in a tent!" Nathan answered the king, "Go, do whatever you have in mind, for the Lord is with you." But that night the Lord spoke to Nathan and said: "Go, tell my servant David, 'Thus says the Lord: Should you build me a house to dwell in?

"'It was I who took you from the pasture and from the care of the flock to be commander of my people Israel. I have been with you wherever you went, and I have destroyed all your enemies before you. And I will make you famous like the great ones of the earth. I will fix a place for my people Israel; I will plant them so that they may dwell in their place without further disturbance. Neither shall the wicked continue to afflict them as they did of old, since the time I first appointed judges over my people Israel. I will give you rest from all your enemies. The Lord also reveals to you that he will establish a house for you. And when your time comes and you rest with your ancestors, I will raise up your heir after you, sprung from your loins, and I will make his kingdom firm. I will be a father to him, and he shall be a son to me. Your house and your kingdom shall endure forever before me; your throne shall stand firm forever.' "

PSALM RESPONSE
Psalm 89:2a

For ever I will sing the goodness of the Lord.

SECOND READING
Romans 16:25–27

Brothers and sisters: To him who can strengthen you, according to my gospel and the proclamation of Jesus Christ, according to the revelation of the mystery kept secret for long ages but now manifested through the prophetic writings and, according to the command of the eternal God, made known to all nations to bring about the obedience of faith, to the only wise God, through Jesus Christ be glory forever and ever. Amen.

The angel Gabriel was sent from God to a town of Galilee called Nazareth, to a virgin betrothed to a man named Joseph, of the house of David, and the virgin's name was Mary. And coming to her, he said, "Hail, full of grace! The Lord is with you." But she was greatly troubled at what was said and pondered what sort of greeting this might be. Then the angel said to her, "Do not be afraid, Mary, for you have found favor with God.

"Behold, you will conceive in your womb and bear a son, and you shall name him Jesus. He will be great and will be called Son of the Most High, and the Lord God will give him the throne of David his father, and he will rule over the house of Jacob forever, and of his kingdom there will be no end." But Mary said to the angel, "How can this be, since I have no relations with a man?" And the angel said to her in reply, "The Holy Spirit will come upon you, and the power of the Most High will overshadow you. Therefore the child to be born will be called holy, the Son of God. And behold, Elizabeth, your relative, has also conceived a son in her old age, and this is the sixth month for her who was called barren; for nothing will be impossible for God." Mary said, "Behold, I am the handmaid of the Lord. May it be done to me according to your word." Then the angel departed from her.

❖ Understanding the Word

David has amassed enough wealth to build a palace for himself, and he is no longer threatened by enemies. The author states very clearly that the peace that David enjoys is not the result of any victory of his own but comes from the good pleasure of the Lord. Now David realizes that the progress he and his people have made politically and socially has not carried over to their religious life. He turns to the prophet Nathan and tells him that he wishes to build a fitting temple for his God. Though God legitimates the Davidic ruling line, it will be Solomon, a descendant of David, not David himself, who will build the temple.

Paul sums up the central theme of his own teaching, namely, that God's new act of revelation in Christ will bring even the Gentiles to the commitment of faith. Paul claims that the revelation of God in Christ was really present in ages past, but as a mystery that was kept secret. This revelation might have been hidden in the past, but those who have eyes of faith today should be able to read these writings and there discover something of God's plan. The purpose of the revelation of this mystery is universal salvation. All, Gentiles included, are to be brought to the commitment of faith.

The account of the Annunciation is cast in a traditional pattern of angelic birth announcements, alerting the reader to the divine significance of future events. Typical in angelic appearances, Mary's reaction is fear. The angel reassures her that everything that will happen in and through her is in God's plan. She does not question that this will happen, but how it will happen, because she is a virgin. The angel assures her that she will be overshadowed by God's Spirit and power. The scene concludes with Mary's acceptance. As a servant of the Lord, she is also a model of openness and receptivity.

In today's first reading King David is settled in his cedar palace, no upcoming battles on the horizon, feeling quite content, glass of wine in hand, chatting with Nathan the prophet about how good life is, when he gets this inspiration: "God should have a house! Certainly more than that old tent we have been dragging around. And I will build it!" Nathan approves.

But that night, God weighs in: "Tell David, 'Thanks, but no thanks. I like the tent.' " We don't know why God said no to David. But it seems that God wanted to make clear not only who was building God's dwelling place but also who really was in charge of everything. God was the kingdom builder and God chose to work with very simple material, like a tent. But this was nothing compared to God's decision a millennium later, on the day when the angel Gabriel was sent to a town of Galilee called Nazareth.

God's plan from the beginning was to take up residence among us closer than any building could be, whether it was as magnificent as Solomon's temple or as humble as the simplest parish church. What God intended was to dwell with us as one of us, taking on human flesh and blood. And in the fullness of time God came asking if one of us would be willing. We don't know how long it took for Mary to answer. We only remember the important thing: she said yes.

✛ Consider/Discuss

- What difference does it make that God chose to dwell among us as one of us?
- Do you think of yourself as a dwelling place of God, as a temple of the Holy Spirit?
- What effect does that have in daily living?

✛ Responding to the Word

O come, O come, Emmanuel. Make your dwelling place in us this day. Let the world recognize that we are a people chosen to be a sign of your loving, merciful, justice-seeking, reconciling presence in the world. Thank you for the many ways you continue to do the impossible in us, through us. Amen.

December 25, 2011

NATIVITY OF THE LORD: AT THE MASS DURING THE DAY

Today's Focus: God's Christmas Card

Throughout history, God's word came through messengers, human and angelic; but in the fullness of time, God said, "Jesus" and God's Word became flesh, "pitching his tent" among us, as his Father had formerly done in the company of Israel—only this time more so: Jesus, truly God, truly human.

FIRST READING
Isaiah 52:7–10

How beautiful upon the mountains
    are the feet of him who brings glad tidings,
announcing peace, bearing good news,
    announcing salvation, and saying to Zion,
    "Your God is King!"

Hark! Your sentinels raise a cry,
    together they shout for joy,
for they see directly, before their eyes,
    the LORD restoring Zion.
Break out together in song,
    O ruins of Jerusalem!
For the LORD comforts his people,
    he redeems Jerusalem.
The LORD has bared his holy arm
    in the sight of all the nations;
all the ends of the earth will behold
    the salvation of our God.

PSALM RESPONSE
Psalm 98:3c

All the ends of the earth have seen the saving power of God.

SECOND READING
Hebrews 1:1–6

Brothers and sisters: In times past, God spoke in partial and various ways to our ancestors through the prophets; in these last days, he has spoken to us through the Son, whom he made heir of all things and through whom he created the universe, who is the refulgence of his glory, the very imprint of his being, and who sustains all things by his mighty word. When he had accomplished purification from sins, he took his seat at the right hand of the Majesty on high, as far superior to the angels as the name he has inherited is more excellent than theirs.

For to which of the angels did God ever say:

You are my son; this day I have begotten you?

Or again:

I will be a father to him, and he shall be a son to me?

And again, when he leads the firstborn into the world, he says:

Let all the angels of God worship him.

In the shorter form of the reading, the passages in brackets are omitted.

GOSPEL
John 1:1–18
or 1:1–5, 9–14

In the beginning was the Word,

and the Word was with God,

and the Word was God.

He was in the beginning with God.

All things came to be through him,

and without him nothing came to be.

What came to be through him was life,

and this life was the light of the human race;

the light shines in the darkness,

and the darkness has not overcome it.

[A man named John was sent from God. He came for testimony, to testify to the light, so that all might believe through him. He was not the light, but came to testify to the light.] The true light, which enlightens everyone, was coming into the world.

He was in the world,

and the world came to be through him,

but the world did not know him.

He came to what was his own,

but his own people did not accept him.

But to those who did accept him he gave power to become children of God, to those who believe in his name, who were born not by natural generation nor by human choice nor by a man's decision but of God.

And the Word became flesh

and made his dwelling among us,

and we saw his glory,

the glory as of the Father's only Son,

full of grace and truth.

[John testified to him and cried out, saying, "This was he of whom I said, 'The one who is coming after me ranks ahead of me because he existed before me.' " From his fullness we have all received, grace in place of grace, because while the law was given through Moses, grace and truth came through Jesus Christ. No one has ever seen God. The only Son, God, who is at the Father's side, has revealed him.]

The proclamation of good news is dramatically portrayed in the scene of the messenger running swiftly over the mountains with the message of peace and salvation. There is excitement here, for the message holds a promise of peace, good news, and salvation. In a second scene, the arm of God is bared, revealing the source of the divine power that brought about the deliverance that the city now enjoys. Just as the messenger heralds peace and salvation to Zion, so the deliverance of the city heralds the mighty power of God to the ends of the earth.

The confessional hymn in the reading from Hebrews celebrates Christ as the agent of revelation, creation, and salvation. As the reflection of God's glory and an exact representation of God's being, Christ is the perfect revelation of God. The author reinterprets the wisdom tradition, where we find that it was through Wisdom that God created. Since Christ is indeed the Wisdom of God, it stands to reason that all things were created through him. The author of this letter has used ancient Israelite religious understanding to illustrate and develop his Christological faith. Jesus is indeed the Son of God, the Wisdom through whom all things came to be and remain in being.

John's lofty presentation of Christ is comparable to that found in the reading from Hebrews. Both characterize Christ as pre-existent; both depict Christ as an agent in the creation of the world. In a free-flowing manner, the author ascribes life-giving power to the Word, the kind of life that gives light. While the Word is the true light that comes into the world, John is merely the witness who testifies to the authenticity and superiority of this light. The Word has entered human history and now dwells in the midst of humankind. Women and men have been greatly enriched by this divine presence, transformed by the love that first prompted God's revelation and Christ's incarnation.

❖ Reflecting on the Word

The beautiful feet of Isaiah's messengers announcing peace and bringing glad tidings can seem distant from our lives. Living in the digital age can diminish any excitement at receiving a message, since they pour in all the time. E-mail, cell phones, and digital intersections like Facebook and LinkedIn bring instantaneous connection, obliterating time and space barriers once crossed by such "antiquated" forms as snail mail, the telegram, and . . . does anyone remember the rotary phone?

But still, at the heart of all communication is the word, and that is the image today's readings present to us in speaking of the mystery of the Incarnation, our God becoming human. Luke's baby of Bethlehem, wrapped in swaddling clothes and laid in a manger, is first presented in John's Gospel as the eternal Word of creation, as life, as light shining in the darkness, as the Father's only Son, full of grace and truth, and finally, as the Word become flesh who dwelled among us, true God and true man.

Give yourself time over these days to *ponder* (a good Christmas word) not only the babe in the crèche but also the profound mystery of the Word of God in whom and through whom all things were made, this Word who became human, revealing the image of the invisible God. The human warmth Luke presents in his Bethlehem story is matched by John's image of Jesus as the only Son, standing (as the *New English Bible* translation has it) "nearest to the Father's heart."

✤ Consider/Discuss

- Do you think about Jesus as the Word of God, the Son "nearest to the Father's heart"? What do these expressions say to you?
- How does the opening prologue of John's Gospel speak to your life?

✤ Responding to the Word

Eternal Word of the Father, you became human so we might become divine. Let your message penetrate deeply into our minds and hearts, and move us to bring your light and life into a world often threatened by darkness and death. Love us today into a new birth. Amen.

January 1, 2012

SOLEMNITY OF MARY, THE HOLY MOTHER OF GOD

Today's Focus: A New Time of Hope

The beginning of a new year usually carries with it a note of hope. Last year is over; whatever joy or sorrow it brought now gives way to new possibilities. We look to Mary today as one who did not merely enter a new year, but a new age. She invites us to join her.

FIRST READING
Numbers 6:22–27

The LORD said to Moses: "Speak to Aaron and his sons and tell them: This is how you shall bless the Israelites. Say to them:

The LORD bless you and keep you!

The LORD let his face shine upon you, and be gracious to you!

The LORD look upon you kindly and give you peace!

So shall they invoke my name upon the Israelites, and I will bless them."

PSALM RESPONSE
Psalm 67:2a

May God bless us in his mercy.

SECOND READING
Galatians 4:4–7

Brothers and sisters: When the fullness of time had come, God sent his Son, born of a woman, born under the law, to ransom those under the law, so that we might receive adoption as sons. As proof that you are sons, God sent the Spirit of his Son into our hearts, crying out, "Abba, Father!" So you are no longer a slave but a son, and if a son then also an heir, through God.

GOSPEL
Luke 2:16–21

The shepherds went in haste to Bethlehem and found Mary and Joseph, and the infant lying in the manger. When they saw this, they made known the message that had been told them about this child. All who heard it were amazed by what had been told them by the shepherds. And Mary kept all these things, reflecting on them in her heart. Then the shepherds returned, glorifying and praising God for all they had heard and seen, just as it had been told to them. When eight days were completed for his circumcision, he was named Jesus, the name given him by the angel before he was conceived in the womb.

❖ Understanding the Word

Often referred to as the Aaronic priestly blessing, the reading from Numbers illustrates various roles, one played by Moses and another played by Aaron and the priests. YHWH, the personal name of God, is repeated three times, demonstrating the power of that name. God is called on to bless with good fortune and to keep from harm; to look favorably toward and to be gracious toward; to look upon and to grant peace. These petitions all ask for the same thing, namely, the blessings that make life worth living. However, they are really all asking for peace, the condition of absolute well-being.

Christ's mission in the world is the major focus of Paul's teaching. "The designated time" refers to that time in history when God brought the messianic expectations to fulfillment by sending the Son into the world. Referring to Christ as God's Son establishes his divine nature; acknowledging that he was born of a woman establishes his human nature. The Christology in this passage is rich and complex. Paul contrasts servitude under the law with freedom in Christ. Still, his attitude toward the law is really not negative. He sees it as a necessary guardian that carefully watches over minors until they are mature enough to take care of themselves.

The Gospel narrative is set within the context of the family. However, the focus is really on the observance of religious practices. Circumcision was the ritual that initiated the males into the community of Israel. As observant Jews, Mary and Joseph fulfilled all of the prescriptions of the law, seeing that the child was circumcised as custom dictated. This was also the time of naming. The child is given the name told to Mary by the angel at the time of his conception. Most of what the angel had announced has now come to pass. But we all will have to wait to see how her son will acquire the throne of his father David and rule the house of Jacob forever.

❖ Reflecting on the Word

What do you seek in a new year? What blessing do you ask of God, who has revealed the depth of divine love in the birth of Jesus? Consider the blessing the Lord ordered Moses to give to Aaron and his sons to speak to the people of Israel. God offered them a blessing that brings divine protection through God's gracious presence, revealing a God who intends to look kindly upon and give peace to the chosen people.

Our annual celebration of Christmas extends these same blessings into God's plan that we become adopted into the family of God by our birth in Christ through baptism. We are given not only the freedom that comes from being made children of God, taken up into a relationship allowing us to call God *Abba* (Father), but also to consider ourselves as heirs and inheritors of our God's kingdom when we pass from this life to eternal life.

The name Jesus means "God saves." This is the message of this season: God became one of us to save us, to seek us out and bring us into communion with the God who is Father, Son, and Holy Spirit. We are invited to think of ourselves as part of the family of the Trinity. Mary is set before us every first day of the new year as the woman who ponders this wonderful mystery of God-become-human from the beginning. She gently extends to us an invitation to quiet reflection, prayer, and praise.

✛ Consider/Discuss

- Why do you think this feast of Mary was chosen for New Year's Day?
- Have you spent time "pondering" God's gift of divine life to you, given in baptism?

✛ Responding to the Word

Mary, mother of Jesus, God's Son and our Savior, you were ever attentive to what God was asking of you, keeping the law of Moses, but also open to hearing and obeying God's ongoing call in your life. Pray for us to be attentive to what God will say and ask of us during this new year of grace. Amen.

January 8, 2012

THE EPIPHANY OF THE LORD

Today's Focus: A Feast for Searchers

Christ came for all, to save all. Many today have set out searching for something, sometimes unnameable, yet recognized as important, even essential, for a full life. Today's feast encourages all searchers, whether in church or not, that there is One waiting for them to arrive. Look for signals being sent out.

FIRST
READING
Isaiah 60:1–6

Rise up in splendor, Jerusalem! Your light has come,
 the glory of the Lord shines upon you.
See, darkness covers the earth,
 and thick clouds cover the peoples;
but upon you the LORD shines,
 and over you appears his glory.
Nations shall walk by your light,
 and kings by your shining radiance.
Raise your eyes and look about;
 they all gather and come to you:
your sons come from afar,
 and your daughters in the arms of their nurses.

Then you shall be radiant at what you see,
 your heart shall throb and overflow,
for the riches of the sea shall be emptied out before you,
 the wealth of nations shall be brought to you.
Caravans of camels shall fill you,
 dromedaries from Midian and Ephah;
all from Sheba shall come
 bearing gold and frankincense,
 and proclaiming the praises of the LORD.

PSALM
RESPONSE
Psalm 72:11

Lord, every nation on earth will adore you.

SECOND
READING
Ephesians
3:2–3a, 5–6

Brothers and sisters: You have heard of the stewardship of God's grace that was given to me for your benefit, namely, that the mystery was made known to me by revelation. It was not made known to people in other generations as it has now been revealed to his holy apostles and prophets by the Spirit: that the Gentiles are coheirs, members of the same body, and copartners in the promise in Christ Jesus through the gospel.

GOSPEL
Matthew 2:1–12

When Jesus was born in Bethlehem of Judea, in the days of King Herod, behold, magi from the east arrived in Jerusalem, saying, "Where is the newborn king of the Jews? We saw his star at its rising and have come to do him homage." When King Herod heard this, he was greatly troubled, and all Jerusalem with him. Assembling all the chief priests and the scribes of the people, he inquired of them where the Christ was to be born. They said to him, "In Bethlehem of Judea, for thus it has been written through the prophet:

And you, Bethlehem, land of Judah,
 are by no means least among the rulers of Judah;
since from you shall come a ruler,
 who is to shepherd my people Israel."

Then Herod called the magi secretly and ascertained from them the time of the star's appearance. He sent them to Bethlehem and said, "Go and search diligently for the child. When you have found him, bring me word, that I too may go and do him homage." After their audience with the king they set out. And behold, the star that they had seen at its rising preceded them, until it came and stopped over the place where the child was.

They were overjoyed at seeing the star, and on entering the house they saw the child with Mary his mother. They prostrated themselves and did him homage. Then they opened their treasures and offered him gifts of gold, frankincense, and myrrh. And having been warned in a dream not to return to Herod, they departed for their country by another way.

❖ Understanding the Word

Isaiah speaks of enlightenment. He cries out to Jerusalem, "Arise!" "Shine!" Jerusalem is not only delivered from its misfortune by God, but also it is reestablished as a thriving city. Its dispersed inhabitants return, its destroyed reputation is restored, and its despoiled prosperity is reconstituted. This is not a promise to be fulfilled in the future; Jerusalem's salvation is an accomplished fact. It is happening before the city's very eyes. Such good fortune is evidence of God's favor. This good favor is another reason why the city is summoned, "Arise and shine forth!"

The Letter to the Ephesians declares that in Christ the Gentiles are coheirs, comembers and copartners with the Jews. According to the author, the status of the Gentiles had to be revealed because it had been secret until now. The apostles and prophets constituted the foundation of the church. Now, it is through this appointed messenger that the Spirit reveals a new revelation to that established church. This new revelation contains a startling message. It claims that in Christ the Gentiles are coheirs, comembers, and copartners with the Jews. This is a radical insight for a church with Jewish roots and traditions.

The story of the Three Kings or Three Wise Men was probably a kind of *haggadah* or popular Jewish story fashioned from diverse biblical material intended to make a spiritual rather than historical point. This does not mean that the story is not true. It means that the truth of it is more in the total story and its meaning than in any or all of its details. The point of the story is that these men were not Israelite, but they were nonetheless open to and in search of God's plan. The story illustrates that people of good will, regardless of their ethnic or religious background, can be responsive to the revelation of God. These men searched for and found the child, and they did not go away disappointed.

✥ Reflecting on the Word

"If there weren't any Wise Men, there should have been," a spiritual mentor once told me. This was at a time when a story's truth was equated with its being factual. The story of the Wise Men is true, whether it is factual in its details or not. From the beginning of time, there have been those who have been searching for "truth" or "light" or other divine signals. This journey often begins when something in our world catches the attention of those looking up or out from themselves, glimpsing a "star" beckoning.

The truth behind the story of the Wise Men affirms that God sends out signals for searchers to pick up on and move further down the road that will take them to God. Sometimes we might get lost for a while, our internal GPS ceasing to function because we have made a sudden turn or gone past a suggested turn-off. But, then, in a moment of grace, we hear a welcome "recalculating," and we are off on our way once again.

Even when "darkness covers the earth and thick clouds cover the peoples," the One we are searching for is present, and will not let us go off the trail completely—at least not for long, and eventually, in "God's good time," we will find our way. The light will return and the Lord's glory will shine upon all seekers and searchers—even some not much interested in seeking or searching. These, especially, are the ones the Son of Man came to save.

✥ Consider/Discuss

- Are you a searcher, a seeker after "something"? Can you name it?
- Have you had any experience of "finding God," or "coming to Christ"?
- Have you ever been a "star" for another?

✥ Responding to the Word

Jesus, send the guiding light we all need to find you. Sometimes there is only darkness and we grow tired, frightened, even hopeless. Be with us then and bring us to that place where you can be found. We pray with St. John Henry Newman: "Lead, kindly Light, amidst th'encircling gloom. Lead thou me on!" Amen.

We are now in Ordinary Time, the time between our celebration of the Incarnation and that of our redemption. Discipleship is the major focus of this period of the liturgical year. The call to discipleship is not reserved for a select few. It accompanies baptismal commitment, and it is issued to all Christians. The readings of this period outline the various stages of this call and provide a sketch of some of the characteristics of each stage. We should not be surprised to see that disciples are very ordinary people. Yet in their ordinariness, they frequently act in extraordinary ways. When they accept this remarkable call, they become radically transformed and are given the power to remain faithful regardless of the difficulties that they must face. In fact, their very suffering becomes an occasion for evangelizing. It is clear that discipleship begins and ends in Christ and in the power of God that is able to transform ordinary people into faithful followers.

Although the readings depict this process of transformation in the lives of others, the messages of these readings are for us today. We are the ones called to discipleship; we are the ones summoned to transformation. A close look at the lives of the prophets and of the disciples shows that, like us, most of them were quite ordinary people. However, with the grace of God they accomplished remarkable feats. Who is to say that we too might not accomplish wonderful things for God? The readings from First and Second Corinthians provide us with instruction for daily living. Were we to live in the ways that Paul outlines in these readings, we would indeed accomplish much.

There is an urgency expressed in some of the readings of this period. They insist that unless we embrace the gospel now and live it fully, we may run out of time. God's call demands a total response. Like the disciples, we must leave the familiarity of our former ways of living and follow the call that we have heard in the depths of our hearts. We may be called from a life that we enjoyed, as the Corinthians were, or we may be called like Jonah to a life from which we try to escape. This may not mean that we actually leave our present lives, but that we live them differently. In any case, God's call to discipleship is persistent, even unrelenting.

As disciples, we are called not only to enter the reign of God but to promote it and to spread it. We are ambassadors of God; we bring the good news of salvation, and we do this wherever we are and in whatever we do.

January 15, 2012

SECOND SUNDAY IN ORDINARY TIME

Today's Focus: Listening for God

If God were trying to "speak" to you, would God get a hearing? Today's readings remind us that God communicates in different ways and we need to be listening for God's voice. Sometimes we might need help—an Eli or a John the Baptist—to recognize God's voice trying to get through.

FIRST READING
1 Samuel 3:3b–10, 19

Samuel was sleeping in the temple of the Lord where the ark of God was. The Lord called to Samuel, who answered, "Here I am." Samuel ran to Eli and said, "Here I am. You called me." "I did not call you," Eli said. "Go back to sleep." So he went back to sleep. Again the Lord called Samuel, who rose and went to Eli. "Here I am," he said. "You called me." But Eli answered, "I did not call you, my son. Go back to sleep."

At that time Samuel was not familiar with the Lord, because the Lord had not revealed anything to him as yet. The Lord called Samuel again, for the third time. Getting up and going to Eli, he said, "Here I am. You called me." Then Eli understood that the Lord was calling the youth. So he said to Samuel, "Go to sleep, and if you are called, reply, Speak, Lord, for your servant is listening." When Samuel went to sleep in his place, the Lord came and revealed his presence, calling out as before, "Samuel, Samuel!" Samuel answered, "Speak, for your servant is listening."

Samuel grew up, and the Lord was with him, not permitting any word of his to be without effect.

PSALM RESPONSE
Psalm 40:8a, 9a

Here am I, Lord; I come to do your will.

SECOND READING
1 Corinthians 6:13c–15a, 17–20

Brothers and sisters: The body is not for immorality, but for the Lord, and the Lord is for the body; God raised the Lord and will also raise us by his power.

Do you not know that your bodies are members of Christ? But whoever is joined to the Lord becomes one Spirit with him. Avoid immorality. Every other sin a person commits is outside the body, but the immoral person sins against his own body. Do you not know that your body is a temple of the Holy Spirit within you, whom you have from God, and that you are not your own? For you have been purchased at a price. Therefore glorify God in your body.

GOSPEL

John 1:35–42

John was standing with two of his disciples, and as he watched Jesus walk by, he said, "Behold, the Lamb of God." The two disciples heard what he said and followed Jesus. Jesus turned and saw them following him and said to them, "What are you looking for?" They said to him, "Rabbi"—which translated means Teacher —, "where are you staying?" He said to them, "Come, and you will see." So they went and saw where Jesus was staying, and they stayed with him that day. It was about four in the afternoon. Andrew, the brother of Simon Peter, was one of the two who heard John and followed Jesus. He first found his own brother Simon and told him, "We have found the Messiah" — which is translated Christ. Then he brought him to Jesus. Jesus looked at him and said, "You are Simon the son of John; you will be called Cephas" —which is translated Peter.

❖ Understanding the Word

The vivid and dynamic account of the call of Samuel is both a call narrative and a theophany or manifestation of God. There is a clear difference between Samuel's relationship with God before this experience and his relationship after it. Though pious, the young Samuel did not know God well; he had received no revelation. His encounter was transformative; a bond was forged between him and God. His responsiveness opened him further, enabling him to receive the word of God and, presumably, to speak it to others. Samuel's influence is attributed to God's direction in his life. It was God who made Samuel's words effective.

Paul furnishes the Corinthian community with instruction on the sanctity of the human body. Since it is through our bodies that union with Christ is possible, this same body is to be revered. God highly values the human body, as evident in the bodily resurrection first of Christ and then of others. Paul goes on to assert that our bodies are temples of the Spirit, the same Spirit with whom we are one through our union with Christ. Paul's final admonition is brief but quite revealing. He calls upon the Corinthians to glorify God in their bodies, which are the means by which we touch the mysteries of God.

There are times when intermediaries play important roles in the lives of others. The Gospel reading describes two such instances of this. John directs two of his own disciples to Jesus. He identifies Jesus as the Lamb of God, a title that may be based on an interpretation of the description of the Suffering Servant found in the prophet Isaiah (cf. Isaiah 53:7). Later in the story, Andrew recognizes something in Jesus and becomes convinced that he is the long-awaited one. Andrew then brings his brother Peter to Jesus. In both instances, the faith of an associate begins another's own journey to discipleship.

✥ Reflecting on the Word

The story of the future prophet Samuel begins by telling us that the voice of the Lord was rarely heard and visions were uncommon. God seemed to have broken off communication, given Israel's spotty record of keeping the Lord's commandments. Or perhaps no one was giving attention to God's voice? One night when Eli the priest and young Samuel were sleeping in the temple, God called Samuel by name. Three times God called, and each time Samuel went in to where Eli was sleeping to see what he wanted. Finally, Eli realized it was the Lord and told Samuel what to say.

When Jesus came to the Jordan to be baptized, John the Baptist pointed him out to those who would be his first disciples. They "heard what he said and followed Jesus." One of them, Andrew, then went and got his brother Peter. Peter listened and followed his brother to meet Jesus.

Sometimes God speaks in the silence of the night, sometimes in the bustle of everyday life. I loved the TV series *Joan of Arcadia*, in which God would show up in various guises—a street performer, an eccentric elderly lady, a child. Scripture reminds us to keep on our toes, lest God walk on by. Even a first recognition of Jesus did not totally reveal all that he was. The disciples called him Rabbi and Messiah, but only John the Baptist knew him for the Lamb of God who would take away the sins of the world.

✥ Consider/Discuss

- In a popular hymn we sing that we have heard God calling in the night. Have you heard God calling lately—night or day?
- Has your response to God's call been more like Samuel's or Andrew's, needing some assistance, or immediate?

✥ Responding to the Word

God who has spoken in times past, help us individually and as a community to listen for your voice in our day. Send us mentors and friends who will help us to know it is your voice, and give us the courage to respond to your call. Amen.

January 22, 2012

THIRD SUNDAY IN ORDINARY TIME

Today's Focus: God's Will: The Conversion of All

God has a plan: that all turn to God and thereby know salvation. To this end, Jesus came preaching a call to turn from sin and believe in the good news of God's loving plan. As with Jonah and the first disciples, God continues to call others to join in this work.

FIRST READING
Jonah 3:1–5, 10

The word of the LORD came to Jonah, saying: "Set out for the great city of Nineveh, and announce to it the message that I will tell you." So Jonah made ready and went to Nineveh, according to the LORD's bidding. Now Nineveh was an enormously large city; it took three days to go through it. Jonah began his journey through the city, and had gone but a single day's walk announcing, "Forty days more and Nineveh shall be destroyed," when the people of Nineveh believed God; they proclaimed a fast and all of them, great and small, put on sackcloth.

When God saw by their actions how they turned from their evil way, he repented of the evil that he had threatened to do to them; he did not carry it out.

PSALM RESPONSE
Psalm 25:4a

Teach me your ways, O Lord.

SECOND READING
1 Corinthians 7:29–31

I tell you, brothers and sisters, the time is running out. From now on, let those having wives act as not having them, those weeping as not weeping, those rejoicing as not rejoicing, those buying as not owning, those using the world as not using it fully. For the world in its present form is passing away.

GOSPEL
Mark 1:14–20

After John had been arrested, Jesus came to Galilee proclaiming the gospel of God: "This is the time of fulfillment. The kingdom of God is at hand. Repent, and believe in the gospel."

As he passed by the Sea of Galilee, he saw Simon and his brother Andrew casting their nets into the sea; they were fishermen. Jesus said to them, "Come after me, and I will make you fishers of men." Then they abandoned their nets and followed him. He walked along a little farther and saw James, the son of Zebedee, and his brother John. They too were in a boat mending their nets. Then he called them. So they left their father Zebedee in the boat along with the hired men and followed him.

The book of Jonah is an unusual story of conversion. Nineveh was Israel's mortal enemy. It was also a symbol for wickedness in the ancient world. Yet when Jonah preached repentance to it, the people heeded the message of the prophet, believed in God, and proclaimed a fast. Jonah was not happy that his enemy repented, but this story demonstrates the universality of divine compassion. It shows that God is willing to forgive even a nation that had been brutal toward Israel, the chosen people. All the people of Nineveh, great and small, put on the garments of penance.

Paul teaches about the endtime. Unlike the regular measure or unfolding of time (*chronos*), this is a different notion of time, *kairos*, a time of greatest significance for God's divine plan. It refers to decisive moments, those that are ordained by God, those that mark the inbreaking of God's action. It is considered the time of fulfillment, of divine revelation. It denotes critical moments in the life of Jesus, his inauguration of the reign of God, his passion and death, his return at the endtime. Paul insists that the *kairos* is fast approaching and so the Christians must live in the present age as though it had already come.

Jesus inaugurates his ministry with this bold declaration: The kingdom of God is at hand. This is an extraordinary time (*kairos*), the time of fulfillment of all expectations. After the initial announcement, Jesus calls for repentance. Just like the prophets of old, he calls for a change of heart, a return to God. This announcement is followed by an account of the call of the fishermen Simon, Andrew, James, and John. The abruptness with which these men leave their familiar lives and all of the relationships and obligations associated with them is a final indication of the radical nature of life in the kingdom of God. This is truly a new way of living in the world.

❖ *Reflecting on the Word*

You might want to read the early part of Jonah's story leading to his ending up in the belly of a "great fish" for three days and nights—a biblical moment distinct in its appeal to the sense of smell, besides bringing out the more playful side of Israel's God. Coming today in mid-story, we miss the struggle between Jonah's stubbornness ("I won't go to Nineveh!") and God's ("Yes, you will!"). But today's emphasis falls on how powerful God's word proves to be, even when uttered by an unwilling prophet who wanted nothing more than to see Nineveh go up in smoke—people, property, and even cows.

Thomas Aquinas once said that when you love a person, their loves become your own. A pleasant enough thought, except when you extend it to God, and realize that it is not given to us to determine what might fall outside of God's loving, enormous embrace and desire to save. While the world that is passing away is often marked by the mess we humans have made of it, God is determined to change this destructive course into a world renewed and wants us engaged in the work.

We get a hint of what this means when we hear the message Jesus proclaimed: God's reign is at hand, so turn away from sin and believe in the gospel—the good news Jesus preached, the good news that is Jesus. We are invited to be part of the solution rather than the problem, joining in the work begun by Jesus and preaching God's offer of salvation to all.

✥ Consider/Discuss

- Do you see yourself called to proclaim that God's kingdom is "at hand"?
- What does this message mean?
- How do you live out this invitation?

✥ Responding to the Word

Loving God, when Jesus proclaimed that your kingdom was near, he was announcing that you were at work in him for the salvation of the world. Help us to trust this message and to hear his call in our lives, respond to it, and communicate this gospel to others. Amen.

January 29, 2012

FOURTH SUNDAY IN ORDINARY TIME

Today's Focus: A New Day Dawns

A prophet is one who speaks in God's name. Moses was the greatest prophet, handing down all that he heard God say to the people God had brought out of Egypt. God's promise to raise up a prophet like Moses is fulfilled in Jesus, whose authoritative word elicits the obedience even of unclean spirits.

FIRST READING
Deuteronomy 18:15–20

Moses spoke to all the people, saying: "A prophet like me will the LORD, your God, raise up for you from among your own kin; to him you shall listen. This is exactly what you requested of the LORD, your God, at Horeb on the day of the assembly, when you said, 'Let us not again hear the voice of the LORD, our God, nor see this great fire any more, lest we die.' And the LORD said to me, 'This was well said. I will raise up for them a prophet like you from among their kin, and will put my words into his mouth; he shall tell them all that I command him. Whoever will not listen to my words which he speaks in my name, I myself will make him answer for it. But if a prophet presumes to speak in my name an oracle that I have not commanded him to speak, or speaks in the name of other gods, he shall die.' "

PSALM RESPONSE
Psalm 95:8

If today you hear his voice, harden not your hearts.

SECOND READING
1 Corinthians 7:32–35

Brothers and sisters: I should like you to be free of anxieties. An unmarried man is anxious about the things of the Lord, how he may please the Lord. But a married man is anxious about the things of the world, how he may please his wife, and he is divided. An unmarried woman or a virgin is anxious about the things of the Lord, so that she may be holy in both body and spirit. A married woman, on the other hand, is anxious about the things of the world, how she may please her husband. I am telling you this for your own benefit, not to impose a restraint upon you, but for the sake of propriety and adherence to the Lord without distraction.

Then they came to Capernaum, and on the sabbath Jesus entered the synagogue and taught. The people were astonished at his teaching, for he taught them as one having authority and not as the scribes. In their synagogue was a man with an unclean spirit; he cried out, "What have you to do with us, Jesus of Nazareth? Have you come to destroy us? I know who you are—the Holy One of God!" Jesus rebuked him and said, "Quiet! Come out of him!" The unclean spirit convulsed him and with a loud cry came out of him. All were amazed and asked one another, "What is this? A new teaching with authority. He commands even the unclean spirits and they obey him." His fame spread everywhere throughout the whole region of Galilee.

✛ *Understanding the Word*
_____

Moses is not normally thought of as a prophet, but today's reading clearly states that he is. In fact, he is considered the prophet *par excellence*. He received the word of the Lord in the form of the Law, and he acted as God's voice, promulgating this Law to the community. He promised that God would not leave the people without a mediator. Rather, just as God chose him to be a prophet, so another will be raised up. This promise of a future prophet led people down through the centuries to wonder whether or not particular individuals might in fact be this promised prophet.

Some today maintain that Paul is opposed to marriage. Though here he seems to prefer the unmarried state, it is because he believes that the endtime is fast approaching, and he wants the Corinthians to be free from the kind of anxieties that accompany marriage. The real contrast that he draws is between commitment to the Lord and over-involvement in the things of this world. Paul knew that those involved in the things of the world can be very committed to the Lord, and those committed to the Lord can possess a very shallow spirituality. He is more concerned with the quality of commitment than with the particular state of life.

The man in the synagogue had an unclean spirit that caused him severe physical suffering. The people of the time believed that evil spirits roamed the world and caused havoc whenever and wherever they could. Such an afflicted person should have been removed from a holy place like a synagogue. However, Jesus does not dismiss the man; instead, he casts out the evil spirit. Just as the people were astonished by the teaching of Jesus, so they are amazed at his power over the evil spirit. Jesus may have been able to silence the spirit, but his fame as a teacher and an exorcist spread throughout Galilee.

Some years ago there was a series of books called A *Day in the Life of* . . . . Sometimes it was a continent like Africa; sometimes a country like America, the Soviet Union, or Thailand; and sometimes a state like Hawaii or California. One hundred top photographers visually captured the experience of this place in a twenty-four-hour period. In today's and next Sunday's Gospels, Mark verbally gives us "A Day in the Life of Jesus, God's Prophet."

The first experience of Jesus as one whose word effects what he says occurs in the synagogue. Here Jesus encounters an unclean spirit. The spirit makes the first move, naming Jesus as the Holy One of God. In biblical thought, naming a person gave you some degree of power over that person. Not here. With a few quick words, Jesus asserts his authority: "Quiet! Come out of him!"

How fitting that Jesus' first public act in the first Gospel to be written down is to free a human being from an evil spirit that has brought him chaos and destruction. This event reveals Jesus as one who came to free us from all that oppresses and beats us down. This liberation continues to be the work of all who follow Jesus.

We don't hear much about evil spirits these days, but can anyone deny their presence in our world? Consider the murder, mutilation, rape, and torture that have taken place in eastern Congo alone for the last twelve years with an estimated death toll of 6.9 million. Change is impossible without God's help.

✜ *Consider/Discuss*

- Do you believe evil spirits continue to dwell in the human heart?
- Does this mean we are not responsible but that "the devil makes us do it"?
- Does this Gospel offer any hope to people today in the face of so much suffering and death in the world?

✜ *Responding to the Word*

Jesus, you are revealed as one who has the power to cast out evil spirits who take up residence in our hearts. May your liberating word free us from all that brings harm, and may we work to bring your healing spirit to touch our world. Amen.

February 5, 2012

FIFTH SUNDAY IN ORDINARY TIME

Today's Focus: A Balanced Life

Today's Gospel continues presenting a day in the life of Jesus, begun last week. In these early days of his ministry, Jesus brings healing into many lives, including Peter's mother-in-law, who then gets up to minister to others. Jesus' healing and preaching are balanced by time spent in prayer with the Father.

FIRST READING
Job 7:1–4, 6–7

Job spoke, saying:
Is not man's life on earth a drudgery?
　Are not his days those of hirelings?
He is a slave who longs for the shade,
　a hireling who waits for his wages.
So I have been assigned months of misery,
　and troubled nights have been allotted to me.
If in bed I say, "When shall I arise?"
　then the night drags on;
　I am filled with restlessness until the dawn.
My days are swifter than a weaver's shuttle;
　they come to an end without hope.
Remember that my life is like the wind;
　I shall not see happiness again.

PSALM RESPONSE
Psalm 147:3a

Praise the Lord, who heals the brokenhearted.

SECOND READING
1 Corinthians 9:16–19, 22–23

Brothers and sisters: If I preach the gospel, this is no reason for me to boast, for an obligation has been imposed on me, and woe to me if I do not preach it! If I do so willingly, I have a recompense, but if unwillingly, then I have been entrusted with a stewardship. What then is my recompense? That, when I preach, I offer the gospel free of charge so as not to make full use of my right in the gospel. Although I am free in regard to all, I have made myself a slave to all so as to win over as many as possible. To the weak I became weak, to win over the weak. I have become all things to all, to save at least some. All this I do for the sake of the gospel, so that I too may have a share in it.

GOSPEL
Mark 1:29–39
On leaving the synagogue Jesus entered the house of Simon and Andrew with James and John. Simon's mother-in-law lay sick with a fever. They immediately told him about her. He approached, grasped her hand, and helped her up. Then the fever left her and she waited on them.

When it was evening, after sunset, they brought to him all who were ill or possessed by demons. The whole town was gathered at the door. He cured many who were sick with various diseases, and he drove out many demons, not permitting them to speak because they knew him.

Rising very early before dawn, he left and went off to a deserted place, where he prayed. Simon and those who were with him pursued him and on finding him said, "Everyone is looking for you." He told them, "Let us go on to the nearby villages that I may preach there also. For this purpose have I come." So he went into their synagogues, preaching and driving out demons throughout the whole of Galilee.

❖❖ *Understanding the Word*

Crushed by the torment of his own situation, Job bemoans the harshness of life itself. It is like hard military service, or like the life of a hireling who has nothing to say about the conditions of work, or like the situation of a slave who is totally dependent upon the slaveholder. These metaphors both describe the tribulations of life and express the helplessness that is experienced in it. Job has nowhere to turn. Life seems to be armed against him and there is neither defense nor escape. So many circumstances are beyond human control, and Job feels helpless in the face of it. It is no wonder that he cries out.

Preaching was the reason Paul was called to follow Christ. In his eyes, he deserved no special credit for this, and therefore he had no grounds for boasting. The issue was not if Paul preached, but how he preached. There were times when he waived his right to financial support and he preached free of charge. He seems to have preferred preaching at no cost, for then he would be beholden to no one and would be able to preach the gospel without being concerned about offending his audience. Still, Paul was willing to conform himself to others without compromising the gospel.

The Gospel reading recounts Jesus' healing of Peter's mother-in-law. Jesus exercises unique authority over the powers of death. The person released from this power then goes about ministering to others. Other healings and exorcisms follow. These two works are connected. The principal message of Jesus' preaching is the long-awaited establishment of the reign of God. However, before God's reign can take firm root and thrive, the reign of evil must be dislodged and cast out. Jesus' fame so spreads that he is compelled to flee to a solitary place to pray. The reading ends with a statement that condenses the entire ministry of Jesus into preaching and driving out demons.

Job's words remind us how weariness, heaviness of heart, sadness, can sweep over us at times and lodge bone-deep. All of our work seems little more than "drudgery." Sometimes these feelings are inexplicable; at other times the loss of a loved one, a sudden change in our lives, the discovery of a serious illness can be the cause.

This second half of a day in the life of Jesus shows us his response to those things that weigh people down, whether it is an illness afflicting the loved one of a disciple, or strangers who were ill or possessed by demons. Jesus responds to those brought before him, curing and driving out many demons. He is the compassion of God present to the people who come to him.

Jesus obviously spent the whole day meeting the needs of the people, long into the evening. Then, perhaps he sat up with Simon and Andrew, James and John, talking with them about what had happened, listening to how this coming of the kingdom of God into their world was affecting them. Then he slept.

We are told that he woke early and went off to a deserted place to pray. This must be how he got the strength to go into another day. As Simon says, "Everyone is looking for you"—whether to thank him or to ask for one more favor we don't know. But Jesus says it is time to move on, to preach and free others from demons.

✥ Consider/Discuss

- Consider how important prayer was for Jesus, so he could keep on doing what he understood as his mission in life.
- Do you have a balanced life: work and prayer, time with family, friends, and sleep?

✥ Responding to the Word

Lord Jesus, you came to show us the face of your Father, who wishes us to be fully alive in the Spirit. Give us the health we need to do the work you have called us to do. Help us to see clearly what our life needs to be open to you and your Father's will. Amen.

February 12, 2012

SIXTH SUNDAY IN ORDINARY TIME

Today's Focus: Bringing Outsiders In

Leprosy was a one way-ticket to exile in the biblical world. A person signaled this affliction with torn garments, disheveled hair, a covered upper lip, and the cry, "Unclean, unclean!" One of the signs that God's kingdom is at hand is the leper being cleansed and restored to the community.

FIRST READING
Leviticus 13:1–2, 44–46

The Lord said to Moses and Aaron, "If someone has on his skin a scab or pustule or blotch which appears to be the sore of leprosy, he shall be brought to Aaron, the priest, or to one of the priests among his descendants. If the man is leprous and unclean, the priest shall declare him unclean by reason of the sore on his head.

"The one who bears the sore of leprosy shall keep his garments rent and his head bare, and shall muffle his beard; he shall cry out, 'Unclean, unclean!' As long as the sore is on him he shall declare himself unclean, since he is in fact unclean. He shall dwell apart, making his abode outside the camp."

PSALM RESPONSE
Psalm 32:7

I turn to you, Lord, in time of trouble, and you fill me with the joy of salvation.

SECOND READING
1 Corinthians 10:31 — 11:1

Brothers and sisters, Whether you eat or drink, or whatever you do, do everything for the glory of God. Avoid giving offense, whether to the Jews or Greeks or the church of God, just as I try to please everyone in every way, not seeking my own benefit but that of the many, that they may be saved. Be imitators of me, as I am of Christ.

GOSPEL
Mark 1:40–45

A leper came to Jesus and kneeling down begged him and said, "If you wish, you can make me clean." Moved with pity, he stretched out his hand, touched him, and said to him, "I do will it. Be made clean." The leprosy left him immediately, and he was made clean. Then, warning him sternly, he dismissed him at once.

He said to him, "See that you tell no one anything, but go, show yourself to the priest and offer for your cleansing what Moses prescribed; that will be proof for them."

The man went away and began to publicize the whole matter. He spread the report abroad so that it was impossible for Jesus to enter a town openly. He remained outside in deserted places, and people kept coming to him from everywhere.

Leprosy included a wide variety of chronic skin diseases. Those with skin ailments were deemed unclean and were banished from the community. The real tragedy of leprosy was less the physical discomfort than the social estrangement and the religious alienation that resulted. Probably because such social and religious alienation was so severe, it was believed that the condition was brought on by some kind of sin. When the conditions that made a person unclean no longer held, it was necessary for the person to undergo some rite of purification before being readmitted into the community. This explains why a priest was involved.

Paul argues that the gospel is demanding enough; people do not need to be burdened with obligations that are extraneous to its message. He insists that neither food laws nor the assertion of one's freedom should be the governing principle in the lives of Christians. The glory of God and sensitivity to others should be the driving force. "Avoid giving offense" is the policy he advocates. The passage ends with a final admonition: Be imitators of me, as I am of Christ. Paul indeed adapted himself to the needs of others, and he did this after the example of Christ. The Corinthians are exhorted to follow Paul, who followed Christ.

The man in the Gospel story was suffering from the kind of skin ailment referred to in the first reading. Despite his condition, he boldly approached Jesus and begged to be made clean. Jesus was moved with pity. He knew that if he touched an unclean man he would become ritually unclean as well. However, his touch actually healed the man and restored him to the state of ritual purity. Jesus then sent him off to the priest for verification of the healing. Once again, the news of his marvelous power causes him to choose the seclusion of solitary places rather than the press of the crowd and their misunderstanding of his mission.

✦ *Reflecting on the Word*

These first days of Jesus' ministry present him preaching, teaching, and healing to bring people to know that God is near. His message and his deeds bring people back to full life in the community. By casting out demons and curing the sick he restores to full humanity those suffering from possession and illness. Today we find Jesus confronting a condition that must have been even more excruciating—leprosy.

To be a leper was to be cut off from others in all ways. You were cast out of the community, isolated, doomed to live in deserted places, no longer part of the human family, unable to participate in any social events, and considered unfit to worship God. It was assumed that if you had leprosy, you had sinned in some way. Your life was summed up in the words the Law of Moses told you to cry out whenever anyone came near, "Unclean, unclean!"

For Jesus to touch a leper meant that in the eyes of others he also became unclean and unfit to associate and worship with others. Even so, when a leper asked for healing, Jesus was unequivocal in his reply: "I do will it. Be made clean." It is easy to hear in his response the authority of the Son of God, set on giving glory to his Father. Yet Jesus, ever respectful of the law, sent the man to the priest, as commanded in the book of Leviticus. In Jesus, pity took precedence over the law, but did not abolish it.

❖ Consider/Discuss

- Have you ever been or seen anyone cut off from a family, a group, or even the community?
- When St Paul says, "Be imitators of me as I am of Christ," how does that speak to your life in terms of Jesus' healing the leper in the Gospel?

❖ Responding to the Word

Jesus, you came to bring us into deeper communion with the Father and one another. Give us the courage to reach out, as you did, to those in need of our compassion and help. Let us not be afraid of the opinions of others when we see that good can be done. Amen.

February 19, 2012

SEVENTH SUNDAY IN ORDINARY TIME

Today's Focus: The Real Agenda—Forgiveness of Sins

God is so endlessly inventive that not even so great an event as Israel's exodus from Egypt was going to be God's final word—or deed—in Israel's life. Freedom from physical slavery was only the prelude to the freedom God wanted all creation to have: from sin and death.

FIRST READING
Isaiah 43:18–19, 21–22, 24b–25

Thus says the Lord:
Remember not the events of the past,
    the things of long ago consider not;
see, I am doing something new!
    Now it springs forth, do you not perceive it?
In the desert I make a way,
    in the wasteland, rivers.
The people I formed for myself,
    that they might announce my praise.
Yet you did not call upon me, O Jacob,
    for you grew weary of me, O Israel.
You burdened me with your sins,
    and wearied me with your crimes.
It is I, I, who wipe out,
    for my own sake, your offenses;
    your sins I remember no more.

PSALM RESPONSE
Psalm 41:5b

Lord, heal my soul, for I have sinned against you.

SECOND READING
2 Corinthians 1:18–22

Brothers and sisters: As God is faithful, our word to you is not "yes" and "no." For the Son of God, Jesus Christ, who was proclaimed to you by us, Silvanus and Timothy and me, was not "yes" and "no," but "yes" has been in him. For however many are the promises of God, their Yes is in him; therefore, the Amen from us also goes through him to God for glory. But the one who gives us security with you in Christ and who anointed us is God; he has also put his seal upon us and given the Spirit in our hearts as a first installment.

GOSPEL
Mark 2:1-12

When Jesus returned to Capernaum after some days, it became known that he was at home. Many gathered together so that there was no longer room for them, not even around the door, and he preached the word to them. They came bringing to him a paralytic carried by four men. Unable to get near Jesus because of the crowd, they opened up the roof above him. After they had broken through, they let down the mat on which the paralytic was lying. When Jesus saw their faith, he said to the paralytic, "Child, your sins are forgiven." Now some of the scribes were sitting there asking themselves, "Why does this man speak that way? He is blaspheming. Who but God alone can forgive sins?" Jesus immediately knew in his mind what they were thinking to themselves, so he said, "Why are you thinking such things in your hearts? Which is easier, to say to the paralytic, 'Your sins are forgiven,' or to say, 'Rise, pick up your mat and walk'? But that you may know that the Son of Man has authority to forgive sins on earth" — he said to the paralytic, "I say to you, rise, pick up your mat, and go home." He rose, picked up his mat at once, and went away in the sight of everyone. They were all astounded and glorified God, saying, "We have never seen anything like this."

❖ *Understanding the Word*

Israel's faith was based on the liberating events of the past. So Isaiah's words, "Remember not . . . consider not," must have been unsettling. The prophet was probably calling the people away from inordinate dependence on the past, a dependence that prevented them from seeing the astonishing new thing that God was accomplishing before their very eyes. Faithful reverence for tradition is one thing, but insistent absorption in it is quite another. While the new way that stretched out before them was truly astounding, most amazing was the transformation that took place within them. Though sinners, the merciful God wiped away their guilt, and once forgiven, they were recreated.

Paul is forced to defend the merit of his apostolic ministry. He does so by basing his defense on the trustworthiness of God. He argues strenuously that his ministry never demonstrated such inconsistency. He offers three examples of God's faithfulness. First, Christ is the center of his preaching. Since there is no inconsistency in Christ, there is no inconsistency in his preaching. Second, all of God's past promises have been fulfilled in Christ. And third, those baptized have been sealed with the Spirit of God. This presentation of God's plan serves as an argument in defense of Paul's ministry.

Jesus' forgiveness of the man who came to him to be healed sets up the conflict between Jesus and the scribes who were present in the witnessing crowd. While they are correct in believing that only God can forgive, they are blind in not recognizing the power of divine forgiveness active in the person of Jesus. Knowing what the incredulous scribes are thinking, Jesus challenges their silent condemnation of him. He points out that forgiving sin is more difficult than healing, so the healing is merely an external sign of internal transformation. The man is sent home forgiven and healed; the crowds are astounded and give glory to God. Only the scribes remain unbelieving.

When Jesus came preaching, teaching, healing, and exorcising, the response was amazement and wonder. He was a "crowd magnet," as we see in today's Gospel. When Jesus showed up, it was standing room only. What would be the next miracle? So when the paralytic came down, there might even have been a little "ho-hum" in the air. "Didn't he do something along these lines that night outside Simon's mother-in-law's house?"

But healing the body and casting out demons were only the first steps in the new creation God had in mind. The next step went to the heart of the matter—salvation. "Child, your sins are forgiven." Alarms went off, at least in the heads of some of the legal experts present. "Did he just say? . . . No, not possible . . . Only God can . . . ." But Jesus, who really could hear people thinking, had no trouble saying it again: "That you may *know* the Son of Man has the authority to forgive sins on earth . . . " then he turned to the paralytic: "Get up and go." And the man got up and went.

All the other things Jesus had been doing were acceptable, except when he did them on a Sabbath, for this was crossing a clearly defined line in the law of Moses. Forgiving sin? Only God could do that. Yes, *that* was the point. And still is. So don't let past actions—even God's, much less yours—lock you in or keep God out. God remains at work in Jesus offering forgiveness, reconciliation, at-one-ment to all who realize they need it.

✦ Consider/Discuss

- How do you feel when you hear Jesus say, "Your sins are forgiven"?
- Do you trust God to do new things? For you? In you? Through you?
- Do you accept that God has put the Spirit in our hearts "as a first installment" of God's desire for total communion?

✦ Responding to the Word

Creator God, in giving us Jesus, you began the final move of a new creation in us and in the world. We thank you for offering through your Son the gift of forgiveness for our sins. May we accept this gift of grace and work to bring others to know its healing power. Amen.

Notes

The themes of these two seasons point to the love that God has for us. Perhaps we should spend more time meditating on that love than on our unworthiness. Covenant is one of the prominent themes found in the first readings for the Sundays of Lent. Here we see that God initiates the covenant-making; the people can do nothing but receive the gift that God offers and allow the covenant relationship to take root in their hearts and in their lives. God does not give up when people turn away from this relationship. In fact, in the second readings we see that Christ's death is the extent to which God goes to ensure the permanence of this relationship. Christ's resurrection is the sign of the richness of God's tender mercy. Mercy and grace are now ours, not through our own works but because of the works of Christ. In this same Christ, we become the handiwork of God. We are called to obey Christ, who was obedient even unto death. We are then invited to have the same self-emptying love in us that was in Christ. With the significance of covenant instilled in our minds and hearts, we can then look to our participation in the promises of the Resurrection.

The entire Easter season celebrates the membership of those who have been newly initiated into the community of believers. The readings constitute a mystagogical catechesis—a formative instruction for the newly baptized—but a teaching that all of us can take to heart. The first readings, all from Acts of the Apostles, create a kind of Easter proclamation announcing the Lord's resurrection. The epistles contain instruction for Christian living. Having been born anew through baptism, the new Christians, and all Christians as well, are exhorted to seek the things that are above, to live as faithful people of God by obeying the commandments, especially the commandment of love. Empowered by the Spirit of God, we are all charged to share the individual gifts that we have received for the good of the entire body of Christ. The various Gospel passages read during this season are woven into a tapestry depicting the Risen Lord's final days on earth.

The presence of the Risen Lord is the central theme of the Easter season. He resides at the heart of the community of believers; he is revealed to us in the breaking of the bread. He not only lives with us, he also lives through us. We make him present to the world as often as we live in actions that mirror his, lives that are truly Spirit-driven. Easter is a time of new beginnings and new hope. It is the time of fulfillment. The entire world cries out: Hallelujah!

February 26, 2012

FIRST SUNDAY OF LENT

Today's Focus: Lent and Beginning Anew

Lent calls our attention to fresh starts. After forty days of rain, creation began anew with Noah. During forty days in the desert, Jesus showed himself to be God's beloved Son by withstanding temptation. Lent offers forty days to prepare for a fresh start at Easter, when we renew the covenant vows of our baptism.

FIRST READING
Genesis 9:8–15

God said to Noah and to his sons with him: "See, I am now establishing my covenant with you and your descendants after you and with every living creature that was with you: all the birds, and the various tame and wild animals that were with you and came out of the ark. I will establish my covenant with you, that never again shall all bodily creatures be destroyed by the waters of a flood; there shall not be another flood to devastate the earth." God added: "This is the sign that I am giving for all ages to come, of the covenant between me and you and every living creature with you: I set my bow in the clouds to serve as a sign of the covenant between me and the earth. When I bring clouds over the earth, and the bow appears in the clouds, I will recall the covenant I have made between me and you and all living beings, so that the waters shall never again become a flood to destroy all mortal beings."

PSALM RESPONSE
Psalm 25:10

Your ways, O Lord, are love and truth to those who keep your covenant.

SECOND READING
1 Peter 3:18-22

Beloved: Christ suffered for sins once, the righteous for the sake of the unrighteous, that he might lead you to God. Put to death in the flesh, he was brought to life in the Spirit. In it he also went to preach to the spirits in prison, who had once been disobedient while God patiently waited in the days of Noah during the building of the ark, in which a few persons, eight in all, were saved through water. This prefigured baptism, which saves you now. It is not a removal of dirt from the body but an appeal to God for a clear conscience, through the resurrection of Jesus Christ, who has gone into heaven and is at the right hand of God, with angels, authorities, and powers subject to him.

GOSPEL
Mark 1:12-15

The Spirit drove Jesus out into the desert, and he remained in the desert for forty days, tempted by Satan. He was among wild beasts, and the angels ministered to him.

After John had been arrested, Jesus came to Galilee proclaiming the gospel of God: "This is the time of fulfillment. The kingdom of God is at hand. Repent, and believe in the gospel."

✤ Understanding the Word

The first reading is an account of the covenant that God entered into after the flood. It was made with Noah, with his descendants, with all the living creatures that were in the ark, and with the earth itself. The covenant was promissory, God pledging that never again would unruly waters destroy the world and its inhabitants. The bow in the sky may well be a reference to the weapon of the divine warrior who was victorious over the forces of primordial chaos. Just as God rested after creation (see Genesis 2:2–3), hanging up the bow is a sign that order has been established in the universe.

The author of First Peter speaks of the efficacy of Christ's death. It was a sin-offering, like the sacrifices of expiation offered daily in the temple, with the blood of the victim sprinkled on the altar. However, Christ's sacrifice was effective for all time and for all people. It was also vicarious, endured for others. Like the servant in Isaiah (Isaiah 53:4–6), Jesus was the innocent man who bore the guilt of the unrighteous. Christ did this so that we might be brought to God and have access to God's saving grace. Finally, after ascending into heaven, Christ occupies the place of honor at the right hand of God.

The account of Jesus' temptation is charged with meaning. The wilderness was the place of trial. Forty days held special meaning. Moses fasted that long as he inscribed the commandments (Exodus 34:28); Elijah fasted for the same length of time as he walked to Horeb (1 Kings 19:8). It was in this same tradition that Jesus fasted. The announcement of his ministry summarizes the content of his preaching. In eschatological thought, the advent of the reign of God called for a change of mind and heart. Since Jesus' interpretation of God's will did not correspond to the predominant understanding of his day, his announcement of such a ministry was fraught with danger.

✥ Reflecting on the Word

A snapshot differs from a TV show or movie, which moves along, demanding that we keep up with the storyline. A snapshot allows us to focus on details, to take as much time as we want. Snapshots allow us to pause, ponder, and meditate. There is no need to rush on to what comes next.

Mark's Gospel opens with a series of snapshots of Jesus, whom Mark proclaims from the start as "Jesus Christ, the Son of God" (1:1). First, he offers a picture of Jesus' baptism when God's voice proclaims, "You are my beloved Son; with you I am well pleased" (1:11). Then, the two pictures presented today: Jesus driven into the desert for forty days to be tested by Satan, and Jesus beginning a new ministry of preaching the gospel.

These snapshots begin the work of drawing us into the mystery of the one proclaimed as the Promised One long awaited, but even more, the one who is the Son of God. In him God's reign comes to us.

Lent is a time for deciding where our loyalty lies in life. To whom or what do we give our allegiance? At the end of the forty days we renew our baptismal promises. We will be called to profess our faith in God who created us and our world out of love, in the Son who died for us and was raised to new life, and in the Spirit who now drives us to confront the power of evil in our world.

✥ Consider/Discuss

- How can this Lent be a time to begin anew? What concrete steps can you take to stop and ponder the shape of your life?
- How does identifying yourself as being a beloved son or daughter of God influence your daily decisions?

✥ Responding to the Word

Loving God, you have spoken to us at our baptism, calling us beloved children, sending your Spirit upon us, making us heirs of the kingdom of God. Help us to be open to your Spirit this Lent and where it leads. Make us content to rest in stillness and hear your voice.

March 4, 2012

SECOND SUNDAY OF LENT

Today's Focus: Seeing in the Dark

Last week's focus was on Jesus tempted; this week, on Jesus transfigured. From testing to transformation is the arc of every believer's life. Our transformation arises out of both God's grace and our efforts to withstand the testing life brings, signaling our ability to be faithful to God—with God's help.

FIRST READING
Genesis 22:1–2, 9a, 10–13, 15–18

God put Abraham to the test. He called to him, "Abraham!" "Here I am!" he replied. Then God said: "Take your son Isaac, your only one, whom you love, and go to the land of Moriah. There you shall offer him up as a holocaust on a height that I will point out to you."

When they came to the place of which God had told him, Abraham built an altar there and arranged the wood on it. Then he reached out and took the knife to slaughter his son. But the LORD's messenger called to him from heaven, "Abraham, Abraham!" "Here I am!" he answered. "Do not lay your hand on the boy," said the messenger. "Do not do the least thing to him. I know now how devoted you are to God, since you did not withhold from me your own beloved son." As Abraham looked about, he spied a ram caught by its horns in the thicket. So he went and took the ram and offered it up as a holocaust in place of his son.

Again the LORD's messenger called to Abraham from heaven and said: "I swear by myself, declares the LORD, that because you acted as you did in not withholding from me your beloved son, I will bless you abundantly and make your descendants as countless as the stars of the sky and the sands of the seashore; your descendants shall take possession of the gates of their enemies, and in your descendants all the nations of the earth shall find blessing—all this because you obeyed my command."

PSALM RESPONSE
Psalm 116:9

I will walk before the Lord, in the land of the living.

SECOND READING
Romans 8:31b–34

Brothers and sisters: If God is for us, who can be against us? He who did not spare his own Son but handed him over for us all, how will he not also give us everything else along with him?

Who will bring a charge against God's chosen ones? It is God who acquits us. Who will condemn? Christ Jesus it is who died—or, rather, was raised—who also is at the right hand of God, who indeed intercedes for us.

Jesus took Peter, James, and John and led them up a high mountain apart by themselves. And he was transfigured before them, and his clothes became dazzling white, such as no fuller on earth could bleach them. Then Elijah appeared to them along with Moses, and they were conversing with Jesus. Then Peter said to Jesus in reply, "Rabbi, it is good that we are here! Let us make three tents: one for you, one for Moses, and one for Elijah." He hardly knew what to say, they were so terrified. Then a cloud came, casting a shadow over them; from the cloud came a voice, "This is my beloved Son. Listen to him." Suddenly, looking around, they no longer saw anyone but Jesus alone with them.

As they were coming down from the mountain, he charged them not to relate what they had seen to anyone, except when the Son of Man had risen from the dead. So they kept the matter to themselves, questioning what rising from the dead meant.

❖❖ Understanding the Word

The story known as "The Sacrifice of Isaac" might be better called "The Testing of Abraham." The story itself states; "God put Abraham to the test." Furthermore, Isaac is never really sacrificed. Abraham, the "father of a multitude" (see Genesis 7:15), is being put to the test. From a human point of view, Abraham's response to God's demand is terrifying, yet demonstrates his unquestioned obedience. Abraham relinquishes his natural claim on the child of promise, and he is blessed with a promise of more children than he can count. God is not outdone in generosity.

Paul wonders who will bring a charge against God's chosen ones, who will condemn them, and who will justify them. He identifies God as this judge. Paul argues that if the sovereign God is on our side, then regardless of what can be mustered against us, it is nothing in comparison to God's power. If God is willing to sacrifice a beloved Son for our sake, it is impossible that God would deny us whatever other trivial things we might need. Finally, if Jesus has willingly died for us, he would certainly not turn around and condemn us. Besides, he is now interceding for us.

The transfiguration of Jesus knits together traditions of Israel's past, insights into Jesus' own identity, and a glimpse into eschatological fulfillment. Moses and Elijah represent the basis of Israel's tradition, the law and the prophets respectively. Furthermore, both prefigure the prophetic dimension of the messianic era. The voice from the cloud identifies Jesus as the beloved Son, reminiscent of Isaac, who was also a beloved son. The connection with Isaac and Jesus suggests that the voice is referring to Jesus' teaching about his death. It may be that the Transfiguration was intended to prepare the inner circle of disciples for Jesus' unthinkable suffering and death in order to strengthen them in advance.

Two of today's readings take us up a mountain. Mountains are sacred plac-es in the scriptures. Moses meets the God of Abraham, Isaac, and Jacob on Mt. Sinai. Elijah has an experience of this same life-giving God on Mt. Horeb. Today Abraham goes up Mt. Moriah in obedience to God's command to "take your son Isaac, your only one, whom you love" (Genesis 22:2) and offer him there as a holocaust.

It is hard to get past this reading today and focus only on the story of the Transfiguration. This story of God testing Abraham to see if Abraham will obey is a story of great anguish. "See" is an important word here: Moriah means "the place of seeing." Abraham responds to Isaac's question about a victim, saying God will provide, a word rooted in the Latin word for seeing. God will see to it that there is a victim, just as God will see that Abraham is obedient in all things.

Seeing also takes place on Mt. Tabor. Peter, James, and John see Jesus in glory, his clothes dazzlingly white; they see him speaking with Moses and Elijah, rep-resenting the law and the prophets; and they see a cloud overshadowing them, and hear a voice calling for their obedience: "This is my beloved Son. Listen to him" (Mark 9:7).

With them, we are invited to see Jesus as the beloved Son whom the Father "did not spare . . . but handed over for us all," as Paul reminds us (Romans 8:32). The mystery of the Cross and Resurrection is an invitation to see God's love for all God's beloved children and trust in it.

✦✦✦ *Consider/Discuss*

- How is there continuity between the God described in Genesis and God in today's Gospel?
- Have you had any glimpse of the glory that awaits those faithful to God?

✦✦✦ *Responding to the Word*

God of Abraham and Sarah, of Isaac and Rebekah, of Jacob and Rachel, God and Father of our Lord, give us a glimpse of the glory that you have prepared for all who trust in you and remain faithful to you. Strengthen us to walk through any darkness that may threaten our ability to believe.

March 11, 2012

THIRD SUNDAY OF LENT, YEAR B

Today's Focus: Jesus as Action Hero

We hear the Ten Commandments given to Moses as God's call to Israel to live worthy lives. We see Jesus acting the prophet as he clears the temple as a sign of his dedication to the holiness of God's dwelling place. Wherever God dwells, whether in buildings or human beings, it is a holy place.

In the shorter form of the reading, the passages in brackets are omitted.

FIRST READING
Exodus 20:1–17 or 20:1–3, 7–8, 12–17

In those days, God delivered all these commandments: "I, the LORD, am your God, who brought you out of the land of Egypt, that place of slavery. You shall not have other gods besides me. [You shall not carve idols for yourselves in the shape of anything in the sky above or on the earth below or in the waters beneath the earth; you shall not bow down before them or worship them. For I, the LORD, your God, am a jealous God, inflicting punishment for their fathers' wickedness on the children of those who hate me, down to the third and fourth generation; but bestowing mercy down to the thousandth generation on the children of those who love me and keep my commandments.]

"You shall not take the name of the LORD, your God, in vain. For the LORD will not leave unpunished the one who takes his name in vain.

"Remember to keep holy the sabbath day. [Six days you may labor and do all your work, but the seventh day is the sabbath of the LORD, your God. No work may be done then either by you, or your son or daughter, or your male or female slave, or your beast, or by the alien who lives with you. In six days the LORD made the heavens and the earth, the sea and all that is in them; but on the seventh day he rested. That is why the LORD has blessed the sabbath day and made it holy.]

"Honor your father and your mother, that you may have a long life in the land which the LORD, your God, is giving you.

You shall not kill.
You shall not commit adultery.
You shall not steal.
You shall not bear false witness against your neighbor.
You shall not covet your neighbor's house.
You shall not covet your neighbor's wife,
    nor his male or female slave, nor his ox or ass,
    nor anything else that belongs to him."

PSALM
RESPONSE
John 6:68c
Lord, you have the words of everlasting life.

SECOND
READING
1 Corinthians
1:22–25

Brothers and sisters: Jews demand signs and Greeks look for wisdom, but we proclaim Christ crucified, a stumbling block to Jews and foolishness to Gentiles, but to those who are called, Jews and Greeks alike, Christ the power of God and the wisdom of God. For the foolishness of God is wiser than human wisdom, and the weakness of God is stronger than human strength.

GOSPEL
John 2:13–25

Since the Passover of the Jews was near, Jesus went up to Jerusalem. He found in the temple area those who sold oxen, sheep, and doves, as well as the money changers seated there. He made a whip out of cords and drove them all out of the temple area, with the sheep and oxen, and spilled the coins of the money changers and overturned their tables, and to those who sold doves he said, "Take these out of here, and stop making my Father's house a marketplace." His disciples recalled the words of Scripture,

Zeal for your house will consume me.

At this the Jews answered and said to him, "What sign can you show us for doing this?" Jesus answered and said to them, "Destroy this temple and in three days I will raise it up." The Jews said, "This temple has been under construction for forty-six years, and you will raise it up in three days?" But he was speaking about the temple of his body. Therefore, when he was raised from the dead, his disciples remembered that he had said this, and they came to believe the Scripture and the word Jesus had spoken.

While he was in Jerusalem for the feast of Passover, many began to believe in his name when they saw the signs he was doing. But Jesus would not trust himself to them because he knew them all, and did not need anyone to testify about human nature. He himself understood it well.

❖ *Understanding the Word*

The Ten Commandments are considered the foundation of Israelite law. They include the basic conditions for covenant membership. They begin with a self-proclamation by the God who has already acted on behalf of the people. The stipulations are absolute and applicable in any situation; sanctions for violation of them are severe. These commandments were really meant to be observed by all. Basically, they provided a sketch of the God with whom the people were in covenant, and they outlined how these covenanted people were to revere their God and live with each other.

In the short reading from First Corinthians, Paul accomplishes several things. He argues that neither the signs and wonders cherished by the Jews nor the philosophy acclaimed by the Greeks is an adequate standard for evaluation. He insists that the crucified Christ is the standard against which everything is judged. The customary wisdom of these two cultures would reject a crucified Christ. However, God's ways frequently reverse human standards. Paul insists that the ridiculed and despised Christ is actually the wisdom of God. What the Jews and the Greeks rejected as foolishness was indeed authentic wisdom, and what they cherished as wisdom was really misguided folly.

Jesus' actions in the temple are acted-out prophecy and his words are prophetic proclamation. He accuses the merchants of making the temple a marketplace. But a part of it was a marketplace. The explanation of his behavior is found both in an allusion to a passage from the prophet Zechariah (14:21), who said that at the endtime there would be no need for merchants in the house of the Lord, and in a psalm text that states that zeal for God's house makes the psalmist vulnerable to the scorn and abuse of others (Psalm 69:9). By driving the merchants out of the temple precincts, Jesus announces the approach of the time of fulfillment. By identifying God as his Father, Jesus affirms his right to make such a claim and to act in accord with it.

✥ Reflecting on the Word

As a boy, I loved this Gospel story. Suddenly Jesus was a superhero. Watch out, Clark Kent! Gentle Jesus is now revealed as Super-J! Red with rage, one strong arm cracking that whip while the other overturns the tables. Sheep and oxen scattering, doves heading for the highest columns of the temple, coins spilling down the steps, some merchants cowering, others heading out the gate. Kapow! Kazaam!

Age has brought me a more refined understanding of this scene. Recorded in all four Gospels, John places it closer to the beginning of Jesus' ministry, rather than during his last days. Some see it as the act of a prophet enraged at the commercialization of the house of the Lord; others as a sign of the coming of the messianic age when anything inappropriate to the true nature of the temple as a place for encountering God will be purged and purified.

For our reflection during Lent, we might take it as a wake-up call to all the compromises we have settled for in our lives that are unworthy of our being the temple of God's Holy Spirit, made so by baptism. In light of the first reading reminding us of God's covenant with Israel at Mt. Sinai, we too are called to live lives that honor God as our only God and to live with all others in a just and loving manner. We do this when we proclaim Christ crucified in our own bodies by living for others.

- How do you react to this portrayal of Jesus cleansing the temple?
- How do you relate this action to the final words today about Jesus not trusting himself to those who were beginning to believe in his name because he "understood human nature well"?

❖ Responding to the Word

Lord Jesus, you call us to live as children of the Father, offering our very lives as a spiritual sacrifice. We do this when we replace our selfish desires with a willingness to listen to the cries of the poor. Continue to shape us into your dwelling place in our world.

March 11, 2012

THIRD SUNDAY OF LENT, YEAR A

Today's Focus: The Woman of Sychar

The Year A readings provide an opportunity to spend time with three important charac-
ters from the Gospel of John, each of whom experienced Jesus in a unique way. Each can
speak to us, encouraging and challenging us. Today we listen to the woman at the well.

FIRST
READING
Exodus 17:3–7

In those days, in their thirst for water, the people grumbled against Moses, saying, "Why did you ever make us leave Egypt? Was it just to have us die here of thirst with our children and our livestock?" So Moses cried out to the LORD, "What shall I do with this people? A little more and they will stone me!" The LORD answered Moses, "Go over there in front of the people, along with some of the elders of Israel, holding in your hand, as you go, the staff with which you struck the river. I will be standing there in front of you on the rock in Horeb. Strike the rock, and the water will flow from it for the people to drink." This Moses did, in the presence of the elders of Israel. The place was called Massah and Meribah, because the Israelites quarreled there and tested the LORD, saying, "Is the LORD in our midst or not?"

PSALM
RESPONSE
Psalm 95:8

If today you hear his voice, harden not your hearts.

SECOND
READING
Romans 5:1–2,
5–8

Brothers and sisters: Since we have been justified by faith, we have peace with God through our Lord Jesus Christ, through whom we have gained access by faith to this grace in which we stand, and we boast in hope of the glory of God.

And hope does not disappoint, because the love of God has been poured out into our hearts through the Holy Spirit who has been given to us. For Christ, while we were still helpless, died at the appointed time for the ungodly. Indeed, only with difficulty does one die for a just person, though perhaps for a good person one might even find courage to die. But God proves his love for us in that while we were still sinners Christ died for us.

In the shorter form of the reading, passages in brackets are omitted.

GOSPEL
John 4:5–42
or 4:5–15,
19b–26, 39a,
40–42

Jesus came to a town of Samaria called Sychar, near the plot of land that Jacob had given to his son Joseph. Jacob's well was there. Jesus, tired from his journey, sat down there at the well. It was about noon.

A woman of Samaria came to draw water. Jesus said to her, "Give me a drink." His disciples had gone into the town to buy food. The Samaritan woman said to him, "How can you, a Jew, ask me, a Samaritan woman, for a drink?"—For Jews use nothing in common with Samaritans—Jesus answered and said to her, "If you knew the gift of God and who is saying to you, 'Give me a drink,' you would have asked him and he would have given you living water." The woman said to him, "Sir, you do not even have a bucket and the cistern is deep; where then can you get this living water? Are you greater than our father Jacob, who gave us this cistern and drank from it himself with his children and his flocks?" Jesus answered and said to her, "Everyone who drinks this water will be thirsty again; but whoever drinks the water I shall give will never thirst; the water I shall give will become in him a spring of water welling up to eternal life." The woman said to him, "Sir, give me this water, so that I may not be thirsty or have to keep coming here to draw water."

[Jesus said to her, "Go call your husband and come back." The woman answered and said to him, "I do not have a husband." Jesus answered her, "You are right in saying, 'I do not have a husband.' For you have had five husbands, and the one you have now is not your husband. What you have said is true." The woman said to him, "Sir,] I can see that you are a prophet. Our ancestors worshiped on this mountain; but you people say that the place to worship is in Jerusalem." Jesus said to her, "Believe me, woman, the hour is coming when you will worship the Father neither on this mountain nor in Jerusalem. You people worship what you do not understand; we worship what we understand, because salvation is from the Jews. But the hour is coming, and is now here, when true worshipers will worship the Father in Spirit and truth; and indeed the Father seeks such people to worship him. God is Spirit, and those who worship him must worship in Spirit and truth."

The woman said to him, "I know that the Messiah is coming, the one called the Christ; when he comes, he will tell us everything." Jesus said to her, "I am he, the one speaking with you."

[At that moment his disciples returned, and were amazed that he was talking with a woman, but still no one said, "What are you looking for?" or "Why are you talking with her?" The woman left her water jar and went into the town and said to the people, "Come see a man who told me everything I have done. Could he possibly be the Christ?" They went out of the town and came to him. Meanwhile, the disciples urged him, "Rabbi, eat." But he said to them, "I have food to eat of which you do not know." So the disciples said to one another, "Could someone have brought him something to eat?" Jesus said to them, "My food is to do the will of the one who sent me and to finish his work. Do you not say, 'In four months the harvest will be here'? I tell you, look up and see the fields ripe for the harvest. The reaper is already receiving payment and gathering crops for eternal life, so that the sower and reaper can rejoice together. For here the saying is verified that 'One sows and another reaps.' I sent you to reap what you have not worked for; others have done the work, and you are sharing the fruits of their work."]

Many of the Samaritans of that town began to believe in him
[because of the word of the woman who testified, "He told me
everything I have done."] When the Samaritans came to him, they
invited him to stay with them; and he stayed there two days. Many
more began to believe in him because of his word, and they said
to the woman, "We no longer believe because of your word; for we
have heard for ourselves, and we know that this is truly the savior
of the world."

✥ Understanding the Word

God responds to the people's murmuring with the miracle of water from the
rock. These were the very people whom God had miraculously delivered out of
Egyptian bondage. Yet they suggest that their rescue was done, not out of God's
loving-kindness, but so that they will die of thirst in the wilderness. In their inso-
lence they cry out their challenge: "Is the LORD in our midst or not?" (Exodus 17:7).
Since the people did not recognize God's reassurance in the signs and wonders of
the past, God performs yet another one. Why does God endure such thankless-
ness, rebellion, and audacity? Because God is kind and merciful.

Paul tells the Christians in Rome that they have not justified themselves. Any
righteousness they might possess originates in God. In fact, they were sinners,
alienated from God, when Christ died for them and gained access for them to the
grace that placed them in right relationship with God. Through his sacrifice, Jesus
opened the way for them to approach God. They may have been brought by Jesus
to the threshold of God's presence, but they themselves must take the step over
that threshold. They do this by faith. With this step of faith they no longer stand
in enmity; they now stand in grace, in peace with God. This is true righteousness.

The story of Jesus' encounter with the Samaritan woman includes the discourse
on living water. He asks for water when in fact he is the one who will give water.
"Living water" refers to divine bounty, suggesting that this living water seems
to have a very special character. The living water metaphor itself has a long and
rich history in the religious tradition of Israel. It was a gift from God when the
people were thirsting in the wilderness (Exodus 17:3–7). The prophets employed
it to refer to the spiritual refreshment that flowed from the temple (Ezekiel 47:1;
Zechariah 14:80). In each of these instances, living water is a principle of spiritual
life.

✥ Reflecting on the Word

When I saw him coming, I was afraid. I had just dropped my bucket into the
well and was pulling it up. What was a Jew doing here? Sychar was not a stopover
for the Jews. It was in Samaritan territory. Jews hated Samaritans, and the feeling
was returned. This went back centuries.

I could tell he was tired. It was almost noon and a scorching day. When he asked for a drink, I couldn't refuse. Even so, I asked him, "How can you, a Jew and a man, ask me, a Samaritan and a woman, for a drink?" "You have the bucket," he said, smiling.

As I was handing him a ladle of water, he said: "If you knew who was saying, 'Give me a drink,' you would have asked me for one." I just stared at this riddle-maker. Then I pointed out the facts: I had the bucket and the well was deep. End of discussion.

But it wasn't. He began to talk about water that satisfies thirst and water that doesn't. And then he said, "Whoever drinks the water I give will never thirst. I will give them water that gushes up into eternal life."

You know, I believed him. I can't explain why. That's not all he said that day. We talked about my life, his work, and a day when Jews and Samaritans would be able to worship together. That was really a dream, I told him. But it wasn't. After his death—and resurrection—it came about. It turned out he was living water after all.

❖ Consider/Discuss

- What do you thirst for?
- How is Jesus life-giving water for you?

❖ Responding to the Word

Jesus, you are life-giving water that quenches our soul's thirst. You continue to meet us during our days, speaking to us so we might know you and what you would do for us. Like the Samaritan woman, may we welcome you and speak to you from our hearts.

March 18, 2012

FOURTH SUNDAY OF LENT, YEAR B

Today's Focus: Going in the Right Direction

God's mercy draws us heavenward. We can mistakenly assume we do not have to do our part. Just as the people in the desert needed to lift up their eyes to see the serpent, we must look with faith on Christ crucified and respond to the mercy of God.

FIRST READING
2 Chronicles 36:14–16, 19–23

In those days, all the princes of Judah, the priests, and the people added infidelity to infidelity, practicing all the abominations of the nations and polluting the LORD's temple which he had consecrated in Jerusalem.

Early and often did the LORD, the God of their fathers, send his messengers to them, for he had compassion on his people and his dwelling place. But they mocked the messengers of God, despised his warnings, and scoffed at his prophets, until the anger of the LORD against his people was so inflamed that there was no remedy. Their enemies burnt the house of God, tore down the walls of Jerusalem, set all its palaces afire, and destroyed all its precious objects. Those who escaped the sword were carried captive to Babylon, where they became servants of the king of the Chaldeans and his sons until the kingdom of the Persians came to power. All this was to fulfill the word of the LORD spoken by Jeremiah: "Until the land has retrieved its lost sabbaths, during all the time it lies waste it shall have rest while seventy years are fulfilled."

In the first year of Cyrus, king of Persia, in order to fulfill the word of the LORD spoken by Jeremiah, the LORD inspired King Cyrus of Persia to issue this proclamation throughout his kingdom, both by word of mouth and in writing: "Thus says Cyrus, king of Persia: All the kingdoms of the earth the LORD, the God of heaven, has given to me, and he has also charged me to build him a house in Jerusalem, which is in Judah. Whoever, therefore, among you belongs to any part of his people, let him go up, and may his God be with him!"

PSALM RESPONSE
Psalm 137:6ab

Let my tongue be silenced, if I ever forget you!

SECOND READING
Ephesians 2:4–10

Brothers and sisters: God, who is rich in mercy, because of the great love he had for us, even when we were dead in our transgressions, brought us to life with Christ—by grace you have been saved—, raised us up with him, and seated us with him in the heavens in Christ Jesus, that in the ages to come he might show the immeasurable riches of his grace in his kindness to us in Christ Jesus. For by grace you have been saved through faith, and this is not from you; it is the gift of God; it is not from works, so no one may boast. For we are his handiwork, created in Christ Jesus for the good works that God has prepared in advance, that we should live in them.

GOSPEL
John 3:14–21

Jesus said to Nicodemus: "Just as Moses lifted up the serpent in the desert, so must the Son of Man be lifted up, so that everyone who believes in him may have eternal life."

For God so loved the world that he gave his only Son, so that everyone who believes in him might not perish but might have eternal life. For God did not send his Son into the world to condemn the world, but that the world might be saved through him. Whoever believes in him will not be condemned, but whoever does not believe has already been condemned, because he has not believed in the name of the only Son of God. And this is the verdict, that the light came into the world, but people preferred darkness to light, because their works were evil. For everyone who does wicked things hates the light and does not come toward the light, so that his works might not be exposed. But whoever lives the truth comes to the light, so that his works may be clearly seen as done in God.

❖ *Understanding the Word*

The first reading is quite poignant as it describes how, despite the sinfulness of the people, God was moved to compassion. Again and again prophets were sent to this corrupt nation, but to no avail. Not only did the people ignore the prophets, they actively derided them. Because of this callous contempt, the avenging anger of God was unleashed. The demise of the monarchy, the collapse of the temple system of worship, and the deportation of the people were the inevitable consequences of this hardhearted obstinacy. The reading ends on a note of hope. The people are told to return to Jerusalem and rebuild the temple.

The image of God that is sketched in the first verses of the reading from Ephesians is very dynamic. God is rich in mercy; has great love for us; has brought us to life, raised us up, and seated us with Christ in glory. Unable to save ourselves, we receive our salvation as a pure gift from God. The contrast between the graciousness of God and human inadequacy is drawn in bold strokes. When we were dead in sin, God made us alive in Christ. Why? Not because we deserved it, but because God is rich in mercy, because God loves us.

Jesus declares that just as healing came to those who looked on the bronze serpent that Moses raised up (Numbers 21:8–9), so life eternal comes to those who believe in the Son of Man, who was raised up in both ignomy and exaltation. Although the world was created good, it often stands in opposition to God and consequently is in need of being saved. God's love for the world is so deep that nothing is spared for its salvation, not even God's only Son. This Son, Jesus Christ, is the true light, and those who choose him live in that light, or live in the truth; those who do not believe are in darkness.

❖ Reflecting on the Word

You rarely hear anyone use the word "hellbent" these days, but it could easily be used to describe the Jewish people before the Babylonian empire destroyed their capital city of Jerusalem in 587 B.C., along with the temple, and then sent its people into exile. Second Chronicles tells a sad story: Judah's princes, priests, and people had all turned away from the Lord. They had become a people hellbent on self-destruction. So finally, the Lord cut them loose.

Of course, the story does not end there. A new dawn comes with the ascendancy of the Persian empire under its leader Cyrus, who looked more kindly on the Jewish people, allowing them to return home to rebuild the temple in Jerusalem. And we are reminded that the hand of a merciful God is behind this.

Ephesians also speaks of a God rich in mercy, who loved us "even when were dead in our transgressions," and who "brought us to life with Christ . . . raised us up with him, and seated us with him in the heavens in Christ Jesus" (Ephesians 2:5–6, 10). For the author of Ephesians this has already happened. It might not feel that way to us much of the time, but faith calls us to see ourselves as "God's handiwork, created in Christ Jesus."

Imagine if we tried living out of that vision for the coming week! Imagine if we really took seriously that God truly loved the world so much that "he gave his only Son" to bring us all eternal life (see John 3:16).

❖ Consider/Discuss

- Do you recognize God as a God of unending mercy who loves us—all of us?
- How can this Lent be a season of conversion for the whole community?

❖ Responding to the Word

Merciful God, you sent your Son to bring us to the fullness of life, now and hereafter. May this season of Lent be a time when we recognize increasingly what it means to choose to live in the light of Christ. Give us the courage to do so each day.

March 18, 2012

FOURTH SUNDAY OF LENT, YEAR A

Today's Focus: The Gift of Sight and Vision

In Jesus' day blindness was seen as a sign that a person, or his ancestors, had sinned. Healing the man born blind allowed Jesus to reveal himself as the light come into the world to deliver us from the darkness of sin and unbelief. Today the blind man speaks to us.

FIRST READING
1 Samuel 16:1b, 6–7, 10–13a

The LORD said to Samuel: "Fill your horn with oil, and be on your way. I am sending you to Jesse of Bethlehem, for I have chosen my king from among his sons."

As Jesse and his sons came to the sacrifice, Samuel looked at Eliab and thought, "Surely the Lord's anointed is here before him." But the LORD said to Samuel: "Do not judge from his appearance or from his lofty stature, because I have rejected him. Not as man sees does God see, because man sees the appearance but the LORD looks into the heart." In the same way Jesse presented seven sons before Samuel, but Samuel said to Jesse, "The LORD has not chosen any one of these." Then Samuel asked Jesse, "Are these all the sons you have?" Jesse replied, "There is still the youngest, who is tending the sheep." Samuel said to Jesse, "Send for him; we will not begin the sacrificial banquet until he arrives here." Jesse sent and had the young man brought to them. He was ruddy, a youth handsome to behold and making a splendid appearance. The LORD said, "There—anoint him, for this is the one!" Then Samuel, with the horn of oil in hand, anointed David in the presence of his brothers; and from that day on, the spirit of the LORD rushed upon David.

PSALM RESPONSE
Psalm 23:1

The Lord is my shepherd; there is nothing I shall want.

SECOND READING
Ephesians 5:8–14

Brothers and sisters: You were once darkness, but now you are light in the Lord. Live as children of light, for light produces every kind of goodness and righteousness and truth. Try to learn what is pleasing to the Lord. Take no part in the fruitless works of darkness; rather expose them, for it is shameful even to mention the things done by them in secret; but everything exposed by the light becomes visible, for everything that becomes visible is light. Therefore, it says:

"Awake, O sleeper,
and arise from the dead,
and Christ will give you light."

In the shorter form of the reading, passages in brackets are omitted.

GOSPEL
John 9:1–41
or 9:1, 6-9,
13–17, 34–38

As Jesus passed by he saw a man blind from birth. [His disciples asked him, "Rabbi, who sinned, this man or his parents, that he was born blind?" Jesus answered, "Neither he nor his parents sinned; it is so that the works of God might be made visible through him. We have to do the works of the one who sent me while it is day. Night is coming when no one can work. While I am in the world, I am the light of the world." When he had said this,] he spat on the ground and made clay with the saliva, and smeared the clay on his eyes, and said to him, "Go wash in the Pool of Siloam"—which means Sent—. So he went and washed, and came back able to see.

His neighbors and those who had seen him earlier as a beggar said, "Isn't this the one who used to sit and beg?" Some said, "It is, " but others said, "No, he just looks like him." He said, "I am." [So they said to him, "How were your eyes opened?" He replied, "The man called Jesus made clay and anointed my eyes and told me, 'Go to Siloam and wash.' So I went there and washed and was able to see." And they said to him, "Where is he?" He said, "I don't know."]

They brought the one who was once blind to the Pharisees. Now Jesus had made clay and opened his eyes on a sabbath. So then the Pharisees also asked him how he was able to see. He said to them, "He put clay on my eyes, and I washed, and now I can see." So some of the Pharisees said, "This man is not from God, because he does not keep the sabbath." But others said, "How can a sinful man do such signs?" And there was a division among them. So they said to the blind man again, "What do you have to say about him, since he opened your eyes?" He said, "He is a prophet."

[Now the Jews did not believe that he had been blind and gained his sight until they summoned the parents of the one who had gained his sight. They asked them, "Is this your son, who you say was born blind? How does he now see?" His parents answered and said, "We know that this is our son and that he was born blind. We do not know how he sees now, nor do we know who opened his eyes. Ask him, he is of age; he can speak for himself." His parents said this because they were afraid of the Jews, for the Jews had already agreed that if anyone acknowledged him as the Christ, he would be expelled from the synagogue. For this reason his parents said, "He is of age; question him."

So a second time they called the man who had been blind and said to him, "Give God the praise! We know that this man is a sinner." He replied, "If he is a sinner, I do not know. One thing I do know is that I was blind and now I see." So they said to him, "What did he do to you? How did he open your eyes?" He answered them, "I told you already and you did not listen. Why do you want to hear it again? Do you want to become his disciples, too?" They ridiculed him and said, "You are that man's disciple; we are disciples of Moses! We know that God spoke to Moses, but we do not know where this one is from." The man answered and said to them, "This is what is so amazing, that you do not know where he is from, yet he opened my eyes. We know that God does not listen to sinners, but if one is devout and does his will, he listens to him. It is unheard of that anyone ever opened the eyes of a person born blind. If this man were not from God, he would not be able to do anything."] They answered and said to him, "You were born totally in sin, and are you trying to teach us?" Then they threw him out.

When Jesus heard that they had thrown him out, he found him and said, "Do you believe in the Son of Man?" He answered and said, "Who is he, sir, that I may believe in him?" Jesus said to him, "You have seen him, the one speaking with you is he." He said, "I do believe, Lord, " and he worshiped him. [Then Jesus said, "I came into this world for judgment, so that those who do not see might see, and those who do see might become blind."

Some of the Pharisees who were with him heard this and said to him, "Surely we are not also blind, are we?" Jesus said to them, "If you were blind, you would have no sin; but now you are saying, 'We see,' so your sin remains."]

❖❖ *Understanding the Word*

The search for the new king and the choice and anointing of David open a new chapter in the story of the Israel. Each step of the way is determined by God, making this a history of salvation. God decided from which family the kings would come, and even which son would be chosen from that family. No one in Jesse's family even considered David as a viable candidate, but God did. It seems that God often chooses the least likely to accomplish great deeds. Once David was anointed king, the spirit of the Lord rushed upon him, confirming the choice of him to rule the people.

The binary opposition of light/darkness is a very significant theme. The Ephesians are told that before they knew Christ, they were so much a part of darkness that they were actually identified with it. Having accepted Christ, they are now identified with the light that comes from the Lord. They are told that they must now live as children of that light. There is a play on the difference between virtuous behavior that can be plainly seen, because it is done in the light, and shameful behavior that is hidden in the secret of darkness. The Ephesians are to hold fast to the new life that has been given to them and live in the light.

The account of the healing of the man born blind is filled with the symbolism of darkness/light, blindness/sight. The man was born blind and so he lived his life in darkness. However, his ultimate insight into the identity of Jesus was rewarded with the gift of sight. In a very real sense, the man is now a new creation, both physically with sight and spiritually with faith. The Pharisees, on the other hand, enjoyed the power of sight, but they were blind to the great powers exercised by Jesus. Furthermore, when given the opportunity to move into the light of faith, they chose the darkness of disbelief.

✤ Reflecting on the Word

My name is Samuel, after the great prophet who anointed our first kings, Saul and David. I used to think my parents showed their sense of humor by naming their blind son after Samuel the seer. But even he didn't always see clearly.

When Samuel went to Jesse's house that day, he thought for sure God wanted him to anoint the eldest, Eliab, tall and handsome, just like Saul had been. But God brought him up short: "No, no, no—not him!" Ended up being the youngest out in the fields tending sheep. A case of the see-er not seeing. Easy to get blinded by appearances,

I could not see Jesus, so I couldn't be blinded by his appearance, or unimpressed if he wasn't that remarkable to look at. But I could tell he had God's power in him. And a fire. After smearing mud on my eyes, he told me to wash in the pool of Siloam. I did. And I saw.

Then the trouble started. My neighbors started arguing, then the Pharisees got into it, and they got my poor parents. Well, I told them he was from God. That's when they threw me out. And suddenly I hear someone say, "Do I believe in the Son of Man?" Without any hesitation, I said: "I do believe, Lord." He said he came into the world so the blind might see and those who saw might be blind.

✤ Consider/Discuss

- Why would Jesus say he came into the world so that those who do see might become blind?
- What kind of seeing does Jesus bring about?

✤ Responding to the Word

Jesus, you are the light come into the world. Sometimes I feel lost in the dark, not sure where I am and which way to go. Enlighten my mind so I may understand more fully the direction you wish me to go in my life. Help me to see so I can serve you.

March 25, 2012

FIFTH SUNDAY OF LENT, YEAR B

Today's Focus: A Heart Renewed

We focus one final time on the word covenant in the reading from the prophet Jeremiah. God speaks of making a new covenant with the people by writing God's law on their hearts. We hear the heart of Jesus being formed as he yields to the hour that has finally come.

FIRST READING
Jeremiah 31:31–34

The days are coming, says the LORD, when I will make a new covenant with the house of Israel and the house of Judah. It will not be like the covenant I made with their fathers the day I took them by the hand to lead them forth from the land of Egypt; for they broke my covenant, and I had to show myself their master, says the LORD. But this is the covenant that I will make with the house of Israel after those days, says the LORD. I will place my law within them and write it upon their hearts; I will be their God, and they shall be my people. No longer will they have need to teach their friends and relatives how to know the LORD. All, from least to greatest, shall know me, says the LORD, for I will forgive their evildoing and remember their sin no more.

PSALM RESPONSE
Psalm 51:12a

Create a clean heart in me, O God.

SECOND READING
Hebrews 5:7–9

In the days when Christ Jesus was in the flesh, he offered prayers and supplications with loud cries and tears to the one who was able to save him from death, and he was heard because of his reverence. Son though he was, he learned obedience from what he suffered; and when he was made perfect, he became the source of eternal salvation for all who obey him.

GOSPEL
John 12:20–33

Some Greeks who had come to worship at the Passover Feast came to Philip, who was from Bethsaida in Galilee, and asked him, "Sir, we would like to see Jesus." Philip went and told Andrew; then Andrew and Philip went and told Jesus. Jesus answered them, "The hour has come for the Son of Man to be glorified. Amen, amen, I say to you, unless a grain of wheat falls to the ground and dies, it remains just a grain of wheat; but if it dies, it produces much fruit. Whoever loves his life loses it, and whoever hates his life in this world will preserve it for eternal life. Whoever serves me must follow me, and where I am, there also will my servant be. The Father will honor whoever serves me.

"I am troubled now. Yet what should I say? 'Father, save me from this hour'? But it was for this purpose that I came to this hour. Father, glorify your name." Then a voice came from heaven, "I have glorified it and will glorify it again." The crowd there heard it and said it was thunder; but others said, "An angel has spoken to him." Jesus answered and said, "This voice did not come for my sake but for yours. Now is the time of judgment on this world; now the ruler of this world will be driven out. And when I am lifted up from the earth, I will draw everyone to myself." He said this indicating the kind of death he would die.

❖ Understanding the Word

Although Jeremiah was a southern prophet who prophesied long after the collapse of the northern kingdom, his message was full of promise for both northern and southern kingdoms. He announced that in the future time of eschatological fulfillment, both kingdoms would be united once again in a new covenant. The old covenant included laws inscribed on stone tablets; the law of the new covenant will be written on their hearts. Each individual will be directed from within. This will require total openness to God and the ability to discern God's will from a myriad of possibilities.

The passage from Hebrews states that Jesus endured torment of body and anguish of soul. He can fully understand human distress and the desire to escape it. He can speak to those in affliction as one who himself was ravaged by sorrow, but who nonetheless clung fast to God's will. From a human point of view, he is one with the human condition. From God's point of view, he is the one who can show others how to accept with docility circumstances over which they have no control. Just as he learned to accept God's designs in his life, so now he teaches others to do the same.

The Gospel reading reports the approach of "some Greeks." This mention of Greeks suggests the inclusion of the Gentile world in the salvation brought by Jesus. Jesus replies to their approach with an announcement: His hour has come! This is both the hour of his glorification and the hour that he dreads. The relationship between his anguish and his exaltation is demonstrated through the image of the grain of wheat that must die if it is to rise. The interior struggle that Jesus endured is revealed in his prayer. Should he ask to be preserved from this hour of anguish/exaltation? But it was for this hour that he came into the world in the first place. Therefore, he accepts it.

✤ Reflecting on the Word

One of the earliest pictures of Jesus I can remember portrayed him at prayer in the garden of Gethsemane. I still see his hands, clasped tight. They spoke to me of an inner struggle long before I knew about his words, "Father, all things are possible to you. Take this cup away from me, but not what I will but what you will" (Mark 14:36). More than any other scene in the Gospels, this one brought home what it meant to say Jesus was truly man.

Today's Gospel has been called John's version of the agony in the garden. The word agony (*agonia* in Greek) means struggle, and we can hear the struggle in Jesus' awareness that "the hour" he has spoken of before in John's Gospel, beginning at Cana, has finally arrived. It is the hour of his being lifted up—the hour of both his glory and his crucifixion. It is why he came into the world, and yet we hear him say, "I am troubled." We hear him wrestling with himself, asking for release from the hour, but then recognizing that it holds "the purpose for which I came."

Hebrews affirms this when it says "he offered prayers and supplications with loud cries and tears to the one able to save him from death, and he was heard because of his reverence" (5:7). He was able to bear the suffering and become the source of eternal salvation for all who listen to him and follow in his steps.

✤ Consider/Discuss

- Do you desire a new heart? What would be different about it?
- How do Jesus' words about the seed falling into the ground, dying, and only then producing fruit challenge you? What needs to die in you?

✤ Responding to the Word

Loving God, give us a new heart in these final days of Lent, a heart that carries within it your loving imprint, that we may always know your will and yield to it, even when it calls for a dying of some kind. In such dying, may we trust that you will bring forth new life.

March 25, 2012

FIFTH SUNDAY OF LENT, YEAR A

Today's Focus: A Sister Speaks

The final witness in the Year A readings is Martha, sister of Lazarus and Mary. In one of the greatest Gospel stories, Lazarus is already in the tomb three days when Martha goes to Jesus to beg him to bring her dead brother back to life. Today she reflects on that occasion.

FIRST READING
Ezekiel 37: 12–14

Thus says the LORD GOD: O my people, I will open your graves and have you rise from them, and bring you back to the land of Israel. Then you shall know that I am the LORD, when I open your graves and have you rise from them, O my people! I will put my spirit in you that you may live, and I will settle you upon your land; thus you shall know that I am the LORD. I have promised, and I will do it, says the LORD.

PSALM RESPONSE
Psalm 130:7

With the Lord there is mercy and fullness of redemption.

SECOND READING
Romans 8:8–11

Brothers and sisters: Those who are in the flesh cannot please God. But you are not in the flesh; on the contrary, you are in the spirit, if only the Spirit of God dwells in you. Whoever does not have the Spirit of Christ does not belong to him. But if Christ is in you, although the body is dead because of sin, the spirit is alive because of righteousness. If the Spirit of the one who raised Jesus from the dead dwells in you, the one who raised Christ from the dead will give life to your mortal bodies also, through his Spirit dwelling in you.

In the shorter form of the reading, passages in brackets are omitted.

GOSPEL
John 11:1–45 or 11:3–7, 17, 20–27, 33b–45

[Now a man was ill, Lazarus from Bethany, the village of Mary and her sister Martha. Mary was the one who had anointed the Lord with perfumed oil and dried his feet with her hair; it was her brother Lazarus who was ill. So] the sisters sent word to Jesus saying, "Master, the one you love is ill." When Jesus heard this he said,
"This illness is not to end in death,
but is for the glory of God,
that the Son of God may be glorified through it."
Now Jesus loved Martha and her sister and Lazarus. So when he heard that he was ill, he remained for two days in the place where he was. Then after this he said to his disciples, "Let us go back to Judea." [The disciples said to him, "Rabbi, the Jews were just trying to stone you, and you want to go back there?" Jesus answered,

"Are there not twelve hours in a day? If one walks during the day, he does not stumble, because he sees the light of this world. But if one walks at night, he stumbles, because the light is not in him." He said this, and then told them, "Our friend Lazarus is asleep, but I am going to awaken him." So the disciples said to him, "Master, if he is asleep, he will be saved." But Jesus was talking about his death, while they thought that he meant ordinary sleep. So then Jesus said to them clearly, "Lazarus has died. And I am glad for you that I was not there, that you may believe. Let us go to him." So Thomas, called Didymus, said to his fellow disciples, "Let us also go to die with him."]

When Jesus arrived, he found that Lazarus had already been in the tomb for four days. [Now Bethany was near Jerusalem, only about two miles away. And many of the Jews had come to Martha and Mary to comfort them about their brother.] When Martha heard that Jesus was coming, she went to meet him; but Mary sat at home. Martha said to Jesus, "Lord, if you had been here, my brother would not have died. But even now I know that whatever you ask of God, God will give you." Jesus said to her, "Your brother will rise." Martha said to him, "I know he will rise, in the resurrection on the last day." Jesus told her,

"I am the resurrection and the life;
whoever believes in me, even if he dies, will live,
and everyone who lives and believes in me will never die.
Do you believe this?" She said to him, "Yes, Lord. I have come to believe that you are the Christ, the Son of God, the one who is coming into the world."

[When she had said this, she went and called her sister Mary secretly, saying, "The teacher is here and is asking for you." As soon as she heard this, she rose quickly and went to him. For Jesus had not yet come into the village, but was still where Martha had met him. So when the Jews who were with her in the house comforting her saw Mary get up quickly and go out, they followed her, presuming that she was going to the tomb to weep there. When Mary came to where Jesus was and saw him, she fell at his feet and said to him, "Lord, if you had been here, my brother would not have died." When] Jesus [saw her weeping and the Jews who had come with her weeping, he] became perturbed and deeply troubled, and said, "Where have you laid him?" They said to him, "Sir, come and see." And Jesus wept. So the Jews said, "See how he loved him." But some of them said, "Could not the one who opened the eyes of the blind man have done something so that this man would not have died?"

So Jesus, perturbed again, came to the tomb. It was a cave, and a stone lay across it. Jesus said, "Take away the stone." Martha, the dead man's sister, said to him, "Lord, by now there will be a stench; he has been dead for four days." Jesus said to her, "Did I not tell you that if you believe you will see the glory of God?" So they took away the stone. And Jesus raised his eyes and said,

"Father, I thank you for hearing me.
I know that you always hear me;
but because of the crowd here I have said this,
that they may believe that you sent me."
And when he had said this, he cried out in a loud voice, "Lazarus, come out!" The dead man came out, tied hand and foot with burial bands, and his face was wrapped in a cloth. So Jesus said to them, "Untie him and let him go."

Now many of the Jews who had come to Mary and seen what he had done began to believe in him.

✤ Understanding the Word

The passage from Ezekiel testifies to God's absolute and unconditional control over the powers of life and death, over destruction and restoration. The prophet employs the metaphor of the restoration of life to dead bodies to illustrate the unbelievable nature of the restoration of the nation. The people probably thought that neither restoration was possible. However, the prophet is insisting that anything is possible with God. If God says it, regardless of how incredible it might appear, it will surely happen. This decisiveness is underscored in the last words of the passage, "I have promised, and I will do it" (37:14).

Paul contrasts two ways of living: life in the flesh and life in the spirit. Life in the flesh (limited human nature) cannot please God. Life in the spirit, on the other hand, is a form of union with God. Paul assures the Christians that they are in the spirit if the Spirit of God dwells within them. In true Trinitarian fashion, he likens the Spirit of God to the Spirit of Christ, and he maintains that it is through this Spirit that resurrection is promised. The Spirit of God raised Jesus, and that same Spirit will raise those who live in the Spirit of Christ.

The death and resurrection of Lazarus point to the future death and resurrection of Jesus and of everyone who believes in him. When Jesus told Martha that her brother would rise, she probably thought that he meant at the general resurrection, a position taught by the Pharisees. Jesus then declared, "I am the resurrection and the life" (John 11:25). The meaning of this claim is the heart of Jesus' teaching here. Belief in Jesus establishes a bond of life that not even death can sever. Although believers die physically, this bond will bring them back to life. Furthermore, this bond will survive physical death and keep believers from an eternal death. A solemn question is posed: "Do you believe?"

So, I'm pushy. At least that's what Mary was always telling me. "Martha, you don't have to say everything that comes into your mind," she would whisper. Like the time when she left me to do all the work in the kitchen while she plopped herself down at Jesus' feet. No sense going into that—you know the story.

But this time being pushy paid off. Our younger and only brother had taken ill with fever. We waited to send word, thinking it would pass, but then early one morning, our beloved Lazarus died. We were heartbroken. He was our protector, our friend, the apple of both our eyes. Never to hear his voice, or pretend annoyance at his silly jokes at our expense. Neither of us could stop crying.

As soon as word came that Jesus had reached the outskirts of the village, I went out to him. I was beside myself with grief: "Where were you? Why didn't you come? If you had, he would not have died." My anger and sorrow broke against him like waves during a summer storm. He listened, then spoke: "He will rise again." "Yes, I know . . . on the last day." His eyes looked into my soul: "I am the resurrection and the life; whoever lives and believes in me will never die, and everyone who lives and believes in me will never die. Do you believe this?"

That is the question, isn't it? Do you believe his words? Do you believe him? Do you believe he is the resurrection and life? Well, do you?

❖ Consider/Discuss

- Is there anything you want to ask Martha? Or say to her?
- What does it mean to believe Jesus is the resurrection and the life?

❖ Responding to the Word

Lord, death seems so merciless, so final. It is hard to believe life can ever be restored. Help us to trust your word and the promise of the Father that death will not be victorious. Help us to place our trust in you as the Lord of life.

April 1, 2012

PALM SUNDAY OF THE PASSION OF THE LORD

Today's Focus: The Purpose of the Palm

As we move from blessing palms to listening to the Passion to praising and giving thanks for the Lord's saving death and resurrection, the human heart can choose to cry "Hosanna." The palm invites us to recognize Jesus as the one who comes in the name of the Lord.

FIRST READING
Isaiah 50:4–7

The Lord GOD has given me
    a well-trained tongue,
that I might know how to speak to the weary
    a word that will rouse them.
Morning after morning
    he opens my ear that I may hear;
and I have not rebelled,
    have not turned back.
I gave my back to those who beat me,
    my cheeks to those who plucked my beard;
my face I did not shield
    from buffets and spitting.

The Lord GOD is my help,
    therefore I am not disgraced;
I have set my face like flint,
    knowing that I shall not be put to shame.

PSALM RESPONSE
Psalm 22:2a

My God, my God, why have you abandoned me?

SECOND READING
Philippians 2:6–11

Christ Jesus, though he was in the form of God,
    did not regard equality with God
    something to be grasped.
Rather, he emptied himself,
    taking the form of a slave,
    coming in human likeness;
    and found human in appearance,
    he humbled himself,
    becoming obedient to the point of death,
    even death on a cross.

Because of this, God greatly exalted him
  and bestowed on him the name
  which is above every name,
  that at the name of Jesus
  every knee should bend,
  of those in heaven and on earth and under the earth,
  and every tongue confess that
  Jesus Christ is Lord,
  to the glory of God the Father.

In the shorter form of the reading, passages in brackets are omitted.

GOSPEL
Mark 14:1 —
15:47 or
15:1–39

[The Passover and the Feast of Unleavened Bread were to take place in two days' time. So the chief priests and the scribes were seeking a way to arrest him by treachery and put him to death. They said, "Not during the festival, for fear that there may be a riot among the people."

When he was in Bethany reclining at table in the house of Simon the leper, a woman came with an alabaster jar of perfumed oil, costly genuine spikenard. She broke the alabaster jar and poured it on his head. There were some who were indignant. "Why has there been this waste of perfumed oil? It could have been sold for more than three hundred days' wages and the money given to the poor." They were infuriated with her. Jesus said, "Let her alone. Why do you make trouble for her? She has done a good thing for me. The poor you will always have with you, and whenever you wish you can do good to them, but you will not always have me. She has done what she could. She has anticipated anointing my body for burial. Amen, I say to you, wherever the gospel is proclaimed to the whole world, what she has done will be told in memory of her."

Then Judas Iscariot, one of the Twelve, went off to the chief priests to hand him over to them. When they heard him they were pleased and promised to pay him money. Then he looked for an opportunity to hand him over.

On the first day of the Feast of Unleavened Bread, when they sacrificed the Passover lamb, his disciples said to him, "Where do you want us to go and prepare for you to eat the Passover?" He sent two of his disciples and said to them, "Go into the city and a man will meet you, carrying a jar of water. Follow him. Wherever he enters, say to the master of the house, 'The Teacher says, "Where is my guest room where I may eat the Passover with my disciples?" ' Then he will show you a large upper room furnished and ready. Make the preparations for us there." The disciples then went off, entered the city, and found it just as he had told them; and they prepared the Passover.

When it was evening, he came with the Twelve. And as they reclined at table and were eating, Jesus said, "Amen, I say to you, one of you will betray me, one who is eating with me." They began to be distressed and to say to him, one by one, "Surely it is not I?" He said to them, "One of the Twelve, the one who dips with me into the dish. For the Son of Man indeed goes, as it is written of him, but woe to that man by whom the Son of Man is betrayed. It would be better for that man if he had never been born."

While they were eating, he took bread, said the blessing, broke it, and gave it to them, and said, "Take it; this is my body." Then he took a cup, gave thanks, and gave it to them, and they all drank from it. He said to them, "This is my blood of the covenant, which will be shed for many. Amen, I say to you, I shall not drink again the fruit of the vine until the day when I drink it new in the kingdom of God." Then, after singing a hymn, they went out to the Mount of Olives.

Then Jesus said to them, "All of you will have your faith shaken, for it is written:

I *will strike the shepherd,*
  and the sheep will be dispersed.

But after I have been raised up, I shall go before you to Galilee." Peter said to him, "Even though all should have their faith shaken, mine will not be." Then Jesus said to him, "Amen, I say to you, this very night before the cock crows twice you will deny me three times." But he vehemently replied, "Even though I should have to die with you, I will not deny you." And they all spoke similarly.

Then they came to a place named Gethsemane, and he said to his disciples, "Sit here while I pray." He took with him Peter, James, and John, and began to be troubled and distressed. Then he said to them, "My soul is sorrowful even to death. Remain here and keep watch." He advanced a little and fell to the ground and prayed that if it were possible the hour might pass by him; he said, "Abba, Father, all things are possible to you. Take this cup away from me, but not what I will but what you will." When he returned he found them asleep. He said to Peter, "Simon, are you asleep? Could you not keep watch for one hour? Watch and pray that you may not undergo the test. The spirit is willing but the flesh is weak." Withdrawing again, he prayed, saying the same thing. Then he returned once more and found them asleep, for they could not keep their eyes open and did not know what to answer him. He returned a third time and said to them, "Are you still sleeping and taking your rest? It is enough. The hour has come. Behold, the Son of Man is to be handed over to sinners. Get up, let us go. See, my betrayer is at hand."

Then, while he was still speaking, Judas, one of the Twelve, arrived, accompanied by a crowd with swords and clubs who had come from the chief priests, the scribes, and the elders. His betrayer had arranged a signal with them, saying, "The man I shall kiss is the one; arrest him and lead him away securely." He came and immediately went over to him and said, "Rabbi." And he kissed him. At this they laid hands on him and arrested him. One of the bystanders drew his sword, struck the high priest's servant, and cut off his ear. Jesus said to them in reply, "Have you come out as against a robber, with swords and clubs, to seize me? Day after day I was with you teaching in the temple area, yet you did not arrest me; but that the Scriptures may be fulfilled." And they all left him and fled. Now a young man followed him wearing nothing but a linen cloth about his body. They seized him, but he left the cloth behind and ran off naked.

They led Jesus away to the high priest, and all the chief priests and the elders and the scribes came together. Peter followed him at a distance into the high priest's courtyard and was seated with the guards, warming himself at the fire. The chief priests and the entire Sanhedrin kept trying to obtain testimony against Jesus in order to put him to death, but they found none. Many gave false witness against him, but their testimony did not agree. Some took the stand and testified falsely against him, alleging, "We heard him say, 'I will destroy this temple made with hands and within three days I will build another not made with hands.' " Even so their testimony did not agree. The high priest rose before the assembly and questioned Jesus, saying, "Have you no answer? What are these men testifying against you?" But he was silent and answered nothing. Again the high priest asked him and said to him, "Are you the Christ, the son of the Blessed One?" Then Jesus answered, "I am;

and 'you will see the Son of Man
    seated at the right hand of the Power
    and coming with the clouds of heaven.' "

At that the high priest tore his garments and said, "What further need have we of witnesses? You have heard the blasphemy. What do you think?" They all condemned him as deserving to die. Some began to spit on him. They blindfolded him and struck him and said to him, "Prophesy!" And the guards greeted him with blows.

While Peter was below in the courtyard, one of the high priest's maids came along. Seeing Peter warming himself, she looked intently at him and said, "You too were with the Nazarene, Jesus." But he denied it saying, "I neither know nor understand what you are talking about." So he went out into the outer court. Then the cock crowed. The maid saw him and began again to say to the bystanders, "This man is one of them." Once again he denied it. A little later the bystanders said to Peter once more, "Surely you are one of them; for you too are a Galilean." He began to curse and to swear, "I do not know this man about whom you are talking." And immediately a cock crowed a second time. Then Peter remembered the word that Jesus had said to him, "Before the cock crows twice you will deny me three times." He broke down and wept.]

As soon as morning came, the chief priests with the elders and the scribes, that is, the whole Sanhedrin, held a council. They bound Jesus, led him away, and handed him over to Pilate. Pilate questioned him, "Are you the king of the Jews?" He said to him in reply, "You say so." The chief priests accused him of many things. Again Pilate questioned him, "Have you no answer? See how many things they accuse you of." Jesus gave him no further answer, so that Pilate was amazed.

Now on the occasion of the feast he used to release to them one prisoner whom they requested. A man called Barabbas was then in prison along with the rebels who had committed murder in a rebellion. The crowd came forward and began to ask him to do for them as he was accustomed. Pilate answered, "Do you want me to release to you the king of the Jews?" For he knew that it was out of envy that the chief priests had handed him over. But the chief priests stirred up the crowd to have him release Barabbas for them instead. Pilate again said to them in reply, "Then what do you want me to do with the man you call the king of the Jews?" They shouted again, "Crucify him." Pilate said to them, "Why? What evil has he done?" They only shouted the louder, "Crucify him." So Pilate, wishing to satisfy the crowd, released Barabbas to them and, after he had Jesus scourged, handed him over to be crucified.

The soldiers led him away inside the palace, that is, the praetorium, and assembled the whole cohort. They clothed him in purple and, weaving a crown of thorns, placed it on him. They began to salute him with, "Hail, King of the Jews!" and kept striking his head with a reed and spitting upon him. They knelt before him in homage. And when they had mocked him, they stripped him of the purple cloak, dressed him in his own clothes, and led him out to crucify him.

They pressed into service a passer-by, Simon, a Cyrenian, who was coming in from the country, the father of Alexander and Rufus, to carry his cross.

They brought him to the place of Golgotha—which is translated Place of the Skull—. They gave him wine drugged with myrrh, but he did not take it. Then they crucified him and divided his garments by casting lots for them to see what each should take. It was nine o'clock in the morning when they crucified him. The inscription of the charge against him read, "The King of the Jews." With him they crucified two revolutionaries, one on his right and one on his left. Those passing by reviled him, shaking their heads and saying, "Aha! You who would destroy the temple and rebuild it in three days, save yourself by coming down from the cross." Likewise the chief priests, with the scribes, mocked him among themselves and said, "He saved others; he cannot save himself. Let the Christ, the King of Israel, come down now from the cross that we may see and believe." Those who were crucified with him also kept abusing him.

At noon darkness came over the whole land until three in the afternoon. And at three o'clock Jesus cried out in a loud voice, "*Eloi, Eloi, lema sabachthani?*" which is translated, "My God, my God, why have you forsaken me?" Some of the bystanders who heard it said, "Look, he is calling Elijah." One of them ran, soaked a sponge with wine, put it on a reed and gave it to him to drink, saying, "Wait, let us see if Elijah comes to take him down." Jesus gave a loud cry and breathed his last.

The veil of the sanctuary was torn in two from top to bottom. When the centurion who stood facing him saw how he breathed his last he said, "Truly this man was the Son of God!" [There were also women looking on from a distance. Among them were Mary Magdalene, Mary the mother of the younger James and of Joses, and Salome. These women had followed him when he was in Galilee and ministered to him. There were also many other women who had come up with him to Jerusalem.

When it was already evening, since it was the day of preparation, the day before the sabbath, Joseph of Arimathea, a distinguished member of the council, who was himself awaiting the kingdom of God, came and courageously went to Pilate and asked for the body of Jesus. Pilate was amazed that he was already dead. He summoned the centurion and asked him if Jesus had already died. And when he learned of it from the centurion, he gave the body to Joseph. Having bought a linen cloth, he took him down, wrapped him in the linen cloth, and laid him in a tomb that had been hewn out of the rock. Then he rolled a stone against the entrance to the tomb. Mary Magdalene and Mary the mother of Joses watched where he was laid.]

❖ Understanding the Word

The prophet's ability to speak and the words that are spoken all come from God, but they are given for the sake of the weary. The speaker suffers both physical attack and personal insult. Despite this, he does not recoil from his call. He willingly accepts what appears to be the consequence of his prophetic ministry to the weary. In the face of his affliction, he maintains that God is his strength. For this reason, he declares that he is not disgraced and he will not be put to shame. There are no grounds to make these claims other than utter confidence in God.

The Philippians hymn states that though in the form of God, Christ chose the form of a slave. Without losing his Godlike being, he took on the likeness of human beings. He did not merely resemble a human being, he really was one. In a sense, Christ's crucifixion, a common punishment for slaves, was inevitable given his controversial teaching. However, his subsequent exaltation is as glorious as his humiliation was debasing. It is important to note that while Christ was the subject of his self-emptying, his superexaltation is attributed directly to God. Now every knee shall do him homage and every tongue shall proclaim his sovereignty.

The entire Passion narrative lays bare the contradiction of Jesus' life and the paradox of God's reign. The initial fear of the religious leaders shows that Jesus had a following among the people, but it was the people who cried for the release of Barabbas and Jesus' own death. Among his intimate followers, only the women remained faithful; one anointed him, others kept watch at his crucifixion and took note of where he was buried. Of the men who knew him well, one betrayed him, another denied him, and the rest fled for safety. It was a foreigner, a centurion, who publicly acclaimed his divinity. At the moment of his greatest agony, he was recognized as the Son of God.

❖ Reflecting on the Word

Someone once told me that people come to church on Palm Sunday because they get something. But I like to think that palm says something they recognize as true.

"He emptied himself, taking the form of a slave, coming in human likeness," writes Paul, quoting the words of an early Christian hymn. "He humbled himself, becoming obedient to the point of death, even death on a cross," follow soon after (Philippians 2:7, 8). Emptying and humbling are the two key words embracing the trajectory of the life of Jesus Christ, the Son of God: from incarnation to passion and death.

He poured himself out for us and for our salvation, certainly suffering physically—from the beating, the scourging, the crowning with thorns, being struck with a reed, spat upon, prodded, pushed, and stumbling up the hill to Golgotha. Then he was stretched out on a crossbeam, nailed to it, and lifted up, his body suspended between heaven and earth. Finally, he suffocated, unable to raise himself to take in more air.

There was also the inner suffering of abandonment, of seeing his disciples run off, of realizing that all those who had cried "Hosanna" a few days ago had either been silent or had cried out, "Crucify him." Only the women had remained with him.

Today, when we take home a piece of palm, it invites us to prepare to renew our baptismal promises on Easter. Then we can add our voices to that solitary voice almost two millennia ago, saying, "Truly, this is the Son of God!"

❖ Consider/Discuss

- Do you have a special place for the blessed palm so it can call you to remember?
- What does Mark's Passion say to you?

❖ Responding to the Word

Loving God, lift up our hearts to give you thanks and praise for all you have done for us through the saving death of your Son. We sing out in our day, "Blessed is he who continues to come in the name of the Lord. Hosanna in the highest."

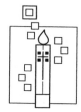

April 8, 2012

EASTER SUNDAY OF THE RESURRECTION OF THE LORD

Today's Focus: He Has Risen! Alleluia!

We define ourselves in many ways—gender, ethnicity, education, profession, tastes, attitudes, and values. But for a Christian, the defining mark is a belief in the resurrection of Jesus from the dead. Today we celebrate this event and enter into the beginning of a fifty-day period of singing "Alleluia!"

FIRST READING
Acts 10:34a, 37–43

Peter proceeded to speak and said: "You know what has happened all over Judea, beginning in Galilee after the baptism that John preached, how God anointed Jesus of Nazareth with the Holy Spirit and power. He went about doing good and healing all those oppressed by the devil, for God was with him. We are witnesses of all that he did both in the country of the Jews and in Jerusalem. They put him to death by hanging him on a tree. This man God raised on the third day and granted that he be visible, not to all the people, but to us, the witnesses chosen by God in advance, who ate and drank with him after he rose from the dead. He commissioned us to preach to the people and testify that he is the one appointed by God as judge of the living and the dead. To him all the prophets bear witness, that everyone who believes in him will receive forgiveness of sins through his name.

PSALM RESPONSE
Psalm 118:24

This is the day the Lord has made; let us rejoice and be glad.

SECOND READING
Colossians 3:1–4

Brothers and sisters: If then you were raised with Christ, seek what is above, where Christ is seated at the right hand of God. Think of what is above, not of what is on earth. For you have died, and your life is hidden with Christ in God. When Christ your life appears, then you too will appear with him in glory.

– or –

1 Corinthians 5:6b–8

Brothers and sisters: Do you not know that a little yeast leavens all the dough? Clear out the old yeast, so that you may become a fresh batch of dough, inasmuch as you are unleavened. For our paschal lamb, Christ, has been sacrificed. Therefore, let us celebrate the feast, not with the old yeast, the yeast of malice and wickedness, but with the unleavened bread of sincerity and truth.

GOSPEL
John 20:1–9

On the first day of the week, Mary of Magdala came to the tomb early in the morning, while it was still dark, and saw the stone removed from the tomb. So she ran and went to Simon Peter and to the other disciple whom Jesus loved, and told them, "They have taken the Lord from the tomb, and we don't know where they put him." So Peter and the other disciple went out and came to the tomb. They both ran, but the other disciple ran faster than Peter and arrived at the tomb first; he bent down and saw the burial cloths there, but did not go in. When Simon Peter arrived after him, he went into the tomb and saw the burial cloths there, and the cloth that had covered his head, not with the burial cloths but rolled up in a separate place. Then the other disciple also went in, the one who had arrived at the tomb first, and he saw and believed. For they did not yet understand the Scripture that he had to rise from the dead.

– *or* –

Mark 16:1–7

When the sabbath was over, Mary Magdalene, Mary, the mother of James, and Salome bought spices so that they might go and anoint him. Very early when the sun had risen, on the first day of the week, they came to the tomb. They were saying to one another, "Who will roll back the stone for us from the entrance to the tomb?" When they looked up, they saw that the stone had been rolled back; it was very large. On entering the tomb they saw a young man sitting on the right side, clothed in a white robe, and they were utterly amazed. He said to them, "Do not be amazed! You seek Jesus of Nazareth, the crucified. He has been raised; he is not here. Behold the place where they laid him. But go and tell his disciples and Peter, 'He is going before you to Galilee; there you will see him, as he told you.' "

✤ Understanding the Word

Peter's teaching regarding the Resurrection includes several important aspects. Clearly a work of God, it is a genuine resurrection from the dead, not merely a resuscitation. That it occurred three days after Jesus' death is evidence of this. That Jesus was seen by some, ate and drank with several of his followers, Peter among them, demonstrates that the appearances of the risen Christ were genuine physical experiences and not some kind of hallucinations. Finally, the fruits of the Resurrection are both transformative and all-encompassing. Thus Peter explains the mystery of Jesus in terms of prophetic expectation, reinterpreting earlier prophetic tradition and developing new religious insight.

Set against the backdrop of ancient cosmology, the passage from Colossians contains the fundamental teaching about the Resurrection and the way it transforms the lives of Christians. Christ rose from the dead and is now in heaven. Enthroned there, Christ both enjoys God's favor and, at God's "right hand," bestows blessings on others and administers God's righteousness. Having gone through the death of human life, Christ has been raised to a new life. In a new and total way, Christ's being is rooted in God. Christians should now turn their attention away from the things of this world and commit themselves to the things of heaven.

The Resurrection stories begin with a report of Mary Magdalene's visit to the tomb. No explanation for her visit is given. Details about the burial wrappings are significant. They are still in the tomb, though the body is not. If the body had been merely transported to another tomb, burial wrappings would still have been needed and taken along. It is unusual that Resurrection faith would spring forth from an experience of the empty tomb rather than from an appearance of the risen Lord, but it is the case here. The reading ends on a curious note: they did not understand the scriptures concerning the resurrection of Jesus.

✣ Reflecting on the Word

"This is the day the Lord has made! Alleluia!" the Church sings today. This is the day that defines who we are as believers. If a belief in the resurrection of Jesus from the dead is not at the top of your list of essential beliefs, then it is time to go back to school for a little remedial Christianity.

From the beginning this belief was what set the followers of Jesus apart from their fellow Jews. Paul even provides a listing of those, including himself, who had had an experience of the risen Lord (see 1 Corinthians 15:5–8). He goes on to make the very clear statement, "If Christ has not been raised, our faith is vain; you are still in your sins" (v. 17).

Peter the denier became Peter the bold proclaimer of the risen Lord, first to the crowds that gathered to hear him on Pentecost, then to the members of the Sanhedrin, and then in the house of Cornelius the Roman centurion. Tradition tells us the others also went about preaching and teaching that God had raised Jesus from the dead.

In the first three Gospels, angels or men dressed in white give the good news of Jesus' resurrection to the women who had come to the tomb. John's Gospel presents Mary Magdalene, who believes the body was stolen; Peter, who sees only an empty tomb and the discarded wrappings; and the beloved disciple. Only this last disciple "saw and believed." He is the model of all who see with the eyes of Easter faith—all who want to.

✤ Consider/Discuss

- With whom do you identify—Peter, Mary Magdalene, or the beloved disciple? Why?
- Why does Paul say that if Christ has not risen, our faith is in vain? Do you see the belief in the resurrection of Jesus as being at the heart of our faith?

✤ Responding to the Word

All powerful, life-giving Father of our Lord Jesus Christ, we are not the first to whom you have sent an angel, we are not the first to see the empty tomb or the garments neatly folded, and still we say: Alleluia! We believe. Deepen our faith in the resurrection of your Son, our Lord.

It's Time to Order
Living the Word 2013: Year C

By now you have discovered what a prayerful and valuable scriptural resource *Living the Word* provides for you each Sunday of the year.

Don't miss a single week! Subscribe to *Living the Word 2013* today for yourself, your staff, parishioners, family, and friends, and share the gift of God's Word.

Order now to receive the same low price as 2012:

100 or more copies	$6.95 each
25–99 copies	$8.95 each
10–24 copies	$9.95 each
2–9 copies	$10.95 each
Single copies	$14.95

MAKE A COPY OF THIS ORDER FORM
AND FAX IT TODAY TO 888-957-3291.
(This will keep your current book intact!)

OR, CALL WLP CUSTOMER CARE AT
800-566-6150 TO PLACE YOUR ORDER.

[ ] Yes, I'd like to order *Living the Word 2013: Year C.* Please send me _____ copies at _____ each, plus shipping, handling and any applicable sales tax.

NAME _____ POSITION _____

PARISH/INSTITUTION _____

ADDRESS _____

CITY _____ STATE _____ ZIP _____

PHONE _____ FAX_____ E-MAIL_____

Please keep a copy of your order for reference.

Living the Word 2013 will be shipped and billed after October 1, 2012.

Add $6.00 for orders up to $20.00. Add 15% of total for orders over $20.00. Payment in U.S. currency only. No cash, please. Make checks payable to World Library Publications. Prices subject to change without notice.
Applicable sales tax will be added to orders based on individual state tax requirements.

World Library Publications
3708 River Road, Suite 400, Franklin Park, IL 60131-2158
800 566-6150 Fax 888 957-3291
www.wlpmusic.com • wlpcs@jspaluch.com

LTWC13

April 15, 2012

SECOND SUNDAY OF EASTER

Today's Focus: A Time to Fathom

Have you ever wondered why the Easter season lasts so long? Why seven Sundays of Easter whereas Christmas usually gets two? We are blessed to have fifty days to fathom the depth of this great mystery of faith, to come to know more fully Jesus as our Lord and God.

FIRST READING
Acts 4:32–35

The community of believers was of one heart and mind, and no one claimed that any of his possessions was his own, but they had everything in common. With great power the apostles bore witness to the resurrection of the Lord Jesus, and great favor was accorded them all. There was no needy person among them, for those who owned property or houses would sell them, bring the proceeds of the sale, and put them at the feet of the apostles, and they were distributed to each according to need.

PSALM RESPONSE
Psalm 118:1

Give thanks to the Lord for he is good, his love is everlasting.

SECOND READING
1 John 5:1–6

Beloved: Everyone who believes that Jesus is the Christ is begotten by God, and everyone who loves the Father loves also the one begotten by him. In this way we know that we love the children of God when we love God and obey his commandments. For the love of God is this, that we keep his commandments. And his commandments are not burdensome, for whoever is begotten by God conquers the world. And the victory that conquers the world is our faith. Who indeed is the victor over the world but the one who believes that Jesus is the Son of God?

This is the one who came through water and blood, Jesus Christ, not by water alone, but by water and blood. The Spirit is the one that testifies, and the Spirit is truth.

GOSPEL
John 20:19–31

On the evening of that first day of the week, when the doors were locked, where the disciples were, for fear of the Jews, Jesus came and stood in their midst and said to them, "Peace be with you." When he had said this, he showed them his hands and his side. The disciples rejoiced when they saw the Lord. Jesus said to them again, "Peace be with you. As the Father has sent me, so I send you." And when he had said this, he breathed on them and said to them, "Receive the Holy Spirit. Whose sins you forgive are forgiven them, and whose sins you retain are retained."

Thomas, called Didymus, one of the Twelve, was not with them when Jesus came. So the other disciples said to him, "We have seen the Lord." But he said to them, "Unless I see the mark of the nails in his hands and put my finger into the nailmarks and put my hand into his side, I will not believe."

Now a week later his disciples were again inside and Thomas was with them. Jesus came, although the doors were locked, and stood in their midst and said, "Peace be with you." Then he said to Thomas, "Put your finger here and see my hands, and bring your hand and put it into my side, and do not be unbelieving, but believe." Thomas answered and said to him, "My Lord and my God!" Jesus said to him, "Have you come to believe because you have seen me? Blessed are those who have not seen and have believed."

Now Jesus did many other signs in the presence of his disciples that are not written in this book. But these are written that you may come to believe that Jesus is the Christ, the Son of God, and that through this belief you may have life in his name.

✤ Understanding the Word

One of the best-known descriptions of the early Christian community states some of its most highly prized values. The picture sketched is probably more spiritually idealized than it is historically accurate. The principal values are unity in mind and heart, the sharing of possessions, and apostolic witness. Unity of mind and heart characterizes the Greek concept of friendship; sharing possessions is a Jewish value. Thus communal harmony espouses values from both cultures. The ideals of this community are noble. They hold out a way of life that might appear to be an ideal, yet through the grace of the Resurrection is attainable.

The reading from the Letter of John is a testimony to Trinitarian faith. It describes God as the One who begets (the Father); it identifies Jesus as the Son of God; and it credits the Spirit as the one who testifies to the triumph of Jesus' death and resurrection. It also sketches the way believers participate in this Trinitarian reality. The reading moves from faith and love to obedience. Jesus alone shares in God's own nature, and thereby can refashion women and men into children of God. It is through faith in him that believers can conquer the evils that threaten them.

Two Resurrection appearances form a kind of diptych. Thomas is the hinge that connects them. Absent for the first event, he is the central character of the second. Thomas is less a doubter than the representative of Christians like us, who are called to believe on the testimony of others. The faith required of him is, in a way, more demanding than that required of those who actually encountered the risen Lord. We may judge him harshly, but Jesus does not. Instead, he invites Thomas to touch him, an invitation not extended earlier to the other disciples. Thomas then declares that the risen Lord is God, a profession of faith that outstrips that of the others.

✢ Reflecting on the Word

Can one "fathom" a mystery? "Fathom" derives from an Old English word meaning "outstretched arms;" eventually it referred to the length from fingertip to fingertip of arms opened wide. As a verb, it means to probe or penetrate in order to understand. Granting the impossibility of ever coming to fathom the Resurrection fully, I like the image of trying to reach out and put my arms around this great mystery—or, better yet, to have the risen Christ put his outstretched arms around me, drawing me into it more fully.

Which brings us to Thomas. He is the original person who tried to fathom the risen Christ, insisting that if his friends in the upper room wanted him to believe what he could only think of as nonsense, he needed to touch the wounds of the risen Lord. Jesus didn't seem to have much of a problem letting him.

We never learn whether Thomas did touch Jesus or not, but every second Sunday of Easter we are told this story about Thomas and the risen Lord. It encourages us to fathom the mystery that is our faith, to learn to penetrate it by confessing Jesus as Lord and God, then allow this belief to flow out into our daily activities, reaching out to embrace others.

Don't you think when Thomas left the upper room that day he knew that the Resurrection was not something to keep to himself? That his whole being was filled with the warmth and light absorbed from being in the presence of the risen Lord? Is it possible that this can happen to us?

✢ Consider/Discuss

- Have you begun to fathom the mystery of the Resurrection?
- What does it mean to say, "My Lord and my God" and make that your daily prayer over the coming weeks?

✢ Responding to the Word

Father of the only-begotten Son, send your Spirit upon us that we might know more deeply the truth of your Son's resurrection and allow it to penetrate our lives. Deepen our faith, hope, and love so the world will know us even now as children of the Resurrection.

April 22, 2012

THIRD SUNDAY OF EASTER

Today's Focus: Recognizing the Lord

To know Christ as risen Lord is the invitation of the Easter season, just as to know Christ as God become fully human is the focus of Christmas time. Today's Gospel offers another encounter where the risen Lord appears but is not recognized. Notice how Jesus opens their minds so they might witness.

FIRST READING
Acts 3:13–15, 17–19

Peter said to the people: "The God of Abraham, the God of Isaac, and the God of Jacob, the God of our fathers, has glorified his servant Jesus, whom you handed over and denied in Pilate's presence when he had decided to release him. You denied the Holy and Righteous One and asked that a murderer be released to you. The author of life you put to death, but God raised him from the dead; of this we are witnesses. Now I know, brothers, that you acted out of ignorance, just as your leaders did; but God has thus brought to fulfillment what he had announced beforehand through the mouth of all the prophets, that his Christ would suffer. Repent, therefore, and be converted, that your sins may be wiped away."

PSALM RESPONSE
Psalm 4:7a

Lord, let your face shine on us.

SECOND READING
1 John 2:1–5a

My children, I am writing this to you so that you may not commit sin. But if anyone does sin, we have an Advocate with the Father, Jesus Christ the righteous one. He is expiation for our sins, and not for our sins only but for those of the whole world. The way we may be sure that we know him is to keep his commandments. Those who say, "I know him," but do not keep his commandments are liars, and the truth is not in them. But whoever keeps his word, the love of God is truly perfected in him.

GOSPEL
Luke 24:35–48

The two disciples recounted what had taken place on the way, and how Jesus was made known to them in the breaking of bread.

While they were still speaking about this, he stood in their midst and said to them, "Peace be with you." But they were startled and terrified and thought that they were seeing a ghost. Then he said to them, "Why are you troubled? And why do questions arise in your hearts? Look at my hands and my feet, that it is I myself. Touch me and see, because a ghost does not have flesh and bones as you can see I have." And as he said this, he showed them his hands and his feet. While they were still incredulous for joy and were amazed, he asked them, "Have you anything here to eat?" They gave him a piece of baked fish; he took it and ate it in front of them.

He said to them, "These are my words that I spoke to you while I was still with you, that everything written about me in the law of Moses and in the prophets and psalms must be fulfilled." Then he opened their minds to understand the Scriptures. And he said to them, "Thus it is written that the Christ would suffer and rise from the dead on the third day and that repentance, for the forgiveness of sins, would be preached in his name to all the nations, beginning from Jerusalem. You are witnesses of these things."

❖ Understanding the Word

Peter stands as a witness to the Resurrection. His attitude toward his Jewish compatriots is hardly a case of anti-Judaism. He is opposed to those who refuse to accept Jesus as Messiah, not to the Jewish nation as a whole. His Christology is rooted in the prophetic tradition of ancient Israel, employing language that is reminiscent of the Suffering Servant tradition of Isaiah. He weaves various thematic threads together, reinterpreting earlier traditions, thus developing his own Christian theology. The power of God to bring life out of death is the point of the passage, not the assignment of blame for Jesus' death.

The major portion of the second reading goes beyond promotion of righteous living. It offers encouragement for those times when believers stray from righteousness and do in fact sin. In these times, Jesus will be an advocate for them before God. Jesus does not assume the role of comforter, a role traditionally assigned to the Spirit. Rather, he is an intercessor, one who atones for the sins of the world. The knowledge of God discussed here is experiential knowledge, knowledge that results in a relationship with God. To know God is to love God. Both knowledge and love of God manifest themselves in obedience to God's commandments.

The risen Lord Jesus addresses a group of women and men with the customary Jewish greeting: Peace be with you! They are terrified, for they think that they are seeing a ghost. Jesus rebukes them for having doubts and then calls attention to the marks of the nails in his hands and feet, demonstrating that it is really he. In a final demonstration of his bodily reality, he eats a piece of cooked fish. Although this is not the official ritual meal of the community, it may have eucharistic overtones. Having assured the disciples of his bodily resurrection, Jesus proceeds to explain his suffering and death by turning to the scriptures.

❖ Reflecting on the Word

Recognizing Jesus as the risen Lord seems to have been something of a problem. Mary Magdalene didn't; she thought he was the gardener. The disciples on the road to Emmaus didn't; they took him for a stranger who had heard nothing about the recent events in Jerusalem. And even in today's Gospel, the apostles thought he was a ghost.

It is instructive to note how Jesus reveals himself in each case. To Mary Magdalene, he simply says her name, "Mary." The two disciples on the road get an instruction on how all these recent events in Jerusalem fulfill the scriptures. And today the apostles are shown his hands and feet, watch him eat, and again, have their minds opened to the meaning of the scriptures. In all cases, Jesus' words play an important role.

How we come to know the risen Lord runs along the same lines. We come to know him through the word of God. He calls us to be disciples, to be friends, to be children of the Father through the scriptures. We come to the table of the Lord each week, where our minds and hearts can be opened.

We recognize him in the breaking of the bread, both the bread of the Eucharist and the bread of God's word. Some preparation on our part can be helpful. By spending some time with the coming Sunday's readings during the week, we are more likely to have God's word penetrate our hearts when we gather to listen together to the scriptures and the preaching.

❖ Consider/Discuss

- Have you had any experience of knowing the presence of Christ and hearing his voice in the readings and preaching at Sunday Eucharist?
- Do you appreciate the Sunday Eucharist as a time when the community continues to experience the presence of the risen Lord?

❖ Responding to the Word

Risen Lord Jesus, by our baptism we began to live with your life and received the gifts of faith, hope, and love. We know you have come to draw us into the life and love of the Trinity. Increase our ability to hear your voice and know you through the scriptures.

April 29, 2012

FOURTH SUNDAY OF EASTER

Today's Focus: Wanted . . . Good Shepherds

Artistic expressions of Jesus as the Good Shepherd were created in the earliest days of the church. This was one of the most comforting images during times of persecution. He called others to shepherd in his name. They were not perfect people, but they became good at shepherding, transformed by the power of Resurrection life. Consider Peter.

FIRST READING
Acts 4:8–12

Peter, filled with the Holy Spirit, said: "Leaders of the people and elders: If we are being examined today about a good deed done to a cripple, namely, by what means he was saved, then all of you and all the people of Israel should know that it was in the name of Jesus Christ the Nazarene whom you crucified, whom God raised from the dead; in his name this man stands before you healed. He is
> the stone rejected by you, the builders,
>   which has become the cornerstone.
There is no salvation through anyone else, nor is there any other name under heaven given to the human race by which we are to be saved."

PSALM RESPONSE
Psalm 118:22

The stone rejected by the builders has become the cornerstone.

SECOND READING
1 John 3:1–2

Beloved: See what love the Father has bestowed on us that we may be called the children of God. Yet so we are. The reason the world does not know us is that it did not know him. Beloved, we are God's children now; what we shall be has not yet been revealed. We do know that when it is revealed we shall be like him, for we shall see him as he is.

GOSPEL
John 10:11–18

Jesus said: "I am the good shepherd. A good shepherd lays down his life for the sheep. A hired man, who is not a shepherd and whose sheep are not his own, sees a wolf coming and leaves the sheep and runs away, and the wolf catches and scatters them. This is because he works for pay and has no concern for the sheep. I am the good shepherd, and I know mine and mine know me, just as the Father knows me and I know the Father; and I will lay down my life for the sheep. I have other sheep that do not belong to this fold. These also I must lead, and they will hear my voice, and there will be one flock, one shepherd. This is why the Father loves me, because I lay down my life in order to take it up again. No one takes it from me, but I lay it down on my own. I have power to lay it down, and power to take it up again. This command I have received from my Father."

Peter responds to the leaders of the Jewish community in Jerusalem who challenged the healing of a crippled man. He claims that it was in the power of Jesus' name that the man was healed, and it will be in the power of this same name that all will be saved. Peter speaks out against the leaders of the people, not because they are Jewish but because they have rejected Jesus. For the crippled man, salvation took the form of healing; for others, it can take the form of spiritual transformation. The name of Jesus is the one and only source of salvation, hence no one can afford to reject it.

The love of which the author of the second reading speaks is generative, transforming; it makes believers children of God. Everything that happens in the lives of believers is a consequence of their having been recreated as God's children. As children of God, they are a new reality and hence not accepted by the world, the old reality. The "now but not yet" of Christian eschatology is clearly stated. Believers have already been reborn as children of God. However, their transformation has not yet been completed. That is dependent on a future manifestation. Promised an even fuller identification with God, believers will see God as God is.

As shepherd, Jesus is committed to the well-being of the sheep. He is willing to protect his flock even to the point of risking his own life for them. He has a mutual, intimate relationship with them based on the mutual, intimate relationship that he has with God. This is true even of sheep that are not now his. The high Christology can be seen in the control that he has not only over his death but also over his resurrection. He has the power to take up his life again. He received this power from God. The universally saving death of Jesus is the work of the Father through the Son.

✦ Reflecting on the Word

Peter is a wonderful example of someone growing into the role of a good shepherd. His calling was evident from the beginning, when Jesus summoned him and his brother Andrew while they were casting their nets into the sea: "Come after me, and I will make you fishers of [people]" (Mark 1:17).

We know Peter as the first to confess Jesus as Messiah, but also as someone who did not understand what this would mean both for Jesus and his followers: the cross. We know Peter was not afraid to ask questions along the lines of "What are we going to get out of being disciples?" or even say the wrong thing ("You shall never wash my feet!"). And, perhaps most importantly, we know Peter folded when the chips were down, denying he ever knew Jesus.

This same Peter boldly preaches Jesus as raised by God for the salvation of all who believe. He preaches not only outside the upper room on Pentecost, but in the synagogue soon after, then twice before the Sanhedrin (the Jewish leaders in Jerusalem), and finally in the house of the Roman centurion Cornelius.

What explains this transformation from denying follower to charismatic leader? Paul tells us in one of his letters (1 Corinthians 15:5) that the risen Lord appeared to Kephas (the Aramaic name for Peter). And Luke records the descent of the Spirit upon those in the upper room (Acts 2:4). All of this reminds us that God's power at work in us is the key to having and being a good shepherd.

✤ Consider/Discuss

- From the beginning, Jesus the Good Shepherd has called others to shepherd in his name. Have you known any good shepherds in your life?
- Do you pray for those called to shepherd God's people?

✤ Responding to the Word

Loving Jesus, you have called many people to shepherd your faithful. We pray for them today, most especially our Holy Father, and all of our bishops, the bishop of this diocese, and all men and women in positions of leadership. Grant them wisdom and give them the gifts needed to guide your people.

May 6, 2012

FIFTH SUNDAY OF EASTER

Today's Focus: The Vitality of the Vine

The tremendous vitality of Jesus as the vine with many branches is seen in the way that the early church grew even in the midst of persecution. The lives of men like Peter, Barnabas, and Saul of Tarsus were some of the earliest manifestations of this vitality revealed in the work they did.

FIRST READING
Acts 9:26–31

When Saul arrived in Jerusalem he tried to join the disciples, but they were all afraid of him, not believing that he was a disciple. Then Barnabas took charge of him and brought him to the apostles, and he reported to them how he had seen the Lord, and that he had spoken to him, and how in Damascus he had spoken out boldly in the name of Jesus. He moved about freely with them in Jerusalem, and spoke out boldly in the name of the Lord. He also spoke and debated with the Hellenists, but they tried to kill him. And when the brothers learned of this, they took him down to Caesarea and sent him on his way to Tarsus.

The church throughout all Judea, Galilee, and Samaria was at peace. It was being built up and walked in the fear of the Lord, and with the consolation of the Holy Spirit it grew in numbers.

PSALM RESPONSE
Psalm 22:26a

I will praise you, Lord, in the assembly of your people.

SECOND READING
1 John 3:18–24

Children, let us love not in word or speech but in deed and truth. Now this is how we shall know that we belong to the truth and reassure our hearts before him in whatever our hearts condemn, for God is greater than our hearts and knows everything. Beloved, if our hearts do not condemn us, we have confidence in God and receive from him whatever we ask, because we keep his commandments and do what pleases him. And his commandment is this: we should believe in the name of his Son, Jesus Christ, and love one another just as he commanded us. Those who keep his commandments remain in him, and he in them, and the way we know that he remains in us is from the Spirit he gave us.

GOSPEL
John 15:1-8

Jesus said to his disciples: "I am the true vine, and my Father is the vine grower. He takes away every branch in me that does not bear fruit, and every one that does he prunes so that it bears more fruit. You are already pruned because of the word that I spoke to you. Remain in me, as I remain in you. Just as a branch cannot bear fruit on its own unless it remains on the vine, so neither can you unless you remain in me. I am the vine, you are the branches. Whoever remains in me and I in him will bear much fruit, because without me you can do nothing. Anyone who does not remain in me will be thrown out like a branch and wither; people will gather them and throw them into a fire and they will be burned. If you remain in me and my words remain in you, ask for whatever you want and it will be done for you. By this is my Father glorified, that you bear much fruit and become my disciples."

❖ Understanding the Word

Saul, the formidable persecutor, has now become a disciple of the risen Lord. Initially he meets resistance, not to his message but to his claim of conversion. It takes another member of the community to witness to the saving grace of God that transformed Saul into a believer. If God can raise Jesus from the dead, surely God can recreate Saul. Saul's rebirth as a disciple is a sign of the grace that has been unleashed by the Resurrection. It was the risen Jesus that Saul encountered and it is that same risen Jesus that he now proclaims. The power of God is unfathomable.

The author of the Letter of John insists that it is not enough to proclaim love for God; it must be demonstrated through concrete action. There seems to have been a sense of guilt somewhere in the community. The writer assures them that God's love far exceeds any guilt that they may experience. They are called to believe this, thus rooting their faith in confidence. This confidence is also manifested in the way they turn to God in prayer. Although only one commandment is placed before them here, its focus is twofold. They are to believe in the name of God's Son, Jesus Christ, and to love one another.

The metaphor of vine and branches characterizes the intimate nature of the relationship between Jesus and his followers. Jesus lives in his branches, and his branches live in his life. The vine is not totally dependent on any one branch or group of branches. Therefore, it can endure pruning without withering and dying. However, there is no vine if there are no branches at all. The basis of this union is acceptance of and fidelity to the words of Jesus, not ethnic or national identity. The vitality expressed by this image is unmistakable. The vine and the branches are alive with the life of God.

Jesus the vine gives flower to some very different branches. Last week we considered Peter, so this week let us turn to Paul. No one would have suspected that Saul of Tarsus, that "breather of murderous threats against the disciples of the Lord," would ever become known as "the Apostle to the Gentiles" and one who would refer to himself as both a loving father and mother to the communities he himself tended. As Peter proved to be a good shepherd of the flock, so Paul was a dedicated worker in the vineyard, tending with such loving care the branches growing from the one vine that is Jesus.

What we see in Paul and hear in his letters is the intimate love of Christ for his church. Take up any of his letters and you will become engaged with the spirit of Paul as an instrument that communicates the spirit of Christ. Paul's letters reveal the many voices he used to preach Christ crucified: the evangelizer and herald, the teacher and witness, the admonishing father and loving midwife, all calling God's children to be fully alive in Christ.

Jesus speaks of himself as a vine with many branches, befitting not only the infinite variety of individuals he called in his own day, but also the many peoples and nations that have come to believe in him. We pray for all who give themselves over to the work of the vineyard, to all who help others to remain in Christ and bear fruit.

✤ Consider/Discuss

- What does the image of Christ as the vine with many branches say to you about today's Church?
- How do you understand Jesus' words about the branches needing to be pruned so that they might bear more fruit?

✤ Responding to the Word

Risen Jesus, you are the vine and we are the branches. Strengthen our resolve as a community to remain in you, so that we might bear more fruit. May your words remain in me, your child; may I, like Paul, recognize the life these words carry within them, and hold them in my heart.

May 13, 2012

SIXTH SUNDAY OF EASTER

Today's Focus: The Falling Spirit

A wonderful image of the Holy Spirit is found in today's first reading. While Peter is preaching to the Roman centurion Cornelius and his family, the Holy Spirit cannot wait for him to finish and then have them ask for baptism, but "[w]hile Peter was still speaking these things the Holy Spirit fell upon all who were listening to the word" (Acts 10:44).

FIRST READING
Acts 10:25–26, 34–35, 44–48

When Peter entered, Cornelius met him and, falling at his feet, paid him homage. Peter, however, raised him up, saying, "Get up. I myself am also a human being."

Then Peter proceeded to speak and said, "In truth, I see that God shows no partiality. Rather, in every nation whoever fears him and acts uprightly is acceptable to him."

While Peter was still speaking these things, the Holy Spirit fell upon all who were listening to the word. The circumcised believers who had accompanied Peter were astounded that the gift of the Holy Spirit should have been poured out on the Gentiles also, for they could hear them speaking in tongues and glorifying God. Then Peter responded, "Can anyone withhold the water for baptizing these people, who have received the Holy Spirit even as we have?" He ordered them to be baptized in the name of Jesus Christ.

PSALM RESPONSE
Psalm 98:2b

The Lord has revealed to the nations his saving power.

SECOND READING
1 John 4:7–10

Beloved, let us love one another, because love is of God; everyone who loves is begotten by God and knows God. Whoever is without love does not know God, for God is love. In this way the love of God was revealed to us: God sent his only Son into the world so that we might have life through him. In this is love: not that we have loved God, but that he loved us and sent his Son as expiation for our sins.

GOSPEL
John 15:9–17

Jesus said to his disciples: "As the Father loves me, so I also love you. Remain in my love. If you keep my commandments, you will remain in my love, just as I have kept my Father's commandments and remain in his love.

"I have told you this so that my joy may be in you and your joy might be complete. This is my commandment: love one another as I love you. No one has greater love than this, to lay down one's life for one's friends. You are my friends if you do what I command you. I no longer call you slaves, because a slave does not know what his master is doing. I have called you friends, because I have told you everything I have heard from my Father. It was not you who chose me, but I who chose you and appointed you to go and bear fruit that will remain, so that whatever you ask the Father in my name he may give you. This I command you: love one another."

⊹ Understanding the Word

Cornelius, the newly converted Roman centurion, recognizes Peter as a messenger of God. The real power of the narrative is seen not in the disposition of Peter but in the action of the Holy Spirit. The event is a kind of Gentile Pentecost. While Peter's companions are surprised that the Spirit is given to the uncircumcised he intervenes on their behalf, insisting that God shows no partiality. Those who received the Spirit at the first Pentecost and those who have received it at this second Pentecost are now joined by a special bond, the shared outpouring of the Spirit. The ritual of baptism is a sign of the church's acceptance of God's action.

The teaching about love is the heart of the message of the second reading. Several dimensions of this reality are examined: Love is of God; love begets others of God; it is revealed in the salvation realized through the sacrifice of the Son of God. The most startling statement about love is: God is love! This divine love is the fundamental reality of our faith. The love described here is neither exemplary piety nor altruistic concern for others. Actually, there is nothing merely human about it. It is divine in its origin and only those who have been begotten of God can have a share in it.

The passage from John's Gospel is one of the best-known discourses on love. The source of this love is divine love itself: "As the Father loves me, so I love you;" "love one another as I love you" (15:9, 12). Jesus promises the disciples that if they abide in his love and obey his commandments, they will abide in his joy as well. Although the passage does not describe the character of this joy, we can presume that it flows from union with God. The love that is described here is active love, reaching out to others—God to Jesus, Jesus to his disciples, the disciples to one another.

If we were going to give a name to this Sunday in the Easter season, we might call it "Love Sunday." No matter which year of readings we hear—A, B, or C—the theme today is love: God's love for Jesus, Jesus' love for God, and God and Jesus' love for us and their desire that we love them in return.

This dynamic picture of divine love is captured powerfully in the first reading when the Holy Spirit "falls upon" Cornelius and his family while Peter is still preaching. The most frequent images for the Holy Spirit in stained glass and paintings are those of a white dove gently hovering, or a flickering flame of fire suspended in mid-air. But here there is a sense of something weightier "falling upon" the listeners, the weight of divine love, intensified by divine impatience. St. Alphonsus spoke of a God "crazy in love" with us. Might we find evidence of such a divine passion at play here?

It is one of the clearest expressions of God's desire for us, of God's great love that yearns for intimate communion. Jesus puts it into words for us: "As the Father loves me, so I love you." Take time and repeat these words of Jesus throughout the week. Then, hear his next words: "Remain in my love." How? "If you keep my commandments, you will remain in my love." And what are those commandments? Just one really: "This I command you: love one another."

✤ *Consider/Discuss*

- How does this command to love relate to the feast of Easter?
- Jesus says that he told us this command to love "so that my joy may be in you and your joy might be complete." Have you known this joy?

✤ *Responding to the Word*

God of love, you call us to know you as love and to live in your love so that your joy may fill us. Draw us into the mystery of the love that binds you, Father, Son, and Spirit, in such intimate communion. Send your Spirit upon us and break down any resistance to knowing and doing your will.

May 17 or 20, 2012

ASCENSION OF THE LORD

Today's Focus: A Return, Not a Retirement

Through the Father's power still at work in him, Jesus ascends to sit at God's right hand. There Jesus intercedes for us as we continue the work of bringing the good news of God's salvation to others. His ascension contains a promise that where he is, those faithful to him will also be.

FIRST READING
Acts 1:1–11

In the first book, Theophilus, I dealt with all that Jesus did and taught until the day he was taken up, after giving instructions through the Holy Spirit to the apostles whom he had chosen. He presented himself alive to them by many proofs after he had suffered, appearing to them during forty days and speaking about the kingdom of God. While meeting with them, he enjoined them not to depart from Jerusalem, but to wait for "the promise of the Father about which you have heard me speak; for John baptized with water, but in a few days you will be baptized with the Holy Spirit."

When they had gathered together they asked him, "Lord, are you at this time going to restore the kingdom to Israel?" He answered them, "It is not for you to know the times or seasons that the Father has established by his own authority. But you will receive power when the Holy Spirit comes upon you, and you will be my witnesses in Jerusalem, throughout Judea and Samaria, and to the ends of the earth." When he had said this, as they were looking on, he was lifted up, and a cloud took him from their sight. While they were looking intently at the sky as he was going, suddenly two men dressed in white garments stood beside them. They said, "Men of Galilee, why are you standing there looking at the sky? This Jesus who has been taken up from you into heaven will return in the same way as you have seen him going into heaven."

PSALM RESPONSE
Psalm 47:6

God mounts his throne to shouts of joy: a blare of trumpets for the Lord.

Brothers and sisters: May the God of our Lord Jesus Christ, the Father of glory, give you a Spirit of wisdom and revelation resulting in knowledge of him. May the eyes of your hearts be enlightened, that you may know what is the hope that belongs to his call, what are the riches of glory in his inheritance among the holy ones, and what is the surpassing greatness of his power for us who believe, in accord with the exercise of his great might, which he worked in Christ, raising him from the dead and seating him at his right hand in the heavens, far above every principality, authority, power, and dominion, and every name that is named not only in this age but also in the one to come. And he put all things beneath his feet and gave him as head over all things to the church, which is his body, the fullness of the one who fills all things in every way.

– or –

In the shorter form of the reading, passages in brackets are omitted.

Ephesians 4:1–13 or 4:1–7, 11–13

Brothers and sisters, I, a prisoner for the Lord, urge you to live in a manner worthy of the call you have received, with all humility and gentleness, with patience, bearing with one another through love, striving to preserve the unity of the spirit through the bond of peace: one body and one Spirit, as you were also called to the one hope of your call; one Lord, one faith, one baptism; one God and Father of all, who is over all and through all and in all.

But grace was given to each of us according to the measure of Christ's gift. [Therefore, it says:
  He *ascended on high and took prisoners captive;*
  he gave gifts to men.
What does "he ascended" mean except that he also descended into the lower regions of the earth? The one who descended is also the one who ascended far above all the heavens, that he might fill all things.]

And he gave some as apostles, others as prophets, others as evangelists, others as pastors and teachers, to equip the holy ones for the work of ministry, for building up the body of Christ, until we all attain to the unity of faith and knowledge of the Son of God, to mature manhood, to the extent of the full stature of Christ.

Jesus said to his disciples: "Go into the whole world and proclaim the gospel to every creature. Whoever believes and is baptized will be saved; whoever does not believe will be condemned. These signs will accompany those who believe: in my name they will drive out demons, they will speak new languages. They will pick up serpents with their hands, and if they drink any deadly thing, it will not harm them. They will lay hands on the sick, and they will recover."

So then the Lord Jesus, after he spoke to them, was taken up into heaven and took his seat at the right hand of God. But they went forth and preached everywhere, while the Lord worked with them and confirmed the word through accompanying signs.

❖ Understanding the Word

The ascension of Jesus brought closure to his earthly activity, while at the same time launching the ministry of the apostles. Thus the Ascension is a turning point in the history of the church. The actual account of the Ascension is brief. Jesus is lifted up and concealed by a cloud. Attention shifts to the men (angels?) who now appear. They rebuke the disciples and assure them that Jesus will return on the clouds just as he left. The church is now in a liminal state. Jesus has left, but the Spirit has not yet come.

The reading from Ephesians is a prayer for spiritual enlightenment. God's power raised Christ from the dead and seated Christ in the place of honor in heaven; God's power made all things subject to Christ and exalted Christ as head of the church. It is this same power that is now called upon. The church is characterized as a body. As members of this exalted body, believers share in the wisdom and insight to grasp these mysteries and to live lives informed by them.

Marks' account of Jesus' ascension ties together many themes found elsewhere in the gospel. It begins with a Resurrection experience in which Jesus commissions the apostles to preach the gospel to all. Jesus is then taken from their sight. The reading clearly states that just as he was raised from the dead by the power of God, so he is taken up today. This reflects the early church's concern to show that it is the power of God that is active in Jesus, not some kind of miraculous force. As exalted Lord, Jesus takes his rightful place of privilege next to God. The concluding verse succinctly summarizes the entire apostolic age: the apostles went into the entire world and preached the gospel; the Lord was with them, confirming their ministry through wondrous signs.

In Bill Davis' play *Mass Appeal*, the young deacon complains about the parish where he grew up, where the "hippy dippy hymn committee" selected "Leaving on a Jet Plane" for the feast of the Ascension. The young deacon did not find it appropriate for the dignity of the event being celebrated. To say the least, it rendered insipid what should be a feast of profound relevance.

Today's feast continues the celebration of the paschal mystery of Christ's suffering, death and resurrection, and return to the Father. It is not just an "afterthought" feast, a bringing down of the curtain on Jesus' life and ministry on earth. We celebrate Jesus' return to the Father to intercede for us and to make possible the sending of the Spirit for the continuation of God's plan of salvation for all people, now taken up by the church under the direction of this same Spirit.

Luke's account of the Ascension places emphasis on the work yet to be done— witnessing to Jesus "to the ends of the earth." This is further highlighted when the two men in white garments suddenly appear after Jesus is taken up and removed from their sight. "Why are you standing there looking up at the sky?" they ask. Time to get moving.

Mark's account has Jesus sending them out to "proclaim the gospel to every creature," and promises that great signs will accompany them. Mark's final word affirms that "the Lord worked with them."

✤ *Consider/Discuss*

- Do you understand the feast of the Ascension only as Jesus' returning to the Father or do you see its connection with the ongoing life and ministry of the Church?
- How does Christ continue to work with us? Are we meant to take literally Jesus' words about being able to pick up serpents and drink deadly poison and heal the sick?

✤ *Responding to the* Word

Jesus, you ascended to the right hand of the Father to intercede for us and to work with us until we are united with you in heaven. Help us to make good use of the gifts you have given for building up your body, the Church, and for making you known throughout the world.

May 20, 2012

SEVENTH SUNDAY OF EASTER

Today's Focus: Replacing Judas

The only time Matthias is mentioned in scripture is in today's story of his being chosen to replace Judas. After prayer, the community offered lots to the two men. Matthias drew the appropriate lot and God was credited with choosing him, because God has knowledge of the human heart.

FIRST READING
Acts 1:15–17, 20a, 20c–26

Peter stood up in the midst of the brothers—there was a group of about one hundred and twenty persons in the one place—. He said, "My brothers, the Scripture had to be fulfilled which the Holy Spirit spoke beforehand through the mouth of David, concerning Judas, who was the guide for those who arrested Jesus. He was numbered among us and was allotted a share in this ministry.

"For it is written in the Book of Psalms:
May another take his office.

"Therefore, it is necessary that one of the men who accompanied us the whole time the Lord Jesus came and went among us, beginning from the baptism of John until the day on which he was taken up from us, become with us a witness to his resurrection." So they proposed two, Judas called Barsabbas, who was also known as Justus, and Matthias. Then they prayed, "You, Lord, who know the hearts of all, show which one of these two you have chosen to take the place in this apostolic ministry from which Judas turned away to go to his own place." Then they gave lots to them, and the lot fell upon Matthias, and he was counted with the eleven apostles.

PSALM RESPONSE
Psalm 103:19a

The Lord has set his throne in heaven.

SECOND READING
1 John 4:11–16

Beloved, if God so loved us, we also must love one another. No one has ever seen God. Yet, if we love one another, God remains in us, and his love is brought to perfection in us.

This is how we know that we remain in him and he in us, that he has given us of his Spirit. Moreover, we have seen and testify that the Father sent his Son as savior of the world. Whoever acknowledges that Jesus is the Son of God, God remains in him and he in God. We have come to know and to believe in the love God has for us.

God is love, and whoever remains in love remains in God and God in him.

Lifting up his eyes to heaven, Jesus prayed, saying: "Holy Father, keep them in your name that you have given me, so that they may be one just as we are one. When I was with them I protected them in your name that you gave me, and I guarded them, and none of them was lost except the son of destruction, in order that the Scripture might be fulfilled. But now I am coming to you. I speak this in the world so that they may share my joy completely. I gave them your word, and the world hated them, because they do not belong to the world any more than I belong to the world. I do not ask that you take them out of the world but that you keep them from the evil one. They do not belong to the world any more than I belong to the world. Consecrate them in the truth. Your word is truth. As you sent me into the world, so I sent them into the world. And I consecrate myself for them, so that they also may be consecrated in truth."

❖ Understanding the Word

After the Ascension, Peter assumes leadership. With the betrayal of Judas, the circle of twelve apostles had been broken and must be restored. The choice of a successor was necessary. It had to be one who was among the company of disciples from the time of Jesus' baptism to his ascension. He also had to be a witness to the Resurrection. The prayer preceding the casting of lots illustrates the faith of the assembly. Since only God can read the human heart, only God knew which of the two should be selected. They were confident that God would determine the outcome. The lot fell to Matthias.

According to the author of the second reading, just as God's love was manifested in the unselfish and redeeming, saving sacrifice of Jesus, so Christians must love others with an unselfish and forgiving love. Such love manifests itself as visible works of love. The reading develops the idea of the mutual abiding of God in believers and believers in God that manifests itself in two ways. First, the Spirit of God that inspires unselfish love is evidence of the abiding presence and love of God. Believers' acknowledgment of Jesus as the Son of God sent to be the savior of the world is further evidence of God's abiding presence.

Jesus' concern for his disciples is plainly stated in his prayer. Prayed shortly before his death, it takes on profound significance. He wishes to share with his followers the union he enjoys with God. Accepting God's word through Jesus, the disciples share in God's holiness. Having sketched the contours of union with God, Jesus acknowledges the resistance that God's word encounters from the world. He is not speaking of the natural world, but of that dimension of society that is antagonistic toward God. Jesus himself was hated by that world and now, because of God's word, his followers will suffer the same fate. It is for this reason that Jesus prays for them.

My friend the storyteller Bob Wilhelm shared an "artful" variation on the story of the choice of Matthias. Both Matthias and Barsabbas were artists, so St. Peter decided on a contest. He divided the upper room where the community gathered for worship with a curtain, giving half to each man to decorate as he saw fit. The community would declare the winner and Judas' successor.

Barsabbas, a painter, sent for his brushes and a rich assortment of paints. All week long he painted lovely scenes of Jesus preaching, teaching, healing, casting out demons. His brush captured the parables, illuminating them. Matthias, a stonecutter and polisher, also toiled all week behind his curtain. People could hear only his humming and soft singing.

The day came and the people entered Barsabbas' half of the church. They broke into applause at his artistry. The uses of color were magnificent. They found themselves depicted in his paintings. They were delighted. Peter became worried. How could Matthias' work possibly compete with this? But he went over to the curtain and turned it back.

Silence filled the room as people turned to see what Matthias had done. His work had been to polish the stone walls of the chapel's other half, allowing people to see themselves as never before. The walls shone like mirrors and every person was given a sense of the beauty of Christ shining within them, a glimpse of the divine spark each one carried within. And so Matthias was chosen to replace Judas. He had revealed Christ by revealing Christ's followers to themselves.

✤ *Consider/Discuss*

- Have you ever left a decision in God's hands?
- Do you believe that God has placed a divine spark within you?

✤ *Responding to the Word*

Loving God, you have made us in your image and placed your truth within our hearts that we might know, love, and serve you. Consecrate us further with the truth of the gospel and direct our feet in the way you wish us to walk. Let us live in your joy.

May 27, 2012

PENTECOST SUNDAY

Today's Focus: Holy Spirit, Speech Teacher

The Spirit blesses us with the gift of speech. The spirit-filled apostles tumble out of the upper room to speak to Jews gathered from many nations, and they all understood, in their own tongues. Paul instructs as to who can say, "Jesus is Lord." The risen Jesus gives us the Spirit so forgiveness can be proclaimed.

FIRST READING
Acts 2:1–11

When the time for Pentecost was fulfilled, they were all in one place together. And suddenly there came from the sky a noise like a strong driving wind, and it filled the entire house in which they were. Then there appeared to them tongues as of fire, which parted and came to rest on each one of them. And they were all filled with the Holy Spirit and began to speak in different tongues, as the Spirit enabled them to proclaim.

Now there were devout Jews from every nation under heaven staying in Jerusalem. At this sound, they gathered in a large crowd, but they were confused because each one heard them speaking in his own language. They were astounded, and in amazement they asked, "Are not all these people who are speaking Galileans? Then how does each of us hear them in his native language? We are Parthians, Medes, and Elamites, inhabitants of Mesopotamia, Judea and Cappadocia, Pontus and Asia, Phrygia and Pamphylia, Egypt and the districts of Libya near Cyrene, as well as travelers from Rome, both Jews and converts to Judaism, Cretans and Arabs, yet we hear them speaking in our own tongues of the mighty acts of God."

PSALM RESPONSE
Psalm 104:30

Lord, send out your Spirit, and renew the face of the earth.

SECOND READING
1 Corinthians 12:3b–7, 12–13

Brothers and sisters: No one can say, "Jesus is Lord," except by the Holy Spirit. There are different kinds of spiritual gifts but the same Spirit; there are different forms of service but the same Lord; there are different workings but the same God who produces all of them in everyone. To each individual the manifestation of the Spirit is given for some benefit.

As a body is one though it has many parts, and all the parts of the body, though many, are one body, so also Christ. For in one Spirit we were all baptized into one body, whether Jews or Greeks, slaves or free persons, and we were all given to drink of one Spirit.

– or –

Galatians 5:16–25   Brothers and sisters, live by the Spirit and you will certainly not gratify the desire of the flesh. For the flesh has desires against the Spirit, and the Spirit against the flesh; these are opposed to each other, so that you may not do what you want. But if you are guided by the Spirit, you are not under the law. Now the works of the flesh are obvious: immorality, impurity, lust, idolatry, sorcery, hatreds, rivalry, jealousy, outbursts of fury, acts of selfishness, dissensions, factions, occasions of envy, drinking bouts, orgies, and the like. I warn you, as I warned you before, that those who do such things will not inherit the kingdom of God. In contrast, the fruit of the Spirit is love, joy, peace, patience, kindness, generosity, faithfulness, gentleness, self-control. Against such there is no law. Now those who belong to Christ Jesus have crucified their flesh with its passions and desires. If we live in the Spirit, let us also follow the Spirit.

GOSPEL   On the evening of that first day of the week, when the doors were
John 20:19–23   locked, where the disciples were, for fear of the Jews, Jesus came and stood in their midst and said to them, "Peace be with you." When he had said this, he showed them his hands and his side. The disciples rejoiced when they saw the Lord. Jesus said to them again, "Peace be with you. As the Father has sent me, so I send you." And when he had said this, he breathed on them and said to them, "Receive the Holy Spirit. Whose sins you forgive are forgiven them, and whose sins you retain are retained."

– *or* –

John 15:26–27;   Jesus said to his disciples: "When the Advocate comes whom I will
16:12–15   send you from the Father, the Spirit of truth that proceeds from the Father, he will testify to me. And you also testify, because you have been with me from the beginning.

"I have much more to tell you, but you cannot bear it now. But when he comes, the Spirit of truth, he will guide you to all truth. He will not speak on his own, but he will speak what he hears, and will declare to you the things that are coming. He will glorify me, because he will take from what is mine and declare it to you. Everything that the Father has is mine; for this reason I told you that he will take from what is mine and declare it to you."

The external manifestations that accompanied the outpouring of the Spirit at the time of Pentecost were all phenomena associated with a theophany or experience of God. As those in the room were filled with the Spirit, they began to speak in other languages, a feat that could only have supernatural origin. Because the Galileans spoke in tongues and those in the crowd heard them in their own speech, some commentators maintain that there was a miracle in hearing as well as in speaking. The exact nature of this marvel is less significant than is its meaning. It was clearly a manifestation of the universal presence and power of the Spirit.

"Lord" (*Kyrios*) was the official title of the Roman emperor. Thus, to proclaim Jesus as Lord was to set up a rivalry between Jesus and the ruling political authority. "Lord" is also the substitute, in the Septuagint or Greek version of the Old Testament, for God's personal name. Paul compares the diversity within the community to the complexity of the human body. Each part has its own unique function, but all parts work for the good of the whole. This metaphor portrays unity in diversity that is far from uniformity. It also underscores the lack of competition among members. Finally, it points up the interdependence that exists within the community.

This Gospel account treats the Resurrection and the bestowal of the Spirit as occurring on the same day. Jesus' wish of peace is a prayer for the eschatological blessings of health, prosperity, and all good things. The image of breathing life into another is reminiscent of the creation of Adam (see Genesis 2:7) and the restoration of Israel after the Exile (see Ezekiel 37:9). By breathing in this way, the risen Lord portrays himself as one who can create or re-create. The disciples are commissioned to go forth, to declare salvation and judgment. With the bestowal of the Spirit, they are authorized to continue the mission of Jesus.

❖ *Reflecting on the Word*

The King's Speech was a movie particularly effective in communicating the torture of not being able to speak one's mind. We first meet Bertie, the man who would become King George VI, as he is about to speak to his people over the radio. Frustration, shame, embarrassment, anger, even terror—all pass over his face as he tries to speak the simplest words, which cannot get past his debilitating stammer. The movie is about a teacher, Lionel Logue, who comes into his life, becomes his friend, and helps him find his voice.

We have all been given the gift of the Holy Spirit who empowers us to speak the language of faith, hope, and love. As Paul reminds the Corinthians (1 Corinthians 12:3b), "No one can say, 'Jesus is Lord,' except by the Holy Spirit." The gift of God's Spirit brings us to articulate our faith in Jesus as the Son of God. And the Spirit keeps the conversation going even when we become tongue-tied, as Paul expresses so beautifully in Romans where he writes that even when we do not know how we ought to pray, "through our inarticulate groans the Spirit is pleading for us" (8:26).

When Jesus breathed on the apostles and said, "Receive the Holy Spirit," he was sending to them the great gift of divine life and making them children of the new creation, empowering them to be carriers of this new life through the gospel of salvation they would preach to the ends of the earth.

- When have you felt the Spirit working through the words of others in everyday life?
- God continues to speak to us at every Eucharist through the readings and the preaching. What helps you to be attentive to what God may be trying to say?

❖❖ *Responding to the Word*

Come, Holy Spirit, come. Give us your wisdom and understanding. Loosen our tongues to bless and praise the Father and the Son for the great gift we received at our baptism, when we came to birth in your life-giving grace. Increase our faith so we might proclaim with all our hearts, "Jesus is Lord!"

After all the excitement of Easter, we are now back in Ordinary Time. Our attention is first turned to two of the most significant tenets of our faith, the fundamental mystery of the Most Holy Trinity, and the eucharistic celebration of the Most Holy Body and Blood of Christ. We then consider aspects of life that meet us day in and day out. The readings offer us a perspective for discovering that ordinary does not mean empty or dull. Ordinary is really the norm, the usual standard, and so we are treated to insights that can deepen our appreciation of the norm.

Once again, though the first readings are rich in theological meaning, in the Lectionary they are in some way linked with their respective Gospels, and it is the Gospel that is normally the focus of consideration. This year we are led through Mark's Gospel. Each selection offers a glimpse of a particular facet of Jesus. We see him wielding the power of the Creator, exercising authority over death, wearing the heavy prophetic mantle, and authorizing his followers to continue his mission after his Ascension. All of these features present him as one who possesses extraordinary power.

As we approach the account of the multiplication of the loaves, we move into the discourse on the "bread of life" from John's Gospel. In it Jesus gradually reveals his true identity and invites us into a life of union with him. He first miraculously feeds the multitude. Next he claims that those who believe in him will not hunger, because he is the bread of life. He concludes with instruction, boldly insisting that if we do not feed on his flesh and blood, we will have no life. Although the claims are incredible, Jesus does not retract them. It is up to us to decide whether or not we will accept him as the one who has the words of eternal life.

Continuous readings from two different Epistles give us glimpses of issues that faced the early Christian communities and the theology that governed the way they were told to handle them. With the Corinthians, we are told that all of our actions, whatever they may be, should be motivated by the love of Christ. When we faithfully act in this way, we are indeed a new creation, fashioned after the pattern of Christ. So fashioned, we will then treat each other with the same love that we have received from Christ, and we will be willing to accept the limitations of our lives, realizing that God's grace is enough.

With the Ephesians we hear this same idea of living our lives in Christ. It is in Christ that all enmity will be overcome, for he is our peace.

June 3, 2012

MOST HOLY TRINITY

Today's Focus: An Enthusiasm for the Divine

Before returning to Ordinary Time, we pause to ponder two great mysteries of faith: God as Trinity and the presence of Christ in the Eucharist. Today's feast of the Most Holy Trinity invites us to a state of enthusiasm for who God is and what God has done for us.

FIRST READING
Deuteronomy 4:32–34, 39–40

Moses said to the people: "Ask now of the days of old, before your time, ever since God created man upon the earth; ask from one end of the sky to the other: Did anything so great ever happen before? Was it ever heard of? Did a people ever hear the voice of God speaking from the midst of fire, as you did, and live? Or did any god venture to go and take a nation for himself from the midst of another nation, by testings, by signs and wonders, by war, with strong hand and outstretched arm, and by great terrors, all of which the LORD, your God, did for you in Egypt before your very eyes? This is why you must now know, and fix in your heart, that the LORD is God in the heavens above and on earth below, and that there is no other. You must keep his statutes and commandments that I enjoin on you today, that you and your children after you may prosper, and that you may have long life on the land which the LORD, your God, is giving you forever."

PSALM RESPONSE
Psalm 33:12b

Blessed the people the Lord has chosen to be his own.

SECOND READING
Romans 8:14–17

Brothers and sisters: Those who are led by the Spirit of God are sons of God. For you did not receive a spirit of slavery to fall back into fear, but you received a Spirit of adoption, through whom we cry, "Abba, Father!" The Spirit himself bears witness with our spirit that we are children of God, and if children, then heirs, heirs of God and joint heirs with Christ, if only we suffer with him so that we may also be glorified with him.

The eleven disciples went to Galilee, to the mountain to which Jesus had ordered them. When they all saw him, they worshiped, but they doubted. Then Jesus approached and said to them, "All power in heaven and on earth has been given to me. Go, therefore, and make disciples of all nations, baptizing them in the name of the Father, and of the Son, and of the Holy Spirit, teaching them to observe all that I have commanded you. And behold, I am with you always, until the end of the age."

❖❖ *Understanding the Word*

Moses admonishes the people to commit themselves to the Lord. He does this by pointing out to them the singular majesty of the God who has taken such a personal interest in their welfare. He reminds them that God chose them out of all the nations and delivered them through numerous signs and wonders, a reference to the Exodus and Sinai events. The monotheism that Moses advocated comes from human experience; since there never had been a god who was able to perform the wonders performed by the God of Israel, there could be no other god.

Paul very clearly states that those who are children of God are so not because they obey the law but because they are led (compelled or constrained) by the Spirit. Furthermore, we can say that it is with and through Christ that we become children of God. If Jesus can call God *Abba*, then we who are joined to him can as well. Finally, as children of God, we are heirs to the inheritance to which Jesus is heir, namely, the glory of God in the coming reign of God. Once again it is our union with Jesus that entitles us to privileges.

The great missionary commission received by Jesus' disciples before his ascension is straightforward and all-encompassing. They are told to make other disciples of all nations. All social or cultural boundaries are dissolved; ethnic and gender restrictions are lifted. The way to accomplish this commission is twofold: by baptizing and by teaching. It is in the name of the Trinitarian God (one name, not three) that the disciples are to baptize. Those to be baptized are plunged into the mystery of that name, and recreated as new beings. Jesus inaugurated the reign of God, at the heart of which is a radically different way of life. This is to be the essence of the teaching of the disciples. Jesus assures them that he will be with them until the end of the age.

❖❖ *Reflecting on the Word*

To be enthusiastic literally means to be "in God" (from the Greek: *en + theos*). A true enthusiast can make you either want to run away or come closer. Listen to the enthusiasm in today's readings.

Moses is bursting with enthusiasm for what the Lord God has done for this once enslaved community. Hear the feeling in his words: "Did anything so great ever happen before? Was it ever heard of? Did a people ever hear the voice of God . . . did any god venture to go and make a nation for himself?" And he wants to pull them into his enthusiasm: "That is why you must now know and fix in your heart, that the LORD is God . . . You must keep his statutes . . . "

And we hear it in Paul's words about the Spirit: "Those led by the Spirit are [children] of God . . . [and] you received a Spirit of adoption, through whom we cry, 'Abba, Father!' " We are children of God and heirs with Christ—if we are willing to suffer with him, so as to be glorified with him. Enter his wonder at what God's gift of the Spirit means for us.

The risen Christ reunites in Galilee with his disciples on a mountain, just as he did early in Matthew's Gospel when he preached the Sermon on the Mount. His work completed, ours begins. Catch the excitement in his words: "All power in heaven and earth has been given to me." Then, he urges: "Go, make disciples . . . baptizing them . . . teaching them . . . and [know] I am with you always."

✣ Consider/Discuss

- When have you felt an enthusiasm that lifted you out of yourself, out of feeling blah or "down"?
- Can this mystery of God as Father, and Son, and Holy Spirit enter more deeply into your life and affect your attitude as you begin the day, be with you as you go through it, and be part of your thoughts before sleep?

✣ Responding to the Word

God who is Father and Son and Spirit, draw me closer into the mystery of your abiding presence in the world and in my life. Help me know the love that has been with me from the first moment of my life, and will remain until I reach my final destiny in you.

June 10, 2012

MOST HOLY BODY AND BLOOD OF CHRIST

Today's Focus: "My Blood Shed for You"

Often this feast focuses our attention on the Body of Christ, most notably the eucharistic bread. This year, the readings speak of blood, the blood of animals that was part of the old covenant and the blood of Christ, shed for our salvation, central to the new covenant.

FIRST READING
Exodus 24:3–8

When Moses came to the people and related all the words and ordinances of the LORD, they all answered with one voice, "We will do everything that the LORD has told us." Moses then wrote down all the words of the LORD and, rising early the next day, he erected at the foot of the mountain an altar and twelve pillars for the twelve tribes of Israel. Then, having sent certain young men of the Israelites to offer holocausts and sacrifice young bulls as peace offerings to the LORD, Moses took half of the blood and put it in large bowls; the other half he splashed on the altar. Taking the book of the covenant, he read it aloud to the people, who answered, "All that the LORD has said, we will heed and do." Then he took the blood and sprinkled it on the people, saying, "This is the blood of the covenant that the LORD has made with you in accordance with all these words of his."

PSALM RESPONSE
Psalm 116:13

I will take the cup of salvation, and call on the name of the Lord.

SECOND READING
Hebrews 9:11–15

Brothers and sisters: When Christ came as high priest of the good things that have come to be, passing through the greater and more perfect tabernacle not made by hands, that is, not belonging to this creation, he entered once for all into the sanctuary, not with the blood of goats and calves but with his own blood, thus obtaining eternal redemption. For if the blood of goats and bulls and the sprinkling of a heifer's ashes can sanctify those who are defiled so that their flesh is cleansed, how much more will the blood of Christ, who through the eternal Spirit offered himself unblemished to God, cleanse our consciences from dead works to worship the living God.

For this reason he is mediator of a new covenant: since a death has taken place for deliverance from transgressions under the first covenant, those who are called may receive the promised eternal inheritance.

GOSPEL

Mark 14:12–16,
22–26

On the first day of the Feast of Unleavened Bread, when they sacrificed the Passover lamb, Jesus' disciples said to him, "Where do you want us to go and prepare for you to eat the Passover?" He sent two of his disciples and said to them, "Go into the city and a man will meet you, carrying a jar of water. Follow him. Wherever he enters, say to the master of the house, 'The Teacher says, "Where is my guest room where I may eat the Passover with my disciples?" ' Then he will show you a large upper room furnished and ready. Make the preparations for us there." The disciples then went off, entered the city, and found it just as he had told them; and they prepared the Passover.

While they were eating, he took bread, said the blessing, broke it, gave it to them, and said, "Take it; this is my body." Then he took a cup, gave thanks, and gave it to them, and they all drank from it. He said to them, "This is my blood of the covenant, which will be shed for many. Amen, I say to you, I shall not drink again the fruit of the vine until the day when I drink it new in the kingdom of God." Then, after singing a hymn, they went out to the Mount of Olives.

❖ Understanding the Word

In preparation for the sacrifice that would seal the covenant, Moses erected symbols that represented the partners of the covenant: an altar, which generally connoted the presence of the deity; and twelve pillars that stood for the totality of the people. Two sacrifices were offered, the holocaust and the peace offering. Blood was poured. This was the most solemn and binding part of the sacrifice that sealed the covenant. Finally the law was read. Moses maintains that the blood ritual ratifies the covenant that the words both describe and fashion. The interplay between word and action is quite clear. Neither can adequately perform its role alone.

Several features of the ritual performed during the Day of Atonement serve as a model of the high priesthood of Christ. He entered the Holy of Holies, just as the high priest did yearly on that solemn occasion to sprinkle blood on the mercy seat. Both ritual acts made amends for sin. However, there is a finality to what Christ did. The new covenant promised by the prophet (see Jeremiah 31:31) has been established, and Christ is its mediator. Since some kind of sacrifice is the foundation of any covenant, the action of Christ not only atones for sin, but also inaugurates a new covenant, one that promises an eternal inheritance

The Gospel reading for today is an account of the institution of the Eucharist, which took place during the Passover meal. The symbolism of the memorial meal recalls the covenant of old and reinterprets it. Eating bread together was an expression of companionship; the reference to the blood of the covenant recalls the ratification of the earlier covenant made through the blood of the sacrifice. Jesus alludes to the messianic banquet of the future, the banquet already present in his body and blood, which will be fully realized when the reign of God is brought to fulfillment.

I can remember becoming "blood brothers" with my best friend, Bunky, when we were six years old. We took something sharp and each of us cut the tip of one finger and put them together, declaring ourselves "blood brothers forever." It remains a sacred memory for me.

The recognition of blood as sacred, as a symbol of life, is probably as old as humanity. All life belonged to God. When Cain slew Abel, God said to him, "Your brother's blood cries out to me from the soil" (Genesis 4:10). It was the blood of animals that Moses sprinkled on the altar and the twelve pillars, symbols of God and the people, and then on the people themselves as they entered into covenant with the God who was leading them to a new life.

Today's second reading presents Christ entering the heavenly sanctuary not with the blood of animals but with his own blood that brought about our redemption, providing cleansing from sin and access to God. Later, this author notes how much more eloquently the blood of Christ speaks than that of Abel; where the latter cried for vengeance, Christ's blood cries for mercy.

Mark puts us in the upper room with Jesus the night before he died, and we hear once again the sacred words: "This is my blood of the covenant, which will be shed for many".

He continues to give the cup to his disciples, so we might have his life in us. Jesus is the Lord of Life.

❖ Consider/Discuss

- How do you experience "giving your blood," whether at the doctor's for a blood test or when contributing to a blood drive?
- What do Jesus' words at Mass mean to you:
  "Take this, all of you, and drink from it,
  for this is the chalice of my Blood,
  the Blood of the new and eternal covenant
  Which will be poured out for you and for many
  for the forgiveness of sins."

❖ Responding to the Word

Lord Jesus, at baptism we were washed in the blood of the Lamb; at every Communion, we eat your Body and drink your Blood. Through the power of the Holy Spirit, we continue to live with your life, sharing in your divinity as you have shared in our humanity. For this we give you praise and thanks.

June 17, 2012

ELEVENTH SUNDAY IN ORDINARY TIME

Today's Focus: Seeds of Hope

Fathering, like mothering, is a vocation dedicated to the growth of something precious, a child. Today's readings use the image of the miracle of growth: a transplanted shoot stretching into a mighty cedar, the kingdom of God flowering into a welcoming shelter, the Christian growing through faith into the fullness of eternal life.

FIRST READING
Ezekiel 17:22–24

Thus says the Lord GOD:
I, too, will take from the crest of the cedar,
    from its topmost branches tear off a tender shoot,
and plant it on a high and lofty mountain;
    on the mountain heights of Israel I will plant it.
It shall put forth branches and bear fruit,
    and become a majestic cedar.
Birds of every kind shall dwell beneath it,
    every winged thing in the shade of its boughs.
And all the trees of the field shall know
    that I, the Lord,
bring low the high tree,
    lift high the lowly tree,
wither up the green tree,
    and make the withered tree bloom.
As I, the LORD, have spoken, so will I do.

PSALM RESPONSE
Psalm 92:2a

Lord, it is good to give thanks to you.

SECOND READING
2 Corinthians 5:6–10

Brothers and sisters: We are always courageous, although we know that while we are at home in the body we are away from the Lord, for we walk by faith, not by sight. Yet we are courageous, and we would rather leave the body and go home to the Lord. Therefore, we aspire to please him, whether we are at home or away. For we must all appear before the judgment seat of Christ, so that each may receive recompense, according to what he did in the body, whether good or evil.

GOSPEL

Mark 4:26–34

Jesus said to the crowds: "This is how it is with the kingdom of God; it is as if a man were to scatter seed on the land and would sleep and rise night and day and through it all the seed would sprout and grow, he knows not how. Of its own accord the land yields fruit, first the blade, then the ear, then the full grain in the ear. And when the grain is ripe, he wields the sickle at once, for the harvest has come."

He said, "To what shall we compare the kingdom of God, or what parable can we use for it? It is like a mustard seed that, when it is sown in the ground, is the smallest of all the seeds on the earth. But once it is sown, it springs up and becomes the largest of plants and puts forth large branches, so that the birds of the sky can dwell in its shade." With many such parables he spoke the word to them as they were able to understand it. Without parables he did not speak to them, but to his own disciples he explained everything in private.

❖ Understanding the Word

Ezekiel pronounces an oracle of salvation employing a fable about a cedar tree. The tender shoot is destined to be planted on the heights of Israel, the very place from which the Davidic dynasty ruled. The words of the Lord describe a reversal performed by God. The twig that was once insignificant and vulnerable will be exalted on a high and lofty mountain. The messianic character of this image is obvious. The divine force of these prophetic words is underscored in the very last verse: The Lord has spoken it, and it is done. The transformation of the tender shoot is but another wonder performed by the sovereign Lord.

Paul instructs the Corinthians on how to live in a time when, though committed to the Lord, they do not see the Lord face to face. This sermon draws a clear distinction between this life and the next. It emphasizes the need to live by faith now, because we cannot live by sight alone. During this life believers are at home in the body, but away from the Lord. In the next life, they will be away from the body and at home with the Lord. Paul ends his exhortation with a sobering thought. At the end of this life, all will stand before Christ to be judged according to whether or not they did in fact live lives of faith after his example.

Jesus' first saying characterizes the reign of God as a seed that takes root, grows, and produces its plant in some secret place within the earth. The seed itself may be quite inconsequential, but deep within itself it possesses great potential. The amazing qualities of a seed are the focus of the parable that follows. The passage ends with a summary statement about Jesus' teaching in parables. They forced his hearers to stretch their imaginations and to make connections that they might not ordinarily make. The presumption was that those who followed Jesus were always willing or able to do this.

✤ Reflecting on the Word

I watch most of the children in my three brothers' families growing into what is called "emerging adulthood." It must be very difficult at times for parents, only being able to watch, hope, and pray as their children start to move away from home and begin to make their own way into the world. Will they be safe, make the right choices, be happy?

Making use of images from nature, scripture reminds us that God gives the growth, whether it is to mighty cedars springing from small shoots, ripened grain sprouting from the blade, or a fully grown mustard plant emerging from the tiniest of seeds to offer its large branches as housing for the birds.

Such poetic language calls us to reflect on the mystery of the kingdom of God, whose seeds were found in the various covenants extended to Noah, Abraham, Moses, and David, and then fully enfleshed in Jesus so many millennia ago. This kingdom continues to sprout in our day, often where least expected.

Sometimes it breaks through like a mighty cedar, but more often it is a quieter blossoming, suddenly emerging like stalks of grain, or the first signs of life carried in a mother's body. I am sure God has worried for all the children of every age who have filled the earth. The kingdom of life won by Christ continues to have the power to carry all God's sons and daughters into the loving arms of the God Jesus taught us to call Father.

✤ Consider/Discuss

- What do you see around you that speaks of the mystery of growth? What encourages or discourages growth?
- What is God presently calling to grow to fullness in your own life? In the life of your parish community? In our world?

✤ Responding to the Word

God of all life, we thank you for the many ways life continues to flourish in our world and in our land. Bless the life you have entrusted to our care. Guide us in raising it to harvest. Remove any obstacles we place in its way. We ask this in Jesus' name.

June 24, 2012

NATIVITY OF SAINT JOHN THE BAPTIST

Today's Focus: A Day for Singing

Some patristic writings claim that the birth of Jesus was placed in the calendar when the days begin to lengthen in the Northern Hemisphere. John's birth marks the time when the days are getting shorter: "He must increase; I must decrease."

FIRST
READING
Isaiah 49:1–6

Hear me, O coastlands
    listen, O distant peoples.
The LORD called me from birth,
    from my mother's womb he gave me my name.
He made of me a sharp-edged sword
    and concealed me in the shadow of his arm.
He made me a polished arrow,
    in his quiver he hid me.
You are my servant, he said to me,
    Israel, through whom I show my glory.

Though I thought I had toiled in vain,
    and for nothing, uselessly, spent my strength,
yet my reward is with the LORD,
    my recompense is with my God.
For now the LORD has spoken
    who formed me as his servant from the womb,
that Jacob may be brought back to him
    and Israel gathered to him;
and I am made glorious in the sight of the LORD,
    and my God is now my strength!
It is too little, he says, for you to be my servant,
    to raise up the tribes of Jacob,
    and restore the survivors of Israel;
I will make you a light to the nations,
    that my salvation my reach to the ends of the earth.

PSALM
RESPONSE
Psalm 139:14a

I praise you for I am wonderfully made.

SECOND READING
Acts 13:22–26

In those days, Paul said: "God raised up David as their king; of him he testified, 'I have found David, son of Jesse, a man after my own heart; he will carry out my every wish.' From this man's descendants God, according to his promise, has brought to Israel a savior, Jesus. John heralded his coming by proclaiming a baptism of repentance to all the people of Israel; and as John was completing his course, he would say, 'What do you suppose that I am? I am not he. Behold, one is coming after me; I am not worthy to unfasten the sandals of his feet.'

"My brothers, children of the family of Abraham, and those others among you who are God-fearing, to us this word of salvation has been sent."

GOSPEL
Luke 1:57–66, 80

When the time arrived for Elizabeth to have her child she gave birth to a son. Her neighbors and relatives heard that the Lord had shown his great mercy toward her, and they rejoiced with her. When they came on the eighth day to circumcise the child, they were going to call him Zechariah after his father, but his mother said in reply, "No. He will be called John." But they answered her, "There is no one among your relatives who has this name." So they made signs, asking his father what he wished him to be called. He asked for a tablet and wrote, "John is his name," and all were amazed. Immediately his mouth was opened, his tongue freed, and he spoke blessing God. Then fear came upon all their neighbors, and all these matters were discussed throughout the hill country of Judea. All who heard these things took them to heart, saying, "What, then, will this child be?" For surely the hand of the Lord was with him.

The child grew and became strong in spirit, and he was in the desert until the day of his manifestation to Israel.

❖ Understanding the Word

The servant of the Lord is commissioned to gather the dispersed people of Israel. However, as important as this might be, it is really too narrow a responsibility. Therefore, the mission of the servant will be expanded to include all of the nations. A mission that originally focused on the rebirth of one nation is broken open to include the salvation of all. It is noteworthy that a people struggling with its own survival after its defeat at the hands of a more powerful nation should envision its God as concerned with the salvation of all, presumably even the nation at whose hands it suffered. Yet this is precisely what "light to the nations" suggests.

Paul provides a brief summary of some of the stages in the unfolding of God's plan of salvation. It began with David, who, though originally overlooked, eventually established the royal dynasty from which came the Messiah. God continued to ready the world for the advent of this messiah through the preaching of John the Baptist. Paul's purpose in reminding his hearers of the roles played by David and John was to place his own preaching squarely within this tradition. Here Paul is speaking to people who would have appreciated his references to David and who might even have had some acquaintance with John the Baptist.

In Israelite society, circumcision was the boy's initiation into the community of the people of God. Here circumcision and naming have been combined. It is clear that this was truly a chosen child, for his father Zechariah was given back his speech when he confirmed that the child was to be named John. John had indeed been set apart by God for a mission to the people of Israel. In preparation for this, he spent his days in the wilderness, the place that was traditionally considered a testing ground. It was there that he was strengthened in spirit for the task before him.

✢ Reflecting on the Word

Luke's infancy narrative would make a wonderful opera. One song leads to another, beginning with Elizabeth's joyful greeting to Mary, then Mary's Magnificat, followed by Zechariah's song at John's birth, climaxing with the angels' hymn at Christ's birth, and gently closing with old Simeon's canticle in the temple.

Today we focus on the event that motivated Zechariah's great song of praise: the birth of John the Baptist. To appreciate this story we must remember the events leading up to what we hear in the Gospel. The archangel Gabriel had appeared to the priest Zechariah as he was offering incense in the temple, telling him that he and his long-barren wife, Elizabeth, would finally have their prayers answered with a son who would do great things for God. Quite taken aback, Zechariah asked how he could know this to be true. Wrong question! For doubting, he was made mute.

Just as Elizabeth gave birth to a son, Zechariah gave birth to a song, one of the most beautiful in scripture, recognizing "the Lord, the God of Israel who has visited and brought redemption to his people," and hailing his infant child as one who would be called "the prophet of the Most High, going before the Lord to prepare his way" (see Luke 1:68–79). John, of course, would go into the desert to sing his own song: "Prepare the way of the Lord, make straight his paths." And, in the fullness of time, Jesus, God's love song to the world, came, and the singing still goes on.

✢ Consider/Discuss

- What song has God given you to sing? (And don't say, "I can't sing!")
- What song does our parish sing to God? Our country? Our world?

✢ Responding to the Word

God of all creation, from the beginning creation sang as you brought the world from chaos into light. Throughout the story of Israel, men and women raised their voices praising your holy name. In Jesus you sang your song of love to us. May our voices join with all the angels and saints in joyful praise.

July 1, 2012

THIRTEENTH SUNDAY IN ORDINARY TIME

Today's Focus: Gracious Living

"Gracious living" can sound like one of those monthly magazines containing recipes and the latest in home design. But it is far more demanding when we understand it from a Pauline perspective as a call to live in imitation of the "gracious action of our Lord Jesus Christ."

FIRST READING
Wisdom 1: 13–15; 2:23–24

God did not make death,
    nor does he rejoice in the destruction of the living.
For he fashioned all things that they might have being;
    and the creatures of the world are wholesome,
and there is not a destructive drug among them
    nor any domain of the netherworld on earth,
    for justice is undying.
For God formed man to be imperishable;
    the image of his own nature he made him.
But by the envy of the devil, death entered the world,
    and they who belong to his company experience it.

PSALM RESPONSE
Psalm 30:2a

I will praise you, Lord, for you have rescued me.

SECOND READING
2 Corinthians 8:7, 9, 13–15

Brothers and sisters: As you excel in every respect, in faith, discourse, knowledge, all earnestness, and in the love we have for you, may you excel in this gracious act also.

For you know the gracious act of our Lord Jesus Christ, that though he was rich, for your sake he became poor, so that by his poverty you might become rich. Not that others should have relief while you are burdened, but that as a matter of equality your abundance at the present time should supply their needs, so that their abundance may also supply your needs, that there may be equality. As it is written:
    Whoever had much did not have more,
      and whoever had little did not have less.

GOSPEL
Mark 5:21–43
or 5:21–24,
35b–43

When Jesus had crossed again in the boat to the other side, a large crowd gathered around him, and he stayed close to the sea. One of the synagogue officials, named Jairus, came forward. Seeing him he fell at his feet and pleaded earnestly with him, saying, "My daughter is at the point of death. Please, come and lay your hands on her that she may get well and live." He went off with him, and a large crowd followed him and pressed upon him.

[There was a woman afflicted with hemorrhages for twelve years. She had suffered greatly at the hands of the many doctors and had spent all that she had. Yet she was not helped but only grew worse. She had heard about Jesus and came up behind him in the crowd and touched his cloak. She said, "If I but touch his clothes, I shall be cured." Immediately her flow of blood dried up. She felt in her body that she was healed of her affliction. Jesus, aware at once that power had gone out from him, turned around in the crowd and asked, "Who has touched my clothes?" But his disciples said to Jesus, "You see how the crowd is pressing upon you, and yet you ask, 'Who touched me?' " And he looked around to see who had done it. The woman, realizing what had happened to her, approached in fear and trembling. She fell down before Jesus and told him the whole truth. He said to her, "Daughter, your faith has saved you. Go in peace and be cured of your affliction."]

While he was still speaking, people from the synagogue official's house arrived and said, "Your daughter has died; why trouble the teacher any longer?" Disregarding the message that was reported, Jesus said to the synagogue official, "Do not be afraid; just have faith." He did not allow anyone to accompany him inside except Peter, James, and John, the brother of James. When they arrived at the house of the synagogue official, he caught sight of a commotion, people weeping and wailing loudly. So he went in and said to them, "Why this commotion and weeping? The child is not dead but asleep." And they ridiculed him. Then he put them all out. He took along the child's father and mother and those who were with him and entered the room where the child was. He took the child by the hand and said to her, "*Talitha koum,*" which means, "Little girl, I say to you, arise!" The girl, a child of twelve, arose immediately and walked around. At that they were utterly astounded. He gave strict orders that no one should know this and said that she should be given something to eat.

The claim that God did not make death calls to mind the story of the first sin, which brought death into the world. The Wisdom author's view of immortality is influenced by both the Jewish idea of covenant bond and the Greek concept of immortality. He claims that "justice is undying." Since this immortal justice characterizes the covenantal relationship of human beings with the immortal God, this relationship is undying as well. The author further argues that, though mortal by nature, as images of God human beings were meant to be imperishable.

Paul pleads with the Corinthian community to come to the assistance of less fortunate Christians. He exhorts them to embrace this new venture with the same enthusiasm that they have shown in other areas of Christian living. He then turns to the example of Jesus, who willingly relinquished life itself for the sake of the Corinthians. He is merely asking that they give out of their abundance, for this is the basis of Christian sharing. Paul assures them that those with whom they are generous have riches to share as well. These may not be material treasures, but they are resources for which the Corinthians have need.

The Gospel reading consists of two healing accounts. A distraught father throws himself at the feet of Jesus and pleads for the life of his daughter. While on his way to heal her, a woman suffering from a hemorrhage seeks a cure by touching Jesus. Both stories demonstrate the faith in the power of God working through Jesus. The healing of the woman, though performed in public, was really a private affair. The raising of the girl, though accomplished in private, was in danger of becoming widely known. At the heart of each of these stories is the invitation to faith in Jesus and his power over sickness and death.

✛ *Reflecting on the Word*

How many times have we taken to heart the opening greeting often used at Sunday Eucharist: "May the grace of our Lord Jesus Christ, the love of God and the fellowship of the Holy Spirit be with you"? To live graciously is to live within and out of the grace of our Lord Jesus Christ.

In today's reading from the Second Letter to the Corinthians, Paul commends the community for excelling in many ways but expresses the hope that they will excel in imitating the gracious act of our Lord Jesus Christ. He is referring to their acting in imitation of Christ's self-emptying. Christ who was rich in divinity became poor by pouring himself out for others. In self-offering, he gave himself both in ministry and especially on the cross, that others might be freed from the power of sickness and death.

Today we see Jesus graciously reach out to two desperate women. One had been hemorrhaging for twelve years, making her continually "unclean," so she could not be in any contact with friends or family, or worship with others. She had lost everything, was truly impoverished. The other was a twelve-year-old girl whose frantic father had come for Jesus to heal her. To both women Jesus showed the gracious love of God, a healing touch restoring them to life.

The book of Wisdom states that God did not make death. God calls us to live graciously, generously. In Christ's death and resurrection we glimpse the divine plan: that we die to self so as to live in God.

✥ Consider/Discuss

- What does being gracious mean?
- How have you known the grace of God?
- Can you see ways in which God's grace can touch others through you?

✥ Responding to the Word

Amazing, gracious God, look kindly on us and fill us with your grace. Expand our hearts so we might be generous to others as you have been to us. Bless our days that we might spread the light of your life to those who feel trapped by the darkness.

July 8, 2012

FOURTEENTH SUNDAY IN ORDINARY TIME

Today's Focus: Open Your Ears, Your Eyes!

At some point, our hearing or seeing falters, perhaps both. This happens not only in the physical sense, but also in more important ways—in terms of listening or comprehending more deeply. The Good News today is that God does not give up on us. Christ keeps knocking on the door of our hearts.

FIRST READING
Ezekiel 2:2–5

As the LORD spoke to me, the spirit entered into me and set me on my feet, and I heard the one who was speaking say to me: Son of man, I am sending you to the Israelites, rebels who have rebelled against me; they and their ancestors have revolted against me to this very day. Hard of face and obstinate of heart are they to whom I am sending you. But you shall say to them: Thus says the LORD God! And whether they heed or resist—for they are a rebellious house—they shall know that a prophet has been among them.

PSALM RESPONSE
Psalm 123:2cd

Our eyes are fixed on the Lord, pleading for his mercy.

SECOND READING
2 Corinthians 12:7–10

Brothers and sisters: That I, Paul, might not become too elated, because of the abundance of the revelations, a thorn in the flesh was given to me, an angel of Satan, to beat me, to keep me from being too elated. Three times I begged the Lord about this, that it might leave me, but he said to me, "My grace is sufficient for you, for power is made perfect in weakness." I will rather boast most gladly of my weaknesses, in order that the power of Christ may dwell with me. Therefore, I am content with weaknesses, insults, hardships, persecutions, and constraints, for the sake of Christ; for when I am weak, then I am strong.

GOSPEL
Mark 6:1–6

Jesus departed from there and came to his native place, accompanied by his disciples. When the sabbath came he began to teach in the synagogue, and many who heard him were astonished. They said, "Where did this man get all this? What kind of wisdom has been given him? What mighty deeds are wrought by his hands! Is he not the carpenter, the son of Mary, and the brother of James and Joses and Judas and Simon? And are not his sisters here with us?" And they took offense at him. Jesus said to them, "A prophet is not without honor except in his native place and among his own kin and in his own house." So he was not able to perform any mighty deed there, apart from curing a few sick people by laying his hands on them. He was amazed at their lack of faith.

Ezekiel has an official mission, with all of the authority that this entails. He is to be the representative of God, sent by God to deliver a message from God. The Israelites, to whom he is being sent, are a rebellious people, "hard of face and obstinate of heart." They have always been rebellious, from the time of their ancestors to the prophet's own day, and so there is little reason to think that they will acquiesce to a message from God now. Still, whether they resist the prophet or heed him, they will know that he is a prophet of God, because dire consequences of their rebelliousness will fall on them.

Paul knows that it is foolish to allow himself to be overly elated or lifted up because of any spiritual favors that he has received. Such self-aggrandizement could easily develop into a personality cult. If he became the center of attention, it might be detrimental to the gospel that he had been sent to preach. Lest this happen, he is stricken with a thorn in the flesh. The nature of this affliction is not clear. Whatever its nature, it humbled him just at the time he might have been exalted. Praying to be relieved of it, he is told: "Power is made perfect in weakness."

The people of Nazareth were not ignorant of Jesus' teaching and the marvelous works that he had accomplished. However, they challenged the source of these wonders. Who did Jesus think he was? The point of the story is the rejection by those who knew Jesus the best, but apparently understood him the least. It was a situation not uncommon for those who have been drawn out of the group by God to speak God's word to that group. The people here lacked the faith required for the power of God to be effective in their midst. Though astonished by Jesus, they were scandalized by him, and he was amazed at this.

✤ *Reflecting on the Word*

What is it that blocks the ears of the heart from hearing? The eyes of the heart from seeing? It even happens with people who are closest to us: family, friends, neighbors, people we work with. We just don't hear what they are trying to tell us, or our ability to see falters. We tend to see people only as they once were and not as who they have become. We stop looking beyond the surface, saying, "Oh, I see" when we really don't.

This seems to have happened with Jesus when he returned to his hometown after preaching and teaching all through the Galilee region up north. He had been working wonders: casting out demons, curing the sick, healing lepers, even raising the dead daughter of a local synagogue official. And yet when he returns home to Nazareth, goes to the synagogue and teaches there, people respond only with astonishment, not faith. We hear two of the saddest lines in the Gospel: "he was not able to perform any mighty deed there, apart from curing a few sick people by laying his hands on them. He was amazed at their lack of faith."

The same thing happened to prophets in the past. Men like Ezekiel were even warned by God that the Israelites were "hard of face and obstinate of heart." And Paul certainly had his problems, even with communities he had founded. Today's readings remind us of two sobering realities: God continues to talk to us and we continue to exercise our freedom not to listen.

✤ Consider/Discuss

- Can you recognize in yourself any tendency to be "hard of face and obstinate of heart"?
- How do you take steps to "listen" for what God might be saying, to "see" how God might be trying to get your attention?

✤ Responding to the Word

God, giver of all good gifts, help us to see you in the world around us, to hear your voice in the many ways you try to speak to us. Give us that gift of faith so that you can continue to work your wonders in our midst and bring life to your creation.

July 15, 2012

FIFTEENTH SUNDAY IN ORDINARY TIME

Today's Focus: The Family Business

God doesn't work alone. From the beginning God engaged others in the works of creation and salvation: Adam named the animals, Noah built the ark, Abraham and Sarah birthed a people, Moses led them to freedom. Prophets, priests, and kings—all were given jobs. Jesus did—and does—the same with his disciples.

FIRST READING
Amos 7:12–15

Amaziah, priest of Bethel, said to Amos, "Off with you, visionary, flee to the land of Judah! There earn your bread by prophesying, but never again prophesy in Bethel; for it is the king's sanctuary and a royal temple." Amos answered Amaziah, "I was no prophet, nor have I belonged to a company of prophets; I was a shepherd and a dresser of sycamores. The LORD took me from following the flock, and said to me, Go, prophesy to my people Israel."

PSALM RESPONSE
Psalm 85:8

Lord, let us see your kindness, and grant us your salvation.

In the shorter form of the reading, the passage in brackets is omitted.

SECOND READING
Ephesians 1:3–14 or 1:3–10

Blessed be the God and Father of our Lord Jesus Christ, who has blessed us in Christ with every spiritual blessing in the heavens, as he chose us in him, before the foundation of the world, to be holy and without blemish before him. In love he destined us for adoption to himself through Jesus Christ, in accord with the favor of his will, for the praise of the glory of his grace that he granted us in the beloved. In him we have redemption by his blood, the forgiveness of transgressions, in accord with the riches of his grace that he lavished upon us. In all wisdom and insight, he has made known to us the mystery of his will in accord with his favor that he set forth in him as a plan for the fullness of times, to sum up all things in Christ, in heaven and on earth.

[In him we were also chosen, destined in accord with the purpose of the One who accomplishes all things according to the intention of his will, so that we might exist for the praise of his glory, we who first hoped in Christ. In him you also, who have heard the word of truth, the gospel of your salvation, and have believed in him, were sealed with the promised holy Spirit, which is the first installment of our inheritance toward redemption as God's possession, to the praise of his glory.]

Jesus summoned the Twelve and began to send them out two by
two and gave them authority over unclean spirits. He instructed
them to take nothing for the journey but a walking stick—no food,
no sack, no money in their belts. They were, however, to wear
sandals but not a second tunic. He said to them, "Wherever you
enter a house, stay there until you leave. Whatever place does
not welcome you or listen to you, leave there and shake the dust
off your feet in testimony against them." So they went off and
preached repentance. The Twelve drove out many demons, and
they anointed with oil many who were sick and cured them.

✣ Understanding the Word

Amos is told to leave the northern shrine of Bethel. The prophet defends his
call from God and, in doing so, his right and responsibility to prophesy in Israel.
He had not chosen to be a prophet, he had been chosen. He was not the kind
of prophet who enjoyed royal patronage, one who was connected with the court
or with a particular shrine, nor had he belonged to any prophetic guild. He was
a prophet of God, independent of any institution. He insists that he had been
summoned by God to be a prophet and then sent to the people of the northern kingdom. His coming to Bethel was due entirely to the command that he
received from God.

The reading from Ephesians argues that salvation in Christ is not an afterthought; it was in God's plan from the beginning. Furthermore, the believers were
not chosen *because* they were holy and blameless, but *that they might become* holy
and blameless. Salvation is the cause and not the consequence of righteousness. Through Christ, believers are chosen for adoption into the family of God.
Destined for adoption through Christ, we have been redeemed by his blood. Our
redemption exacted a ransom, for we were being redeemed from sin. The author
insists that all of this was done so that God's plan would finally be brought to
fulfillment in Christ.

Jesus prepares the Twelve for their first missionary venture. They are given the
power to drive out unclean spirits, but they can only do this through the authority
of Jesus. They must participate in this mission in a truly self-sacrificing manner.
Jesus prepares them for possible rejection and failure. If this happens they are
to shake the dust of the place from their sandals as a symbolic act of ridding
themselves of any unclean substance that might profane the land of Israel. They
are to preach repentance, drive out demons, and heal the sick. In this way, the
reign of God will be inaugurated.

Working for God doesn't always guarantee a welcome. When the prophet Amos, from the south, showed up at the sanctuary in Bethel, about fourteen miles north of Jerusalem, the priest Amaziah was not thrilled to see him. "Go home," he shouted. "Prophesy there and leave us alone." Amos' response is interesting. "Not my idea to be here, nor to be doing this," he says. "I was a shepherd and a dresser of sycamores. The Lord told me to do this."

Perhaps Jesus' disciples knew the story, since many of them were from up north—the fishermen Peter and Andrew, James and John, to be sure. And more than likely most of the others. When God calls you, you go. The same happened when Jesus came along. All he said was "Follow me" and they did. Now he sends them out, preaching, teaching, healing, and casting out demons. Travel light, he says. Stay where you land. Keep to the message. If they don't want it, move along.

The Lord continues to send us out, as God did with prophets and as Jesus did with those first disciples. The world needs the message more than ever: God wants a family that will be faithful to God, loving to each other and caring for the earth once entrusted to Adam and Eve for tending. God wants a holy people. This holiness comes as a gift from God, if we accept it. For this message to get out, messengers are needed, witnesses in word and deed. That's us.

✛ Consider/Discuss

- Do you see yourself as "sent" to witness to your faith by word and action?
- How do the instructions Jesus gives his disciples carry over into our world?

✛ Responding to the Word

Jesus, Risen Lord, you continue to call men and women to join you in the work of preaching the gospel and delivering the world from the power of evil. Give us generous hearts that we might respond willingly to your invitation and faithfully fulfill the work to which you have called us.

July 22, 2012

SIXTEENTH SUNDAY IN ORDINARY TIME

Today's Focus: A Shepherd's Heart

In the face of leaders who fail to shepherd God's people, Jeremiah proclaims that God will be their shepherd. God, then, promises to raise up one who will shepherd them. This promised is fulfilled when Jesus comes; today we see him as the one who shepherds by teaching the crowd many things.

FIRST READING
Jeremiah 23:1–6

Woe to the shepherds who mislead and scatter the flock of my pasture, says the LORD. Therefore, thus says the LORD, the God of Israel, against the shepherds who shepherd my people: You have scattered my sheep and driven them away. You have not cared for them, but I will take care to punish your evil deeds. I myself will gather the remnant of my flock from all the lands to which I have driven them and bring them back to their meadow; there they shall increase and multiply. I will appoint shepherds for them who will shepherd them so that they need no longer fear and tremble; and none shall be missing, says the LORD.

> Behold, the days are coming, says the LORD,
> when I will raise up a righteous shoot to David;
> as king he shall reign and govern wisely,
> he shall do what is just and right in the land.
> In his days Judah shall be saved,
> Israel shall dwell in security.
> This is the name they give him:
> "The LORD, our justice."

PSALM RESPONSE
Psalm 23:1

The Lord is my shepherd; there is nothing I shall want.

SECOND READING
Ephesians 2:13–18

Brothers and sisters: In Christ Jesus you who once were far off have become near by the blood of Christ.

For he is our peace, he who made both one and broke down the dividing wall of enmity, through his flesh, abolishing the law with its commandments and legal claims, that he might create in himself one new person in place of the two, thus establishing peace, and might reconcile both with God, in one body, through the cross, putting that enmity to death by it. He came and preached peace to you who were far off and peace to those who were near, for through him we both have access in one Spirit to the Father.

GOSPEL
Mark 6:30–34

The apostles gathered together with Jesus and reported all they had done and taught. He said to them, "Come away by yourselves to a deserted place and rest a while." People were coming and going in great numbers, and they had no opportunity even to eat. So they went off in the boat by themselves to a deserted place. People saw them leaving and many came to know about it. They hastened there on foot from all the towns and arrived at the place before them.

When he disembarked and saw the vast crowd, his heart was moved with pity for them, for they were like sheep without a shepherd; and he began to teach them many things.

❖ Understanding the Word

Jeremiah's indictment of the leaders of the people is terse and decisive. They have not only neglected the people of God, they have actually misled them. Because the shepherds had not cared for the flock, God would definitely care for the punishment of these derelict leaders. They had scattered the sheep; God would gather them up again. They had been false shepherds; God would be the true shepherd. God promises to raise up a new royal shepherd, a righteous leader who will govern the nation wisely and justly. The coming king will reestablish both Israel and Judah, and he will do it in the righteousness that comes from God.

The reading from Ephesians speaks of the union, accomplished in Christ, of two different groups of people. The author declares that a change has taken place in the Ephesians. Previously they had been far off from faith, but now, through the blood of Christ, they have been brought near to all those who believed in Christ before they did. Christ is their peace; in Christ they are one people. The passage ends with a Trinitarian proclamation of faith. Jesus has died and risen from the dead and now lives in the Spirit. Through him, in the Spirit, all believers have access to the Father.

Either the apostles were quite successful in their mission, or the fame of Jesus had spread abroad, or both, for the people were coming in such numbers that the missionaries had to get away from the crowds. However, their departure did not deter the crowds, who seemed to know where they were going and arrived there before Jesus and the apostles did. Seeing them, Jesus was moved with pity, for they were like sheep without a shepherd, searching for someone or something that they could follow. Seeing that the people were bereft of strong and dependable leadership, Jesus began to teach them.

Recently I heard some statistics that said for every person coming into the Catholic Church, four are leaving it. It is estimated that 33 per cent of those baptized Catholic already have left. This is staggering news. Where are they going? Some join other churches; others just drift away. Why do they leave? Different reasons are given, but many said they left because they were not being nourished spiritually.

In the Gospel the disciples have returned from their work of preaching and casting out demons. They brought many stories back with them, telling about all that had happened, all that God had done through them. Jesus noticed they were tired, so he invited them for a rest, a little "R and R." But when they arrived at their destination, they discovered that a huge crowd had followed them there.

Mark presents Jesus as one whose "heart was moved with pity for them, for they were like sheep without a shepherd." And so he began to teach them. Jesus is a good shepherd, in contrast to the religious leaders Jeremiah speaks of. The religious leaders of his day made God angry. "Woe" is the equivalent of "Damn you." And for good reason: they were misleading the people, causing them to scatter.

Every age has had its bad shepherds as well as the good ones who have served faithfully. Today more than ever we need good shepherds, as many of those who have served faithfully for years are no longer in active ministry.

✤✤ Consider/Discuss

- Is God refusing to send good shepherds to lead the people, or are there other reasons for the lack of clergy in the United States?
- Have you ever considered inviting someone to contemplate a vocation to ordination or professed religious life?

✤✤ Responding to the Word

God, you spoke through Jeremiah, saying you would appoint shepherds to care for your people. In your Son Jesus you gave us a shepherd who laid down his life for us. Answer our need today for shepherds who will be faithful servants, shepherding with compassion and perseverance.

July 29, 2012

SEVENTEENTH SUNDAY IN ORDINARY TIME

Today's Focus: Looking More Deeply

Today begins a five-week encounter with Chapter 6 of John's Gospel and its Bread of Life discourse. Every Gospel recounts the miraculous feeding of the five thousand (Matthew and Mark have two, with Jesus feeding the Jews first, then the Gentiles). But John's Gospel lingers over this event, giving us time to go deeper into its meaning.

FIRST READING
2 Kings 4:42–44

A man came from Baal-shalishah bringing to Elisha, the man of God, twenty barley loaves made from the firstfruits, and fresh grain in the ear. Elisha said, "Give it to the people to eat." But his servant objected, "How can I set this before a hundred people?" Elisha insisted, "Give it to the people to eat. For thus says the LORD, 'They shall eat and there shall be some left over.'" And when they had eaten, there was some left over, as the LORD had said.

PSALM RESPONSE
Psalm 145:16

The hand of the Lord feeds us; he answers all our needs.

SECOND READING
Ephesians 4:1–6

Brothers and sisters: I, a prisoner for the Lord, urge you to live in a manner worthy of the call you have received, with all humility and gentleness, with patience, bearing with one another through love, striving to preserve the unity of the spirit through the bond of peace: one body and one Spirit, as you were also called to the one hope of your call; one Lord, one faith, one baptism; one God and Father of all, who is over all and through all and in all.

GOSPEL
John 6:1–15

Jesus went across the Sea of Galilee. A large crowd followed him, because they saw the signs he was performing on the sick. Jesus went up on the mountain, and there he sat down with his disciples. The Jewish feast of Passover was near. When Jesus raised his eyes and saw that a large crowd was coming to him, he said to Philip, "Where can we buy enough food for them to eat?" He said this to test him, because he himself knew what he was going to do. Philip answered him, "Two hundred days' wages worth of food would not be enough for each of them to have a little." One of his disciples, Andrew, the brother of Simon Peter, said to him, "There is a boy here who has five barley loaves and two fish; but what good are these for so many?" Jesus said, "Have the people recline." Now there was a great deal of grass in that place. So the men reclined, about five thousand in number. Then Jesus took the loaves, gave thanks, and distributed them to those who were reclining, and also as much of the fish as they wanted. When they had had their fill, he said to his disciples, "Gather the fragments left over, so that nothing will be wasted." So they collected them, and filled twelve wicker baskets with fragments from the five barley loaves that had been more than they could eat. When the people saw the sign he had done, they said, "This is truly the Prophet, the one who is to come into the world." Since Jesus knew that they were going to come and carry him off to make him king, he withdrew again to the mountain alone.

❖ Understanding the Word

Elisha directs that bread and grain be given to the people who have gathered at the shrine. Those who ministered at the shrine objected, because the bread was intended for cultic use. Elisha insisted, and one hundred people were fed by a mere twenty loaves. The miracle is the result of the words spoken by the Lord through the prophet. The original intent of the story is uncertain. It cannot be a reference to the manna in the wilderness, where God miraculously fed the multitude, for there the people took only what they needed and nothing was left over. This miracle reveals the bounteous generosity of God.

From prison Paul admonishes the Ephesians to lead the kind of life that has resulted in his own captivity. Rather than deterring them from following his example, his imprisonment demonstrates the price he is willing to pay for having been invited into a life of Christian virtue. He insists that only such a life is worthy of the call that they too have received from God. All the virtues he proposes are relational and foster community harmony. This is the kind of conduct that engenders peace within the community and provides the members with the inner dispositions needed to preserve the unity that comes from the Spirit.

Jesus took the barley loaves and fish, gave thanks, and distributed them. The eucharistic reference here is obvious. Once again the crowds were overwhelmed by Jesus, following him to the other side of the lake in order to witness his exceptional power. They were not disappointed. They now recognize him as more than a wonder-worker. He is the long-awaited prophet like Moses, the one who will usher in the messianic age. The event took place at the time of the Passover, the feast that coincided with the Feast of Unleavened Bread, feasts that celebrated the saving events of the past and looked forward in hope to the final age of fulfillment.

❖ Reflecting on the Word

Each Gospel presents this event with its own unique details. Philip and Andrew play a special role in John's account. Each looks at the same situation, but their focus differs. Philip sees the immensity of the crowd and the impossibility of feeding so many, but Andrew spies a boy with five barley loaves and two fish, and senses another possibility. So much depends on where you direct your gaze.

The first half of John's Gospel is called the Book of Signs (John 1:19 — 12:50), recording a series of events, beginning with the miracle at the marriage feast at Cana, that reveal God at work in Jesus. This feeding is the fourth sign, serving to remind us that the God who once fed Israel with manna in the desert is now feeding people through Jesus. But not only food for the body is involved here.

However, earthly food is what captures the crowd, leading them to recognize Jesus as the prophet Moses predicted, then to acclaim him as king (Messiah)— the long-awaited leader who would bring them freedom. Jesus flees from the crowd and this understanding of who he is.

This fourth "sign" continues to speak to us. It signals God's desire both to nourish us and to satisfy the deepest hungers of the heart. Also, it reminds us that Jesus continues to work with what is at hand, even when neither the quality nor quantity seem adequate. Finally, this event will lead to a deeper appreciation of who Jesus is and why he came.

⬥ Consider/Discuss

- Do you tend to see problems (Philip) or possibilities (Andrew)?
- What are some of the ways God feeds you?

⬥ Responding to the Word

Nourishing God, you continue to feed us, often in surprising and unexpected ways. Help us to be attentive to our true hungers and to turn to you for the bread that will satisfy them. May we also recognize the hungers of our world and respond to them in the spirit of Jesus.

August 5, 2012

EIGHTEENTH SUNDAY IN ORDINARY TIME

Today's Focus: What Are You Eating?

We have been called a "fast-food nation." Recently voices have been raised about the quality of our food, the obesity of our people, and especially the dangers of a fast-food diet for children. God's word directs our attention to food that truly nourishes us, the bread come down from heaven.

FIRST READING
Exodus 16:2–4, 12–15

The whole Israelite community grumbled against Moses and Aaron. The Israelites said to them, "Would that we had died at the LORD's hand in the land of Egypt, as we sat by our fleshpots and ate our fill of bread! But you had to lead us into this desert to make the whole community die of famine!"

Then the LORD said to Moses, "I will now rain down bread from heaven for you. Each day the people are to go out and gather their daily portion; thus will I test them, to see whether they follow my instructions or not.

"I have heard the grumbling of the Israelites. Tell them: In the evening twilight you shall eat flesh, and in the morning you shall have your fill of bread, so that you may know that I, the LORD, am your God."

In the evening quail came up and covered the camp. In the morning a dew lay all about the camp, and when the dew evaporated, there on the surface of the desert were fine flakes like hoarfrost on the ground. On seeing it, the Israelites asked one another, "What is this?" for they did not know what it was. But Moses told them, "This is the bread that the LORD has given you to eat."

PSALM RESPONSE
Psalm 78:24b

The Lord gave them bread from heaven.

SECOND READING
Ephesians 4:17, 20–24

Brothers and sisters: I declare and testify in the Lord that you must no longer live as the Gentiles do, in the futility of their minds; that is not how you learned Christ, assuming that you have heard of him and were taught in him, as truth is in Jesus, that you should put away the old self of your former way of life, corrupted through deceitful desires, and be renewed in the spirit of your minds, and put on the new self, created in God's way in righteousness and holiness of truth.

GOSPEL
John 6:24–35
When the crowd saw that neither Jesus nor his disciples were there, they themselves got into boats and came to Capernaum looking for Jesus. And when they found him across the sea they said to him, "Rabbi, when did you get here?" Jesus answered them and said, "Amen, amen, I say to you, you are looking for me not because you saw signs but because you ate the loaves and were filled. Do not work for food that perishes but for the food that endures for eternal life, which the Son of Man will give you. For on him the Father, God, has set his seal." So they said to him, "What can we do to accomplish the works of God?" Jesus answered and said to them, "This is the work of God, that you believe in the one he sent." So they said to him, "What sign can you do, that we may see and believe in you? What can you do? Our ancestors ate manna in the desert, as it is written:

He gave them bread from heaven to eat."

So Jesus said to them, "Amen, amen I say to you, it was not Moses who gave the bread from heaven; my Father gives you the true bread from heaven. For the bread of God is that which comes down from heaven and gives life to the world."

So they said to him, "Sir, give us this bread always." Jesus said to them, "I am the bread of life; whoever comes to me will never hunger, and whoever believes in me will never thirst."

✤ Understanding the Word

The Israelites' murmuring in the wilderness highlights more than their discouragement in the face of hunger. Their very real need for food put their faith in God to the test. The entire Israelite community grumbled to Moses and Aaron. Although it is God's leadership that is being challenged, it is God's appointed leaders who are being blamed. It is not the complaint itself but its content that is disturbing. The people prefer their former situation of oppression in Egypt with food, rather than their present freedom without food. God hears their rebellious grumbling and responds, not with punishment, but with provisions. Once again God's divine power and mercy are demonstrated.

The admonition that Paul gives to the Ephesians is a wisdom teaching in which contrasts are drawn in an uncompromising manner. There are only two ways of living: the way of the wise or righteous, and the way of the foolish or wicked. Paul contrasts the life the Ephesians lived before their conversion with the one to which they have now committed themselves. This new life demands a radical change. However, this is not out of the reach of the Ephesians. They must further choose the path they will follow. Will it be the way of futility, or will they be recreated in God's own righteousness and holiness?

Jesus' discourse on the bread of life is actually a response to the challenge from the people who demand a sign that will verify his authority. Knowing that the crowds followed him for food, Jesus makes this an opportunity to teach them about food that would endure. Just as God gave their ancestors manna from heaven, so God gives them the true bread from heaven, the bread that gives life to the world. Through careful explanation, Jesus has led them away from a superficial search for physical satisfaction to a desire for the deeper things of God. More than that, he has prepared them for his self-proclamation: I am the bread of life.

❖ Responding to the Word

Israel's complaining can sound childish to us. Did the people really think that the God who brought them out of Egypt with such great signs and wonders was going to let them die? But God responds graciously to their complaints with a diet of manna in the morning and quail at suppertime. Scholars say the manna (the word means "What-is-this?") was an excretion of desert insects, a kind of "bug juice." Whatever it was, it came faithfully until Israel entered the Promised Land. Israel had to learn to trust God and eat what was put before them.

The Letter to the Ephesians speaks of "learning Christ," learning the truth that is in Jesus, indeed, that *is* Jesus. Learning Christ calls for a different way of living, being made new "in the spirit of your minds," and "putting on a new self." We are talking about a different perspective on life. To learn Christ is to accept him as the one sent by the Father, the one who feeds our deepest hunger for the wisdom that brings life to our world. It's another way of eating what is set before us.

John's Gospel calls us to absorb into our minds and hearts the wisdom of the signs Jesus offers the people. While they focused on the surface event—Jesus providing bread to eat—Jesus calls them to "work for the food that endures for eternal life." Jesus is that food. Jesus, who embodies God's wisdom, is the bread come down from heaven. Are we eating what he sets before us?

❖ Consider/Discuss

- Do you give much thought to what you are feeding your mind? Your spirit?
- What is the wisdom that Jesus brings to our lives?

❖ Reflecting on the Word

Jesus, you are the bread that comes from heaven to give life to our world. You invite us to eat at the table of your wisdom, that we might grow into the maturity that marks us as true children of the Father, healthy in mind, heart, and spirit. We thank you.

August 12, 2012

NINETEENTH SUNDAY IN ORDINARY TIME

Today's Focus: Even Prophets Get the Blues

More murmuring and grumbling this week, this time from one of the greatest prophets who just wants "out," and from those who have been listening to Jesus' claim that he is the bread come down from heaven. Both God and Jesus hold fast to God's plan, which remains good news for all.

FIRST READING
1 Kings 19:4–8

Elijah went a day's journey into the desert, until he came to a broom tree and sat beneath it. He prayed for death, saying: "This is enough, O LORD! Take my life, for I am no better than my fathers." He lay down and fell asleep under the broom tree, but then an angel touched him and ordered him to get up and eat. Elijah looked and there at his head was a hearth cake and a jug of water. After he ate and drank, he lay down again, but the angel of the LORD came back a second time, touched him, and ordered, "Get up and eat, else the journey will be too long for you!" He got up, ate, and drank; then strengthened by that food, he walked forty days and forty nights to the mountain of God, Horeb.

PSALM RESPONSE
Psalm 34:9a

Taste and see the goodness of the Lord.

SECOND READING
Ephesians 4:30 — 5:2

Brothers and sisters: Do not grieve the Holy Spirit of God, with which you were sealed for the day of redemption. All bitterness, fury, anger, shouting, and reviling must be removed from you, along with all malice. And be kind to one another, compassionate, forgiving one another as God has forgiven you in Christ.

So be imitators of God, as beloved children, and live in love, as Christ loved us and handed himself over for us as a sacrificial offering to God for a fragrant aroma.

GOSPEL
John 6:41–51

The Jews murmured about Jesus because he said, "I am the bread that came down from heaven," and they said, "Is this not Jesus, the son of Joseph? Do we not know his father and mother? Then how can he say, 'I have come down from heaven'?" Jesus answered and said to them, "Stop murmuring among yourselves. No one can come to me unless the Father who sent me draw him, and I will raise him on the last day. It is written in the prophets:

> They shall all be taught by God.

Everyone who listens to my Father and learns from him comes to me. Not that anyone has seen the Father except the one who is from God; he has seen the Father. Amen, amen, I say to you, whoever believes has eternal life. I am the bread of life. Your ancestors ate the manna in the desert, but they died; this is the bread that comes down from heaven so that one may eat it and not die. I am the living bread that came down from heaven; whoever eats this bread will live forever; and the bread that I will give is my flesh for the life of the world."

❖ Understanding the Word

The prophet Elijah goes into the desert, not to pray or to recommit himself to the service of the Lord, but in the hope that he will die. The office of prophet has become too heavy to bear. He sits under a broom tree, hoping to die. His prayer is not heard; his mission has not yet been completed. Instead, an angel of the Lord brings him food and drink. Then in the strength of this mysterious food and water, he walks forty days and forty nights, arriving at Horeb, the mountain of revelation. A story that begins in desperation ends with the prophet once again actively involved in God's affairs.

The second reading opens with a plea directed to the Christians not to grieve the Holy Spirit of God. They have been sealed by this Spirit, a seal that is a pledge of the fulfillment of their redemption. The author then urges the Christians to live lives of generosity of heart, compassion, tolerance, and patience. They are to forgive others as God has forgiven them, by accepting the sacrifice of Christ on their behalf. The Trinitarian theology is obvious. As imitators of God, and after the example of Christ, they have been called to live according to the Spirit.

The exchange between Jesus and his opponents was meant to enhance the status of one member of the exchange as it diminished the status of the other. In a clever turn of phrase, Jesus declares that only those drawn by God will be drawn to the one who was sent by God. If one does not come to him, it is probably a sign that person was never called by God. This argument ends with a declaration of Jesus' ultimate authority and power. Not only is he the one who came down from heaven, but he is the one who will raise people up from the dead, for whoever believes this has eternal life.

A favorite aunt once said to me, "We are living too long." Her words stemmed from heart congestion that had sent her again and again to the hospital to have fluid drained from her lungs.

She was tired of it all and weary of life. She was having an Elijah moment.

The prophet Elijah became weary of life. His recent work had brought on the wrath of the infamous Queen Jezebel (for the story, read 1 Kings 18:1 — 19:3), and she wanted his head. So Elijah goes out to the desert, asking God to let him die. But God still had work for him and dispatched an angel with food, drink, and a message: "Get up, eat, and move on. You're not finished yet." And Elijah found he had enough strength to walk for forty days to meet God on Mount Horeb. (My aunt also found she had the strength to go on.)

All of which goes to prove that God is the One in charge.

Jesus tells the Jews that his Father is in charge and that, if they listen to the Father, they will learn that he sent Jesus to bring eternal life. They think they know who Jesus is, reducing him to "the son of Joseph." But Jesus is making it clear who he is to those murmuring and to us who might murmur: the One sent by the Father, who will raise us up on the last day, who has seen the Father, who is the bread of life.

❖ Consider/Discuss

- Have you had any "Elijah moments" lately?
- Where did Elijah get his strength to go on?
- Did you recognize who gave it to him?

❖ Responding to the Word

Father, we ask you for whatever strength we need to do the work you have given us to do. Send your Spirit into our hearts to remove any bitterness, anger, or malice that has taken up residence there. Help us to be imitators of your Son, Jesus Christ.

August 19, 2012

TWENTIETH SUNDAY IN ORDINARY TIME

Today's Focus: Eat, Drink, Live

The image of divine Wisdom setting a table of meat and wine so we may eat and live is matched by Jesus inviting the crowds to the table of his body and blood so they might have eternal life. Ephesians calls us to drink of the Spirit so as to live wisely. Quite a menu!

FIRST READING
Proverbs 9:1–6

Wisdom has built her house,
　she has set up her seven columns;
she has dressed her meat, mixed her wine,
　yes, she has spread her table.
She has sent out her maidens; she calls
　from the heights out over the city:
"Let whoever is simple turn in here;
　to the one who lacks understanding, she says,
Come, eat of my food,
　and drink of the wine I have mixed!
Forsake foolishness that you may live;
　advance in the way of understanding."

PSALM RESPONSE
Psalm 34:9a

Taste and see the goodness of the Lord.

SECOND READING
Ephesians 5:15–20

Brothers and sisters: Watch carefully how you live, not as foolish persons but as wise, making the most of the opportunity, because the days are evil. Therefore, do not continue in ignorance, but try to understand what is the will of the Lord. And do not get drunk on wine, in which lies debauchery, but be filled with the Spirit, addressing one another in psalms and hymns and spiritual songs, singing and playing to the Lord in your hearts, giving thanks always and for everything in the name of our Lord Jesus Christ to God the Father.

GOSPEL
John 6:51–58

Jesus said to the crowds: "I am the living bread that came down from heaven; whoever eats this bread will live forever; and the bread that I will give is my flesh for the life of the world."

The Jews quarreled among themselves, saying, "How can this man give us his flesh to eat?" Jesus said to them, "Amen, amen, I say to you, unless you eat the flesh of the Son of Man and drink his blood, you do not have life within you. Whoever eats my flesh and drinks my blood has eternal life, and I will raise him on the last day. For my flesh is true food, and my blood is true drink. Whoever eats my flesh and drinks my blood remains in me and I in him. Just as the living Father sent me and I have life because of the Father, so also the one who feeds on me will have life because of me. This is the bread that came down from heaven. Unlike your ancestors who ate and still died, whoever eats this bread will live forever."

❖ Understanding the Word

Wisdom prepares a lavish banquet. Everything is ready, and servants are sent out to call in the guests. Wisdom always invites, cajoles, persuades; she never commands. She feeds the desire for knowledge and insight; she satisfies the hunger for learning. Wisdom is interested in the simple, the innocent, the child-like, those who are eager to learn. She oversees all of the mysteries of the universe; in her hands are the secrets of life. These are the delicacies with which she spreads her table; this is the fare that she offers her guests. No one can survive without Wisdom. The way of understanding is the way to life.

The wisdom theme continues in the second reading. Christians are encouraged to live like the wise, not like the foolish. The wise are those who know how to make the most out of every opportunity. They can recognize the decisive point of the moment, and they can seize it. The ignorance against which the author warns is the inability to draw prudent conclusions in practical situations. Some people just do not seem to be able to learn from experience. As a remedy to this, Christians are urged to seek God's will for them and to live in accordance with it.

The bread of life discourse ends with a eucharistic reinterpretation of the manna tradition. Jesus' flesh is food and his blood is drink. His flesh and blood are the source of life for those who partake of it. Just as we become one with what we eat and drink, so Jesus and those who feed on him form an intimate union. Those who share in the Eucharist already possess eternal life. For them, the future holds fullness of life that will be enjoyed after the general resurrection on the last day. Jesus, not manna, is the bread that came, not from the sky, but from the very being of God. Those who ate manna died; those who feed on Jesus live forever.

As a boy, I was often sent to Kauder's Bakery on the corner of Preston and Ensor Streets in Baltimore. There was nothing like the variety of breads today, but whether it was white, rye, or Vienna, the smell of fresh baked bread and especially the crunch of the crust stays with me more than sixty years later.

Kauder's came to mind after reading today's Gospel. Biblical scholars point out that the crowds would have been appalled at Jesus' words: "Unless you eat the flesh of the son of Man and drink his blood, you do not have life within you." The word used for "eat" is a very physical word, the equivalent of munching or chewing. To hear "eat my flesh" would have been repulsive. An invitation to cannibalism! The same with "drink my blood." Jewish law was very clear that no blood should remain in any animal slaughtered for eating. Blood was the "seat of life" and life belonged only to God.

But this is precisely the point. Behind this "sign" is God's wondrous life-giving plan: to bring us into intimate communion when we partake of the very life of the Word made flesh, Jesus Christ. We are not to get drunk on the wine of this world but on the divinized drink of everlasting life. Not mundane manna but the bread that mediates an encounter with the Lord of our salvation. This is truly Wisdom's house, where we eat both the bread of God's word and the bread that is the Lamb of God.

✦ Consider/Discuss

- Can you appreciate the shocking impact of Jesus' words on those listening?
- Do these words have any impact on you or have they become too familiar to shock?

✦ Responding to the Word

Lord Jesus, you call us to the banquet table to eat the food that will nourish us for eternal life, bringing us into communion with you, the Father, and the Holy Spirit. Give us an appetite for this food you so generously offer. May we not turn away from it for other food that neither nourishes nor satisfies.

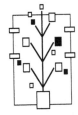

August 26, 2012

TWENTY-FIRST SUNDAY IN ORDINARY TIME

Today's Focus: R.S.V.P.

The sign was given, the words spoken. Then came the time to respond. Many walked away at Jesus' words. From that time until now, the invitation to the Lord's table has been extended, offering an ongoing covenantal relationship with the Father through Jesus Christ in the power of the Spirit. Your response, please!

FIRST READING
Joshua 24:1–2a, 15–17, 18b

Joshua gathered together all the tribes of Israel at Shechem, summoning their elders, their leaders, their judges, and their officers. When they stood in ranks before God, Joshua addressed all the people: "If it does not please you to serve the LORD, decide today whom you will serve, the gods your fathers served beyond the River or the gods of the Amorites in whose country you are now dwelling. As for me and my household, we will serve the LORD."

But the people answered, "Far be it from us to forsake the LORD for the service of other gods. For it was the LORD, our God, who brought us and our fathers up out of the land of Egypt, out of a state of slavery. He performed those great miracles before our very eyes and protected us along our entire journey and among the peoples through whom we passed. Therefore we also will serve the LORD, for he is our God."

PSALM RESPONSE
Psalm 34:9a

Taste and see the goodness of the Lord.

In the shorter form of the reading, the passage in brackets is omitted

SECOND READING
Ephesians 5:21–32 or 5:2a, 25–32

Brothers and sisters: [Be subordinate to one another out of reverence for Christ. Wives should be subordinate to their husbands as to the Lord. For the husband is head of his wife just as Christ is head of the church, he himself the savior of the body. As the church is subordinate to Christ, so wives should be subordinate to their husbands in everything.] Husbands, love your wives, even as Christ loved the church and handed himself over for her to sanctify her, cleansing her by the bath of water with the word, that he might present to himself the church in splendor, without spot or wrinkle or any such thing, that she might be holy and without blemish. So also husbands should love their wives as their own bodies. He who loves his wife loves himself. For no one hates his own flesh but rather nourishes and cherishes it, even as Christ does the church, because we are members of his body.

> For this reason a man shall leave his father and his mother
> and be joined to his wife,
> and the two shall become one flesh.

This is a great mystery, but I speak in reference to Christ and the church.

GOSPEL
John 6:60–69

Many of Jesus' disciples who were listening said, "This saying is hard; who can accept it?" Since Jesus knew that his disciples were murmuring about this, he said to them, "Does this shock you? What if you were to see the Son of Man ascending to where he was before? It is the spirit that gives life, while the flesh is of no avail. The words I have spoken to you are Spirit and life. But there are some of you who do not believe." Jesus knew from the beginning the ones who would not believe and the one who would betray him. And he said, "For this reason I have told you that no one can come to me unless it is granted him by my Father."

As a result of this, many of his disciples returned to their former way of life and no longer accompanied him. Jesus then said to the Twelve, "Do you also want to leave?" Simon Peter answered him, "Master, to whom shall we go? You have the words of eternal life. We have come to believe and are convinced that you are the Holy One of God."

✤ Understanding the Word

In his address to the assembly, Joshua places before them a choice that will shape their own self-identity, and will determine the path that they will travel for the rest of their lives and the lives of their descendants. Whom will they serve? They can continue to serve their ancestral gods; they can opt for the gods of the people in whose land they are now dwelling; or they can worship the Lord. Speaking for his own family, Joshua declares: We will serve the Lord. The rest of the people make the same decision. Their choice of a god is determined by the personal involvement of God in their lives.

The responsibilities of husbands in contrast to a traditional patriarchal marriage are the subject of the Ephesian reading. First, Christ loved the church enough to give his life for it. This is the degree of spousal commitment envisioned for husbands. Following the example of Christ who sacrificed his divine privileges for the sake of the church, husbands are told to sacrifice their patriarchal privileges for the sake of their wives. In Genesis the husband and wife constitute one flesh (2:24). Building on this concept, the author argues that when husbands love their spouses, they are really loving themselves. This transformed understanding of marriage is then used to characterize the mysterious union of Christ and the church.

Jesus' words or deeds were met with disbelief. He responds to the challenge of these unbelievers with one of his own. If they were troubled by the thought of him descending from heaven, what would they think about him ascending back to where he had originated? Both descending and ascending imply that he is a heavenly being, the very claim that scandalized his hearers in the first place. Jesus continues his defense by setting the notion of flesh against that of spirit. He insists that the flesh (the human way of being in the world) cannot give life. On hearing this, some no longer followed him.

❖ Reflecting on the Word

"Does it please you to serve the Lord?" Joshua asked at Shechem. "Decide today." And the people answered: "Far be it from us to forsake the LORD for the service of other gods," going on to name the deeds the Lord had done for them.

Centuries later, after hearing Jesus call himself bread to be eaten, descendants of those at Shechem said: "This saying is hard; who can accept it?" And they "no longer accompanied him." Jesus then asked the Twelve if they would leave, too. Simon answered for all: "We have come to believe and are convinced you are the Holy One of God."

Our response is a simple but weighty *Amen* (meaning "So be it"). When the consecrated host is held up, accompanied by "The Body of Christ," and the cup offered with "The Blood of Christ," we are asked to put our faith on the line and say, "Amen."

Has familiarity bred contentment? Are we so used to this mystery that we rarely have a sense of awe or wonder? The first act of faith is believing that God is present in things as ordinary as this bread and wine. We believe that the bread and wine are changed into the Body and Blood of Christ. What is the change in us that should accompany receiving them?

But of such stuff dreams are made—God's dream of a family, loving daughters and sons, gathered around a table to say "Amen," then to live Communion in a world of broken bodies, shed blood, wounded hearts, and crushed spirits. When you say "Amen" to this mystery, who knows what might happen?

❖ Consider/Discuss

- What meaning does "Amen" have for you?
- Is it a response in word only, or in word and in deed, so that you not only "receive" Communion with Christ and his body but live it daily?

❖ Responding to the Word

Jesus, you came from the Father and returned to the Father and remain ever near the Father's heart. You remain the Father's Word of love to us, the Word of the Father's commitment to us, draw us into being "Amen" as you were also "Amen" to the Father's will. Amen.

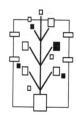

September 2, 2012

TWENTY-SECOND SUNDAY IN ORDINARY TIME

Today's Focus: What Dwells Within?

The issue in the Gospel can seem silly to us. We find the scribes and Pharisees criticizing Jesus' disciples for not washing their hands before eating and therefore not keeping the traditions of the elders. The underlying issue? What renders a person "clean" or pure before the Lord? It's a matter of the heart.

FIRST READING
Deuteronomy 4:1–2, 6–8

Moses said to the people: "Now, Israel, hear the statutes and decrees which I am teaching you to observe, that you may live, and may enter in and take possession of the land which the LORD, the God of your fathers, is giving you. In your observance of the commandments of the LORD, your God, which I enjoin upon you, you shall not add to what I command you nor subtract from it. Observe them carefully, for thus will you give evidence of your wisdom and intelligence to the nations, who will hear of all these statutes and say, 'This great nation is truly a wise and intelligent people.' For what great nation is there that has gods so close to it as the LORD, our God, is to us whenever we call upon him? Or what great nation has statutes and decrees that are as just as this whole law which I am setting before you today?"

PSALM RESPONSE
Psalm 15:1a

The one who does justice will live in the presence of the Lord.

SECOND READING
James 1:17–18, 21b–22, 27

Dearest brothers and sisters: All good giving and every perfect gift is from above, coming down from the Father of lights, with whom there is no alteration or shadow caused by change. He willed to give us birth by the word of truth that we may be a kind of first-fruits of his creatures.

Humbly welcome the word that has been planted in you and is able to save your souls.

Be doers of the word and not hearers only, deluding yourselves.

Religion that is pure and undefiled before God and the Father is this: to care for orphans and widows in their affliction and to keep oneself unstained by the world.

GOSPEL
Mark 7:1–8,
14–15, 21–23

When the Pharisees with some scribes who had come from Jerusalem gathered around Jesus, they observed that some of his disciples ate their meals with unclean, that is, unwashed, hands. — For the Pharisees and, in fact, all Jews, do not eat without carefully washing their hands, keeping the tradition of the elders. And on coming from the marketplace they do not eat without purifying themselves. And there are many other things that they have traditionally observed, the purification of cups and jugs and kettles and beds. — So the Pharisees and scribes questioned him, "Why do your disciples not follow the tradition of the elders but instead eat a meal with unclean hands?" He responded, "Well did Isaiah prophesy about you hypocrites, as it is written:

This people honors me with their lips,
  but their hearts are far from me;
in vain do they worship me,
  teaching as doctrines human precepts.

You disregard God's commandment but cling to human tradition." He summoned the crowd again and said to them, "Hear me, all of you, and understand. Nothing that enters one from outside can defile that person; but the things that come out from within are what defile.

"From within people, from their hearts, come evil thoughts, unchastity, theft, murder, adultery, greed, malice, deceit, licentiousness, envy, blasphemy, arrogance, folly. All these evils come from within and they defile."

❖ Understanding the Word

Moses calls the people to hear (*shema*). It is a solemn summons used to assemble the people of God for consultation, worship, or war. It is used here to stress the significance of the proclamation of the law that is to follow. Obedience to the law is not for Israel's sake alone. Israel's compliance will serve to witness to the other nations the extraordinary character of these statutes and decrees. Such obedience is, then, a sign of Israel's wisdom. The nations will recognize the wisdom contained in this law, and conclude that only a great people would merit so great a God.

Three characteristics of God are praised in the Letter of James. God is first described as the fountain of giving and the source of all the gifts themselves. Furthermore, God's goodness is constant, not intermittent. God is the source of both our birth and our re-birth or salvation. Finally, the Christians are admonished to avoid those practices of the world that challenge Christian values. They are also to intervene on behalf of the community's most vulnerable, the widows and orphans who have no legal status in the patriarchal society. When they do this, the word of truth will take concrete form in their lives.

The conflict between Jesus and some of his opponents concerns ritual cleansing. The custom of hand washing originated as a regulation observed by priests when offering sacrifice, and over time developed into an obligation for everyone. Jesus' disciples were not observing this custom. Jesus' response to criticism is swift and incisive. He explicitly draws a comparison between those whom the prophet condemns and the scribes and Pharisees who condemn the disciples. The very ones who demand strict observance of their law fail to observe God's law. Jesus uses this encounter to teach a deeper lesson. He insists that defilement originates from the innermost recesses of the heart, not from some external behavior.

✢ *Reflecting on the Word*

"Be careful what you allow to dwell in your hearts," Archbishop Edward Gilbert of the Trinidad and Tobago archdiocese once preached during an ordination. This thought clearly flows from the words of Jesus today. The criticism of the scribes and Pharisees about his disciples not washing must have sparked something in Jesus because he lands a verbal body-blow on them, calling them hypocrites and then quoting Isaiah against them for saying one thing with their lips but keeping their hearts distant from God.

All the readings come together harmoniously today. Moses calls the people to keep God's law, to observe all the commandments carefully, not only for their own sakes but so the people might draw others to God. James calls his listeners to welcome God's word that has been planted in their hearts, and to act on it by taking care of those most vulnerable in society: the widows and orphans.

My brother's pastor weaves his Sunday preaching into themes that run several weeks. Last Lent he began a series he called "Christian Atheism," asking whether those who come to church on Sunday act is if they didn't believe the rest of the week. Sometime we get used to living with two creeds competing for our attention: what we say we believe, even want to believe, and what we act out daily. Jesus reminds us that our actions spring from within. So be careful what you allow to dwell in your hearts. From the heart comes forth good or evil.

✢ *Consider/Discuss*

- What are the commandments that really govern your behavior? Are they God's or merely commands of human tradition?
- Can you think of any time "human tradition" has assumed greater importance than God's commands?

✢ *Responding to the Word*

God of truth, we pray for the courage to take inventory of what we truly treasure. Help us to recognize the values that are more reflective of our culture than of your Son. Give us the strength to pursue what you would have us do, and thus honor you as the Father of lights.

166

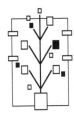

September 9, 2012

TWENTY-THIRD SUNDAY
IN ORDINARY TIME

Today's Focus: The Tender Touch of Healing

The book of the prophet Isaiah has been called the fifth Gospel because it contains so much good news about what God will do for creation, especially for those in need of healing. We see those promises fulfilled in the ministry of Jesus, whose healing touch restores speech and sound.

FIRST READING
Isaiah 35:4–7a

Thus says the LORD:
Say to those whose hearts are frightened:
    Be strong, fear not!
Here is your God,
    he comes with vindication;
with divine recompense
    he comes to save you.
Then will the eyes of the blind be opened,
    the ears of the deaf be cleared;
then will the lame leap like a stag,
    then the tongue of the mute will sing.
Streams will burst forth in the desert,
    and rivers in the steppe.
The burning sands will become pools,
    and the thirsty ground, springs of water.

PSALM RESPONSE
Psalm 146:1b

Praise the Lord, my soul!

SECOND READING
James 2:1–5

My brothers and sisters, show no partiality as you adhere to the faith in our glorious Lord Jesus Christ. For if a man with gold rings and fine clothes comes into your assembly, and a poor person in shabby clothes also comes in, and you pay attention to the one wearing the fine clothes and say, "Sit here, please," while you say to the poor one, "Stand there," or "Sit at my feet," have you not made distinctions among yourselves and become judges with evil designs?

Listen, my beloved brothers and sisters. Did not God choose those who are poor in the world to be rich in faith and heirs of the kingdom that he promised to those who love him?

Again Jesus left the district of Tyre and went by way of Sidon to the Sea of Galilee, into the district of the Decapolis. And people brought to him a deaf man who had a speech impediment and begged him to lay his hand on him. He took him off by himself away from the crowd. He put his finger into the man's ears and, spitting, touched his tongue; then he looked up to heaven and groaned, and said to him, "*Ephphatha!*"—that is, "Be opened!" —And immediately the man's ears were opened, his speech impediment was removed, and he spoke plainly. He ordered them not to tell anyone. But the more he ordered them not to, the more they proclaimed it. They were exceedingly astonished and they said, "He has done all things well. He makes the deaf hear and the mute speak."

❖ *Understanding the Word*

Isaiah depicts two ways in which the renewal promised by God is manifested: those who suffer physical maladies will be healed of their infirmities, and the barren wilderness will be filled with the promise of new life. Just as deprivation and infirmity were considered signs of evil in the world, so this restoration was perceived as a sign of the transformation that only God can effect. It was a testimony to God's presence in the world and to God's victory over evil. Once again God reestablished the original order of creation, and all life began again to flourish.

In broad and clear strokes, the author of the Letter of James paints a picture of unacceptable discrimination. He condemns the preference for the man dressed in fine clothing and the contemptuous way the poor man is treated, thus exposing the community's bias. Such discrimination is not only an example of social snobbery, but it is also in direct opposition to the basis upon which the church was founded, namely, the gathering of all into the reign of God. Such behavior is condemned for two reasons. First, the people are reestablishing distinctions where God has eliminated them. Second, their partiality jeopardizes the justice that they are called to administer.

Jesus is in Gentile territory. There he heals a deaf man. In an oral culture such as his, those who cannot hear are at a great disadvantage. They are marginalized in ways that others are not. Furthermore, hearing symbolizes openness to God. Jesus unstops the ears of a man who was unable to hear his words, so that now the man can hear them and can be open to their message. Those who witnessed this miracle relate the wonders that Jesus can perform to the prophetic promise of regeneration that will take place during the new age of the reign of God. They proclaim that Jesus has accomplished here exactly what was to be accomplished in that time of fulfillment.

Perhaps you saw the movie *The King's Speech* about the future king of England, George VI, whose speech impediment was so severe that it reduced him to tears of anger and humiliation. His wife, Elizabeth, found a speech therapist who was able to help him by using some unorthodox methods, such as rolling around on the floor, cursing, and singing. It is a profoundly moving experience when King George finally addresses his people over the radio and delivers a speech flawlessly, giving courage to his people on the eve of World War II.

The story in this Gospel tells us how Jesus helped a man to find his voice. The man whose tongue Jesus touched with his spittle (an element believed to ward off demons) came to speak "plainly." Another word for "plainly" would be "rightly," in the sense of correctly or truly. "Be opened," Jesus says, and it happens. The man then spoke the truth of what Jesus did for him, and honored him.

As we hold firm to our faith in the Lord, Jesus calls us to both speak and act "rightly" in the eyes of the world, caring for those who have little and treating them with the same dignity as those who have much. We are called to imitate Jesus by reaching out tenderly to touch those who have been wounded by life and burdened by the rejection of others. Helping others to hear the sound of love can be done in many quiet ways and with little fanfare.

❖ Consider/Discuss

- Has anyone ever helped you hear something you were unable to hear up until then, or to find your voice so that you could speak what was in your heart?
- Consider how Jesus has touched your life and enabled you to hear his voice and sing his praise.

❖ Responding to the Word

Lord, open our ears to hear the many ways you speak to us in our lives, to listen for the gentle sound of your voice that often comes to us in stillness. May we be still and know that you are our God, ever ready and desiring to draw closer.

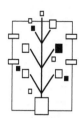

September 16, 2012

TWENTY-FOURTH SUNDAY IN ORDINARY TIME

Today's Focus: Not Your Father's Messiah

We hear Jesus questioning his disciples about what others think of him, then asking what they think of him. Peter rushes to answer: "You are the Christ." Peter is both right and wrong. Jesus does prove to be the Messiah, but not exactly the one Peter thought was coming.

FIRST READING
Isaiah 50:5–9a

The Lord GOD opens my ear that I may hear;
    and I have not rebelled,
    have not turned back.
I gave my back to those who beat me,
    my cheeks to those who plucked my beard;
my face I did not shield
    from buffets and spitting.

The Lord GOD is my my help,
    therefore I am not disgraced;
I have set my face like flint,
    knowing that I shall not be put to shame.
He is near who upholds my right;
    if anyone wishes to oppose me,
    let us appear together.
Who disputes my right?
    Let that man confront me.
See, the Lord GOD is my help;
    who will prove me wrong?

PSALM RESPONSE
Psalm 116:9

I will walk before the Lord, in the land of the living.

SECOND READING
James 2:14–18

What good is it, my brothers and sisters, if someone says he has faith but does not have works? Can that faith save him? If a brother or sister has nothing to wear and has no food for the day, and one of you says to them, "Go in peace, keep warm, and eat well," but you do not give them the necessities of the body, what good is it? So also faith of itself, if it does not have works, is dead.

Indeed someone might say, "You have faith and I have works." Demonstrate your faith to me without works, and I will demonstrate my faith to you from my works.

170

GOSPEL
Mark 8:27–35

Jesus and his disciples set out for the villages of Caesarea Philippi. Along the way he asked his disciples, "Who do people say that I am?" They said in reply, "John the Baptist, others Elijah, still others one of the prophets." And he asked them, "But who do you say that I am?" Peter said to him in reply, "You are the Christ." Then he warned them not to tell anyone about him.

He began to teach them that the Son of Man must suffer greatly and be rejected by the elders, the chief priests, and the scribes, and be killed, and rise after three days. He spoke this openly. Then Peter took him aside and began to rebuke him. At this he turned around and, looking at his disciples, rebuked Peter and said, "Get behind me, Satan. You are thinking not as God does, but as human beings do."

He summoned the crowd with his disciples and said to them, "Whoever wishes to come after me must deny himself, take up his cross, and follow me. For whoever wishes to save his life will lose it, but whoever loses his life for my sake and that of the gospel will save it."

❖ Understanding the Word

The opening verse of the passage from Isaiah sets the stage for what follows: "My ears are open!" Hearing is an ability that is most intimate. The ear catches the sound and carries it into the very core of the person. Because of its importance, openness to sound carries the symbolic meaning of openness before God. At the outset, the speaker acknowledges that his ears are open to hear, but it is God who opened them. In other words, though he stands ready to accept God's will in his life, the readiness itself comes from God. The speaker takes credit for nothing; he is totally dependent on God.

The Letter of James addresses a misunderstanding that has arisen in the church regarding the nature of true faith. Some were satisfied with correct belief expressed in orthodox doctrine. James insists that genuine faith must be practical, expressed in action. Furthermore, it must manifest itself in more than acts of authentic worship. While the issue here is certainly ethical, it pertains to our salvation as well: What kind of faith will save? James' opponents, whether real or imaginary, wanted to separate faith and good works. James insists that such a separation is impossible.

Jesus asks the disciples what people are saying about him. The question is not self-serving. It seeks to discover how Jesus' words and actions are understood, and it prepares the disciples for their own assessment of him. The people believe that Jesus is a prophetic figure who has come back from the dead. Peter speaks in the name of the others when he proclaims that Jesus is the Christ, the Messiah, the anointed one of God. Hearing this, Jesus states that he will be a messiah in the tradition of the Son of Man, the enigmatic figure who will come on the clouds at the end of this age. Jesus then bluntly announces that he will be rejected, will suffer and die, but will rise again.

"Who am I for you?" is a question we might ask another when a relationship becomes more serious. We want those we love to know and value who we are, just as we want to know and value them. A relationship deepens and grows from such exchanges.

At this mid-point in Mark's Gospel, Jesus asks those who have been with him since the beginning of his ministry what they think of him. They have heard him preaching and teaching; they have seen him casting out demons and curing those with various ailments of body and spirit. They have even seen him raise a young girl who had died. So they have been with him long enough to have formed an impression.

Peter's answer is not given the warm welcome in Mark's Gospel that it gets in Matthew's, where Jesus responds by affirming that his heavenly Father has revealed this to Peter. Here Jesus gives a warning "not to tell anyone about him," and then begins to teach him his own self-understanding.

The notion of a messiah was so caught up with military might and kingly authority that Jesus counters it with a different understanding, rooted in the Servant Songs of Isaiah. (We heard one today as our first reading.) Jesus sees himself as destined to be a suffering messiah, something incomprehensible to his followers, as we shall see. But if they want to be his followers, they must take up the cross in their own life and lose their life for Jesus' sake.

❖❖ *Consider/Discuss*

- What does Jesus mean when he tells Peter he is "thinking not as God does but as human beings do"?
- How does losing my life for Jesus' sake lead to saving it?
- Did God want Jesus to suffer? Does God want us to suffer?

❖❖ *Responding to the Word*

Jesus, you call us to know you as one who gave himself for us, so we might be saved and have fullness of life. Help us to recognize where the cross is to be found and teach us how to embrace it, so that we can continue your work of redeeming the world.

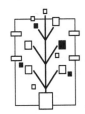

September 23, 2012

TWENTY-FIFTH SUNDAY IN ORDINARY TIME

Today's Focus: Continuing Ed

Education is not a once-and-for-all experience when you go to school to become one of Jesus' disciples. It continues throughout our lives. In today's Gospel, Jesus continues to educate his somewhat resistant disciples into what it means to follow him, turning to a child as his primary visual aid.

FIRST READING
Wisdom 2:12, 17–20

The wicked say:
> Let us beset the just one, because he is obnoxious to us;
>   he sets himself against our doings,
> reproaches us for transgressions of the law
>   and charges us with violations of our training.
> Let us see whether his words be true;
>   let us find out what will happen to him.
> For if the just one be the son of God, God will defend him
>   and deliver him from the hand of his foes.
> With revilement and torture let us put the just one to the test
>   that we may have proof of his gentleness
>   and try his patience.
> Let us condemn him to a shameful death;
>   for according to his own words, God will take care of him.

PSALM RESPONSE
Psalm 54:6b

The Lord upholds my life.

SECOND READING
James 3:16 — 4:3

Beloved: Where jealousy and selfish ambition exist, there is disorder and every foul practice. But the wisdom from above is first of all pure, then peaceable, gentle, compliant, full of mercy and good fruits, without inconstancy or insincerity. And the fruit of righteousness is sown in peace for those who cultivate peace.

Where do the wars and where do the conflicts among you come from? Is it not from your passions that make war within your members? You covet but do not possess. You kill and envy but you cannot obtain; you fight and wage war. You do not possess because you do not ask. You ask but do not receive, because you ask wrongly, to spend it on your passions.

GOSPEL
Mark 9:30–37

Jesus and his disciples left from there and began a journey through Galilee, but he did not wish anyone to know about it. He was teaching his disciples and telling them, "The Son of Man is to be handed over to men and they will kill him, and three days after his death the Son of Man will rise." But they did not understand the saying, and they were afraid to question him.

They came to Capernaum and, once inside the house, he began to ask them, "What were you arguing about on the way?" But they remained silent. They had been discussing among themselves on the way who was the greatest. Then he sat down, called the Twelve, and said to them, "If anyone wishes to be first, he shall be the last of all and the servant of all." Taking a child, he placed it in their midst, and putting his arms around it, he said to them, "Whoever receives one child such as this in my name, receives me; and whoever receives me, receives not me but the One who sent me."

❖ Understanding the Word

The ungodly speak in this passage from Wisdom. They conspire to assault the righteous one who has become a living reproach to them. Three matters in particular plague them. This honorable person stands in opposition to the wrong-doings of the wicked; he denounces them for their sin; and he accuses them of not being faithful to their upbringing. The mistreatment that is being planned is extreme, even fatal. The righteous one, described as gentle and patient, is now an innocent victim of the evildoers' resentment. The reading ends on a note of apprehension. Will the righteous one succumb to the persecution of the wicked? Or will God intervene on behalf of this just person?

Two styles of behavior are described in the Letter of James. Foolishness shows itself in various forms of social unrest—jealousy, selfish ambition, etc. A life motivated by wisdom generates harmony and peace, which give birth to all of the manifestations of love. While wisdom is generally thought to proceed from reflection on experience, it is also believed to be a gift from God. It is this latter dimension of wisdom that James addresses. The wisdom of which he speaks is pure, totally committed to what pertains to God; it is peaceable, drawing the members of the community together in unity; it is fruitful, producing good works in abundance.

Identifying himself as the mysterious Son of Man who comes on the clouds to announce the end of one age and the beginning of the other, Jesus tells his closest associates that he will be handed over and killed, but that he will rise from the dead after three days. It is not surprising that the disciples do not understand. What is surprising is their competitiveness. Without reprimanding them, Jesus seizes the moment to teach an important lesson. He insists that, following his example, those who hold the highest positions within the community must be willing to take the lowest place.

✦ *Reflecting on the Word*

The disciples may have been a bit slow to understand how Jesus was re-defining the Messiah he was going to be, but they were not stupid on all accounts. They picked up on the reaction Peter got when he rebuked Jesus for talking about suffering rejection and death. So, when Jesus brought up the subject for a second time in today's Gospel, they just listened politely, then dropped back out of earshot and changed the subject to a more pleasant one: themselves— and who was the greatest.

Things must have gotten quite animated because when they got home, Jesus asked about it. Their silence surely disappointed him, since he could surmise what had engaged them. But like a good teacher, he tries another way to make his point. There must have been a child nearby, because he calls her over and places his arms protectively around her, and says to them, "If you want to be first, then be last. If you want to be in charge, then serve. When you take in the least, you take in not only me but my Father." Class dismissed.

It has proven a hard lesson to learn. Or maybe few of us really want to learn it. When you look out at the world, most seem to want to be first, the greatest, the one with the most and best toys, a wielder of power and influence and authority. Choosing to serve the least doesn't make the top ten on most people's "to do" list.

✦ *Consider/Discuss*

- What area(s) of your life does this Gospel direct you to consider?
- What do you find most difficult about Jesus' call to be "the last of all and the servant of all"?

✦ *Responding to the Word*

Lord, help us to follow your call by serving the "little ones," especially those more likely to be subject to the cruelty and indifference of the world. Sustain us in this work with the assurance that when we receive them, we receive not only you but the One who sent you.

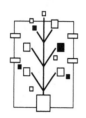

September 30, 2012

TWENTY-SIXTH SUNDAY IN ORDINARY TIME

Today's Focus: Extending Boundaries

We like knowing where God is at work—to such a degree that when God does something outside of our comfort zone, we can find it hard to accommodate. Both Moses' aide Joshua and John the apostle have difficulty when God works outside of the lines they have drawn. Moses and Jesus attend to more important issues.

FIRST READING
Numbers 11:25–29

The LORD came down in the cloud and spoke to Moses. Taking some of the spirit that was on Moses, the LORD bestowed it on the seventy elders; and as the spirit came to rest on them, they prophesied.

Now two men, one named Eldad and the other Medad, were not in the gathering but had been left in the camp. They too had been on the list, but had not gone out to the tent; yet the spirit came to rest on them also, and they prophesied in the camp. So, when a young man quickly told Moses, "Eldad and Medad are prophesying in the camp," Joshua, son of Nun, who from his youth had been Moses' aide, said, "Moses, my lord, stop them." But Moses answered him, "Are you jealous for my sake? Would that all the people of the LORD were prophets! Would that the LORD might bestow his spirit on them all!"

PSALM RESPONSE
Psalm 19:9a

The precepts of the Lord give joy to the heart.

SECOND READING
James 5:1–6

Come now, you rich, weep and wail over your impending miseries. Your wealth has rotted away, your clothes have become moth-eaten, your gold and silver have corroded, and that corrosion will be a testimony against you; it will devour your flesh like a fire. You have stored up treasure for the last days. Behold, the wages you withheld from the workers who harvested your fields are crying aloud; and the cries of the harvesters have reached the ears of the Lord of hosts. You have lived on earth in luxury and pleasure; you have fattened your hearts for the day of slaughter. You have condemned; you have murdered the righteous one; he offers you no resistance.

GOSPEL
Mark 9:38–43,
45, 47–48 At that time, John said to Jesus, "Teacher, we saw someone driving out demons in your name, and we tried to prevent him because he does not follow us." Jesus replied, "Do not prevent him. There is no one who performs a mighty deed in my name who can at the same time speak ill of me. For whoever is not against us is for us. Anyone who gives you a cup of water to drink because you belong to Christ, amen, I say to you, will surely not lose his reward.

"Whoever causes one of these little ones who believe in me to sin, it would be better for him if a great millstone were put around his neck and he were thrown into the sea. If your hand causes you to sin, cut it off. It is better for you to enter into life maimed than with two hands to go into Gehenna, into the unquenchable fire. And if your foot causes you to sin, cut it off. It is better for you to enter into life crippled than with two feet to be thrown into Gehenna. And if your eye causes you to sin, pluck it out. Better for you to enter into the kingdom of God with one eye than with two eyes to be thrown into Gehenna, where 'their worm does not die, and the fire is not quenched.' "

❖ Understanding the Word

Moses is portrayed as a prophet, a spokesperson of God. The spirit of prophecy that was upon him was bestowed as well on some elders so that the burden of prophecy would not be so heavy on his own shoulders. Despite the fact that Eldad and Medad had been preordained to receive the spirit, Joshua felt that their absence from the group disqualified them. Moses questioned the sharpness of Joshua's opposition. Was he concerned with probity or was he protecting the privilege that official prophesying often brought with it? Moses believed that the work of God took precedence over the institutional ordering of the community.

According to James, the wealthy have foolishly and ravenously hoarded the treasures of the earth. They have been busy accruing money rather than sharing it with the poor, and this selfish attitude will be a testimony against them. Some of the rich have even gained their wealth at the expense of those in their employ. Such victimization is particularly loathsome in Israel, since the very event that shaped them into a people was their deliverance from slavery in Egypt. The author depicts the unscrupulous people foolishly enjoying their wealth and comfort, oblivious of the fact that they are really being fattened for the day of slaughter, the impending day of judgment.

The Gospel reading is a collection of pronouncements of Jesus on the topics of acceptance, hospitality, and scandal. Jesus authenticates the right of a man to cast out demons. It is important that the work of the reign of God be done; it is not important who does it. Jesus justifies all works of mercy that are performed in his name. He then warns against giving scandal. Those who cause others to sin will be severely punished. Jesus instructs his disciples to take even drastic means if necessary as a precaution against falling into sin. Nothing should jeopardize the possibility of enjoying life in the reign of God.

Close ties can enrich life, whether due to blood, loyalty, or faith in God. However, any close tie can become overly exclusive. "She won't fit into our family." "He's not for our group." This also happens in God's family. People want to draw lines, decide who is "in," who is "out." God doesn't work that way.

Today we have Joshua upset that the spirit of Moses has been given to two men who weren't at the appointed place at the appointed time. Moses, who knows what it means to be both "in" and "out," has the wisdom to know that God will give the spirit to whomever God wishes. Moses was about extending boundaries.

The apostle John notices a man casting out demons in Jesus' name. "We tried to prevent him because he does not follow us." "Us?" Jesus asks. "Us? Who decides who drives out demons? No one who performs a deed in my name can speak ill of me. Whoever is not against us is for us." Jesus was about extending boundaries.

Human boundaries don't fence in the Holy Spirit. God's open arms extend beyond our imaginations. Isaiah sings, "All the tribes shall go up to worship the Lord. All nations shall stream to God's holy mountain."

So stretch out your hands in generosity. Give drinks of water to whoever thirsts. Protect the little ones. The only restrictions concern whatever causes you to sin and lose the kingdom. Otherwise, expect God to work in unexpected places, in unexpected people, in unexpected ways.

❖ Consider/Discuss

- Have you ever been surprised by God working in someone, someplace, in an unexpected way?
- Jesus' words about giving scandal are to be taken very seriously. Do they speak to your life in any way?

❖ Responding to the Word

Lord, help us recognize the working of your Spirit in our world. May we see your hand in anything done to liberate others from oppression and to bring peace and reconciliation. Never let us bring any of your little ones to harm. And give true contrition to those who have caused others harm.

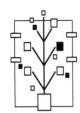

October 7, 2012

TWENTY-SEVENTH SUNDAY IN ORDINARY TIME

Today's Focus: True Family Values

When questioned about divorce, Jesus the teacher holds up the vision of marriage found in Genesis. Mark joins this to Jesus' teaching on the place of children in the kingdom of God. Neither teaching is based on sentimentality but on a recognition of the God-given dignity of those concerned.

FIRST READING
Genesis 2:18–24

The Lord God said: "It is not good for the man to be alone. I will make a suitable partner for him." So the Lord God formed out of the ground various wild animals and various birds of the air, and he brought them to the man to see what he would call them; whatever the man called each of them would be its name. The man gave names to all the cattle, all the birds of the air, and all wild animals; but none proved to be the suitable partner for the man.

So the Lord God cast a deep sleep on the man, and while he was asleep, he took out one of his ribs and closed up its place with flesh. The Lord God then built up into a woman the rib that he had taken from the man. When he brought her to the man, the man said:
"This one, at last, is bone of my bones
and flesh of my flesh;
this one shall be called 'woman,'
for out of 'her man' this one has been taken."
That is why a man leaves his father and mother and clings to his wife, and the two of them become one flesh.

PSALM RESPONSE
Psalm 128:5

May the Lord bless us all the days of our lives.

SECOND READING
Hebrews 2:9–11

Brothers and sisters: He "for a little while" was made "lower than the angels," that by the grace of God he might taste death for everyone.

For it was fitting that he, for whom and through whom all things exist, in bringing many children to glory, should make the leader to their salvation perfect through suffering. He who consecrates and those who are being consecrated all have one origin. Therefore, he is not ashamed to call them "brothers."

GOSPEL
Mark 10:2–16
or 10:2–12

The Pharisees approached Jesus and asked, "Is it lawful for a husband to divorce his wife?" They were testing him. He said to them in reply, "What did Moses command you?" They replied, "Moses permitted a husband to write a bill of divorce and dismiss her." But Jesus told them, "Because of the hardness of your hearts he wrote you this commandment. But from the beginning of creation,

God made them male and female.

For this reason a man shall leave his father and mother
and be joined to his wife,
and the two shall become one flesh.

So they are no longer two but one flesh. Therefore what God has joined together, no human being must separate." In the house the disciples again questioned Jesus about this. He said to them, "Whoever divorces his wife and marries another commits adultery against her; and if she divorces her husband and marries another, she commits adultery."

[And people were bringing children to him that he might touch them, but the disciples rebuked them. When Jesus saw this he became indignant and said to them, "Let the children come to me; do not prevent them, for the kingdom of God belongs to such as these. Amen, I say to you, whoever does not accept the kingdom of God like a child will not enter it." Then he embraced them and blessed them, placing his hands on them.]

❖ Understanding the Word

In the second creation account no animal was found fit to serve as a suitable partner for the human being. The word for partner (*'ezer*) denotes a source of blessing after some kind of deliverance. It is not good that the human creature be alone, but the other animals are not suitable partners, so God creates the woman. The detail that she was built from one of the man's ribs stems from an ancient source in which the word for "woman of life," comes from the same root word as "woman of the rib." Since she is united to him in "bone and flesh," a typical way of expressing comprehensiveness, the man now has a suitable partner.

Jesus' solidarity with the rest of the human family is outlined in the second reading. While in his human nature, Jesus shared the status that human beings enjoyed. However, assuming human nature was for him a humbling experience. In accepting the human condition, he emptied himself of his divine privileges, and if this were not humbling enough, he did so in order to empty himself radically in death for the sake of us all, thus reconciling the human race with God. Jesus' self-emptying death shows that he is not ashamed of the human nature that he shares with all humanity.

The Pharisees test Jesus with a question about divorce. They were probably probing to see if Jesus would disagree with Moses, who allowed it. They challenge Jesus: Is divorce ever acceptable? If so, on what grounds? Jesus does not undermine the authority of Moses, but he points out its concession to human weakness. He insists that in God's original design the couple become one flesh and should not be separated. Jesus' teaching does not make the demands of marriage easier, but it does place the marriage partners on an equal footing. Speaking of the reign of God, he states that one can only enter it with the unpretentiousness of children.

❖ *Reflecting on the Word*

Jesus' teaching on divorce can sound harsh to our ears and even cause pain to anyone who has suffered the trauma of a divorce. It is important to understand that the scribes are testing Jesus the rabbi/teacher and his understanding of the law of Moses on marriage and divorce. Maybe they simply wanted to know what Jesus thought, but it is more probable they wanted to get him in trouble either with the authorities (consider the preaching of John the Baptist on Herod's marital situation) or with the people who revered Moses and the law that allowed for divorce.

Two rabbinic schools of thought had weighed in on this matter. Rabbi Shammai allowed divorce only for adultery; Rabbi Hillel allowed it for just about anything. In Jesus' day a more liberal interpretation prevailed, and divorce was allowed for trivial reasons.

Jesus the teacher becomes Jesus the prophet here, going back to Genesis and proclaiming the intent of the Creator: that a man leave his mother and father's home and cling to his wife, the two becoming one. Here the woman was equal to the man, not subordinate, made "from (a rib) nearest his heart to be alongside him, equal to him, loved by him, and from beneath his arm to be protected by him."

The Church's teaching flows from that of Jesus. God's plan is that marriage be graced and life-giving, a community of love and life. Children, the fruit of marriage, are to be cherished, blessed, and protected, never neglected or abused in any way.

❖ *Consider/Discuss*

- How do the teachings of Jesus and Genesis relate to the contemporary experience of marriage?
- Why does the kingdom of God belong to children and what does it mean to accept this kingdom like a child?

❖ *Responding to the Word*

Loving God, you created man and woman in your image, and have called many to the vocation of marriage as a witness to and participation in the love that binds you, Father, with the Son and Holy Spirit. Hear our prayer for all married couples; make their love faithful, fruitful, and forever.

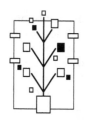

October 14, 2012

TWENTY-EIGHTH SUNDAY IN ORDINARY TIME

Today's Focus: Seek Wisdom

What do you seek? What are you looking for in life? We hear today the prayer, often attributed to Solomon, of one who seeks and receives first prudence, then wisdom. Mark tells us about a man seeking to inherit eternal life. We are all seeking something, not always what we need most.

FIRST READING
Wisdom 7:7–11

I prayed, and prudence was given me;
    I pleaded, and the spirit of wisdom came to me.
I preferred her to scepter and throne,
and deemed riches nothing in comparison with her,
    nor did I liken any priceless gem to her;
because all gold, in view of her, is a little sand,
    and before her, silver is to be accounted mire.
Beyond health and comeliness I loved her,
and I chose to have her rather than the light,
    because the splendor of her never yields to sleep.
Yet all good things together came to me in her company,
    and countless riches at her hands.

PSALM RESPONSE
Psalm 90:14

Fill us with your love, O Lord, and we will sing for joy!

SECOND READING
Hebrews 4:12–13

Brothers and sisters: Indeed the word of God is living and effective, sharper than any two-edged sword, penetrating even between soul and spirit, joints and marrow, and able to discern reflections and thoughts of the heart. No creature is concealed from him, but everything is naked and exposed to the eyes of him to whom we must render an account.

the shorter form of the reading, the passage in brackets is omitted.

GOSPEL
Mark 10:17–30 or 10:17–27

As Jesus was setting out on a journey, a man ran up, knelt down before him, and asked him, "Good teacher, what must I do to inherit eternal life?" Jesus answered him, "Why do you call me good? No one is good but God alone. You know the command-ments: *You shall not kill;*
    you shall not commit adultery;
    you shall not steal;
    you shall not bear false witness;
    you shall not defraud;
    honor your father and your mother."

He replied and said to him, "Teacher, all of these I have observed from my youth." Jesus, looking at him, loved him and said to him, "You are lacking in one thing. Go, sell what you have, and give to the poor and you will have treasure in heaven; then come, follow me." At that statement his face fell, and he went away sad, for he had many possessions.

Jesus looked around and said to his disciples, "How hard it is for those who have wealth to enter the kingdom of God!" The disciples were amazed at his words. So Jesus again said to them in reply, "Children, how hard it is to enter the kingdom of God! It is easier for a camel to pass through the eye of a needle than for one who is rich to enter the kingdom of God." They were exceedingly astonished and said among themselves, "Then who can be saved?" Jesus looked at them and said, "For human beings it is impossible, but not for God. All things are possible for God." [Peter began to say to him, "We have given up everything and followed you." Jesus said, "Amen, I say to you, there is no one who has given up house or brothers or sisters or mother or father or children or lands for my sake and for the sake of the gospel who will not receive a hundred times more now in this present age: houses and brothers and sisters and mothers and children and lands, with persecutions, and eternal life in the age to come."]

❖ Understanding the Word

Wisdom is personified as a woman and she is praised as a priceless treasure beyond compare. The speaker is depicted as a king who prayed for wisdom that would enable him to rule judiciously. He proclaims that he prefers her to riches, to health, to beauty, to everything that women and men normally cherish. Of all the wonders that life has to offer, in his eyes Wisdom is the most precious treasure. In fact, in comparison with her, other riches are of little value. Though he has spurned riches, in the end he received them along with the wisdom he sought.

The word of God is extolled in the Letter to the Hebrews for both its creative and its juridical force. It is living and effective, because it is the expression of the God who is living and effective. As performative speech, it accomplishes what it describes; as juridical speech, it passes judgment on what it discovers. God's word is incisive and probing, sharper than a sword that cuts both ways. It can pierce the inner recesses of a person, cutting cleanly amid soul and spirit and body, and penetrating the most secret thoughts of the heart. God's word has both a comprehensive and a profound effect; nothing can escape it.

The initial exchange between Jesus and the rich man raises an important theological question: Can one gain eternal life, or is it a gift from God? The man's question implies that he believes that he can do something to deserve eternal life. Jesus argues that it is a gift. However, a particular way of living is indeed called forth for those who desire eternal life. The man is not putting Jesus to the test; he has approached him with great respect. This is an honest and upright man, one who has been observant from his youth, but who realizes that there is still something missing in his life. Jesus recognizes his goodness, and he loves him.

The wisdom prayed for in the first reading is a gift from God. Perhaps the first question that confronts us today is whether we consider wisdom worth our energy and effort, or whether we are busy pursuing what are considered more "practical" objectives. Consider, however, that the wisdom of God has been described as knowledge of how to do things—in Solomon's case, ruling wisely.

Scripture also connects the pursuit of wisdom with the pursuit of eternal life that the man is seeking in the Gospel. He has come to recognize that eternal life is the supreme value, and he wants to know what he must do to inherit it. Again, wisdom as doing. When Jesus points him toward keeping the commandments, he quickly responds that he's been doing this "from my youth."

He wins Jesus' heart with this response, so Jesus invites him to join his disciples, to be part of a new family, leaving behind his property, possessions, and all that binds him to the past. All too much! He walks away sad. "Who can be saved?" asks Peter. "Impossible for humans, but not for God. All things are possible for God." Which brings us back to prayer. Ask for wisdom, the ability to do what is necessary, and more will be given than you can imagine.

God's word is spoken of as living and effective, a two-edged sword that penetrates our heart, enables discernment, brings light, leads to right action. What does God's word illuminate today?

✤ Consider/Discuss

- What do you seek? What do you ask for in prayer? Wisdom? Eternal life? Or . . . ?
- Do you trust Jesus' promise that one who chooses to be part of his family will receive a hundred times more even now?

✤ Responding to the Word

God of wisdom and life, "teach us to number our days aright, that we may gain wisdom of heart." Send us your Spirit of wisdom and understanding that we may know the difference between what the world holds up as riches and what is of true value in your sight.

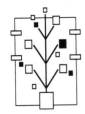

October 21, 2012

TWENTY-NINTH SUNDAY IN ORDINARY TIME

Today's Focus: To Lord or Not to Lord

The request James and John make of Jesus—to seat them at his right and left when he enters into glory—follows immediately upon Jesus' third prediction of his passion and death. While the rest of the Twelve get upset at the two brothers, Jesus offers yet another lesson in what it means to follow him.

FIRST READING
Isaiah 53:10–11

The LORD was pleased
    to crush him in infirmity.

If he gives his life as an offering for sin,
    he shall see his descendants in a long life,
    and the will of the LORD shall be accomplished through him.

Because of his affliction
    he shall see the light in fullness of days;
through his suffering, my servant shall justify many,
    and their guilt he shall bear.

PSALM RESPONSE
Psalm 33:22

Lord, let your mercy be on us, as we place our trust in you.

SECOND READING
Hebrews 4:14–16

Brothers and sisters: Since we have a great high priest who has passed through the heavens, Jesus, the Son of God, let us hold fast to our confession. For we do not have a high priest who is unable to sympathize with our weaknesses, but one who has similarly been tested in every way, yet without sin. So let us confidently approach the throne of grace to receive mercy and to find grace for timely help.

In the shorter form of the reading, the passage in brackets is omitted.

GOSPEL
Mark 10:35–45
or 10:42–45

[James and John, the sons of Zebedee, came to Jesus and said to him, "Teacher, we want you to do for us whatever we ask of you." He replied, "What do you wish me to do for you?" They answered him, "Grant that in your glory we may sit one at your right and the other at your left." Jesus said to them, "You do not know what you are asking. Can you drink the cup that I drink or be baptized with the baptism with which I am baptized?" They said to him, "We can." Jesus said to them, "The cup that I drink, you will drink, and with the baptism with which I am baptized, you will be baptized; but to sit at my right or at my left is not mine to give but is for those for whom it has been prepared." When the ten heard this, they became indignant at James and John.] Jesus summoned [them] the Twelve and said to them, "You know that those who are recognized as rulers over the Gentiles lord it over them, and their great ones make their authority over them felt. But it shall not be so among you. Rather, whoever wishes to be great among you will be your servant; whoever wishes to be first among you will be the slave of all. For the Son of Man did not come to be served but to serve and to give his life as a ransom for many."

❖ *Understanding the Word*

The role that God plays in suffering has long plagued religious people. The misfortune of sinners may be just punishment for their offenses, but the suffering of the righteous is always disturbing. In the reading from Isaiah, the servant gives himself as a sin offering; he endures his agony so that others can be justified. His death will win life for others, and in this way he will accomplish God's will. The violence inflicted upon him is accepted, embraced, and put to rest. With the offering of this innocent scapegoat, reconciliation with God is accomplished.

In order to demonstrate Jesus' preeminence, the author of the second reading compares him to the high priest. Just as the high priest passed through the curtain into the presence of God in the Holy of Holies, there to sprinkle sacrificial blood on the mercy seat, so Christ, exalted after shedding his own blood, passed through the heavens into the presence of God. His sacrifice far exceeds anything that the ritual performed by the high priest might have actually accomplished or hoped to accomplish. Unlike previous high priests who approached the mercy seat alone and only on the Day of Atonement, Christ enables each one of us to approach God, and to do so continually.

James and John seek places of prominence in Jesus' kingdom and Jesus informs them that real prominence is found in service, not in wielding authority over others. The proclaimed willingness of the sons of Zebedee to accept the cup that Jesus will eventually drink and be baptized in his baptism is another example of their misunderstanding. Even if they had grasped the meaning of his words, they could hardly have imagined their implications. Since they believed that Jesus would reign in glory, they could certainly not conceive of his ignominious suffering and death. Jesus assures them that they will indeed face what he must face, but they will not do so willingly as they now presume they will.

186

❖ Reflecting on the Word

One of the temptations in having younger siblings is the felt need to remind them of their place in the family "pecking order," especially when it comes to certain privileges that belong to the eldest sibling(s). Every social, political, or family group has "elders," either by age or rank, who claim certain privileges as their due. Another way to put this is "lording it over others."

Jesus works to undermine this approach to community life. He has been teaching his disciples that he must suffer, die, and then be raised to eternal life. He has just finished telling this to them for the third time when James and John come up to claim a seat at his right and left when he comes into his kingdom. After all, they were among the first to be called! No wonder the others were about to throttle them—not because James and John should not have made such a claim, but because they beat the others to it. It's hard to give up "lording" when the opportunity arrives.

The Letter to the Hebrews speaks of Jesus as the great high priest able to sympathize with us in our weaknesses, similarly tested, yet without sin. This Jesus calls us to service, warning us, as he did the disciples, against lording it over one another and making our authority felt. We too are to follow him in the way of service and self-giving, caring for our brothers and sisters, humbly and without regard for reward.

❖ Consider/Discuss

- Are there particular circumstances that tempt you to "lord it over" someone else? What do you do?
- Do you believe that Jesus really was tested in every way and yet was without sin? Which part of this do you find hardest to believe?

❖ Responding to the Word

Lord Jesus Christ, you teach us that we will find honor in serving each other, not in seeking positions of superiority or power over others. You came to give your life as a ransom for "the many"—meaning "for all." Give us a share in this spirit of generous service.

October 28, 2012

THIRTIETH SUNDAY IN ORDINARY TIME

Today's Focus: Saving Faith

Should we call the blind beggar St. Bartimaeus? He is presented as an ideal disciple in today's Gospel, a bookend to another blind man Jesus heals earlier in Mark's Gospel (8:22–25). Bartimaeus models the difference between saving face and a saving faith. A faith that saves is a faith that sees.

FIRST READING
Jeremiah 31:7–9

Thus says the LORD:
Shout with joy for Jacob,
    exult at the head of the nations;
    proclaim your praise and say:
The LORD has delivered his people,
    the remnant of Israel.
Behold, I will bring them back
    from the land of the north;
I will gather them from the ends of the world,
    with the blind and the lame in their midst,
the mothers and those with child;
    they shall return as an immense throng.
They departed in tears,
    but I will console them and guide them;
I will lead them to brooks of water,
    on a level road, so that none shall stumble.
For I am a father to Israel,
    Ephraim is my first-born.

PSALM RESPONSE
Psalm 126:3

The Lord has done great things for us; we are filled with joy.

SECOND READING
Hebrews 5:1–6

Brothers and sisters: Every high priest is taken from among men and made their representative before God, to offer gifts and sacrifices for sins. He is able to deal patiently with the ignorant and erring, for he himself is beset by weakness and so, for this reason, must make sin offerings for himself as well as for the people. No one takes this honor upon himself but only when called by God, just as Aaron was. In the same way, it was not Christ who glorified himself in becoming high priest, but rather the one who said to him:
    You are my son:
      this day I have begotten you;
just as he says in another place:
    You are a priest forever
      according to the order of Melchizedek.

GOSPEL
Mark 10:46–52

As Jesus was leaving Jericho with his disciples and a sizable crowd, Bartimaeus, a blind man, the son of Timaeus, sat by the roadside begging. On hearing that it was Jesus of Nazareth, he began to cry out and say, "Jesus, son of David, have pity on me." And many rebuked him, telling him to be silent. But he kept calling out all the more, "Son of David, have pity on me." Jesus stopped and said, "Call him." So they called the blind man, saying to him, "Take courage; get up, Jesus is calling you." He threw aside his cloak, sprang up, and came to Jesus. Jesus said to him in reply, "What do you want me to do for you?" The blind man replied to him, "Master, I want to see." Jesus told him, "Go your way; your faith has saved you." Immediately he received his sight and followed him on the way.

❖ Understanding the Word

The procession of returnees seems to be retracing the very path taken when the people were exiled to the land in the north. They had left their cherished homeland in tears, but they would return amid shouts of joy. Jeremiah states that only a remnant will return, and this remnant will consist of the most vulnerable of the people. It will include those who are blind or lame, who are mothers or who are pregnant, all people who are utterly dependent upon God. It will be through them that the nation will be restored. Restoration is a work of God, not of human endeavor.

Patterned after the model of Aaron, the prospective high priest must be able to empathize with the frailty of the people, and he must have been called by God. Jesus did not trace his ancestry to a priestly family, and there was no need for him to make sin offerings for himself. Therefore, his right to function as high priest had to be explained. The author of the Letter to the Hebrews does this by referring to him as Christ, and then reinterpreting two very familiar biblical passages that have messianic significance. Since both kings and priests were anointed, the title Christ, or "anointed one," carries both royal and priestly connotations. To call Jesus by this title is to make a claim about his messianic identity.

The faith of the blind man in the Gospel is both demonstrated by his actions and explicitly recognized by Jesus. When he hears that it is Jesus of Nazareth who is passing by him, he cries out to him using a title that has strong messianic connotations. Son of David identifies Jesus not only as a descendant of this royal figure, but also as the long-awaited one who was to fulfill both the religious and the political expectations of the people. The man who was blind already had eyes of faith and he acted on this faith, publicly proclaiming it.

◆◆◆ *Reflecting on the Word*

A saving faith is one that knows it needs a savior. Bartimaeus must have been told that Jesus was going by, so he begins to cry out, a true cry from the heart: "Jesus, son of David, have pity on me." The crowd rebukes him at first. Why are they telling him to be silent? Do they want him to save face, preserve his dignity? Or does he embarrass them, annoy them?

Bartimaeus is not interested in saving face, his or theirs. He has a saving faith that keeps him shouting. Though blind, he sees what he has to do to get a response from Jesus. An unambiguous cry for mercy, along with a special name, "Jesus, son of David." It carries his prayer right into Jesus' heart. He stops and calls the blind man over. The crowd now encourages Bartimaeus: "Take courage. Get up, Jesus is calling you." A saving faith trumps saving face.

Then, in a gesture that speaks Bartimaeus' faith as much as his words, he throws aside his cloak. This cloak is his greatest possession; he sits on it, begging all day, and wraps himself in it to sleep at night. He now leaves it and his past behind, going to Jesus.

"What do you want me to do?" Jesus asks. "Master, I want to see," he says, already acknowledging himself a disciple of the "Master." Jesus speaks: "Go your way; your faith has saved you." Then, Mark's perfect ending: "Immediately he received his sight and followed him on the way."

◆◆◆ *Consider/Discuss*

- What does your faith allow you to see?
- What do you still need to see in order to "follow Jesus on the way"?

◆◆◆ *Responding to the Word*

Lord Jesus, you heard the cry of a blind man and answered his plea, giving him a new life with you. In our blindness, we sometimes fail to remember how near you always are. Remove any obstacles that prevent us from calling out, trusting in your mercy and love.

November 1, 2012

ALL SAINTS

Today's Focus: All in the Family

All Saints is a day to revel in God's creativity, to stop and remember all those who have touched our lives with truth, beauty, goodness, and holiness—all signals of the living God at work in our world. The only limits are those due to our memory, awareness, and imagination.

FIRST READING
Revelation 7:2–4, 9–14

I, John, saw another angel come up from the East, holding the seal of the living God. He cried out in a loud voice to the four angels who were given power to damage the land and the sea, "Do not damage the land or the sea or the trees until we put the seal on the foreheads of the servants of our God." I heard the number of those who had been marked with the seal, one hundred and forty-four thousand marked from every tribe of the Israelites.

After this I had a vision of a great multitude, which no one could count, from every nation, race, people, and tongue. They stood before the throne and before the Lamb, wearing white robes and holding palm branches in their hands. They cried out in a loud voice:

"Salvation comes from our God, who is seated on the throne, and from the Lamb."

All the angels stood around the throne and around the elders and the four living creatures. They prostrated themselves before the throne, worshiped God, and exclaimed:

"Amen. Blessing and glory, wisdom and thanksgiving, honor, power, and might be to our God forever and ever. Amen."

Then one of the elders spoke up and said to me, "Who are these wearing white robes, and where did they come from?" I said to him, "My lord, you are the one who knows." He said to me, "These are the ones who have survived the time of great distress; they have washed their robes and made them white in the blood of the Lamb."

PSALM RESPONSE
Psalm 24:6

Lord, this is the people that longs to see your face.

Beloved: See what love the Father has bestowed on us that we
may be called the children of God. Yet so we are. The reason
the world does not know us is that it did not know him. Beloved,
we are God's children now; what we shall be has not yet been
revealed. We do know that when it is revealed we shall be like
him, for we shall see him as he is. Everyone who has this hope
based on him makes himself pure, as he is pure.

When Jesus saw the crowds, he went up the mountain, and after
he had sat down, his disciples came to him. He began to teach
them, saying:

"Blessed are the poor in spirit,
for theirs is the kingdom of heaven.
Blessed are they who mourn,
for they will be comforted.
Blessed are the meek,
for they will inherit the land.
Blessed are they who hunger and thirst for righteousness,
for they will be satisfied.
Blessed are the merciful,
for they will be shown mercy.
Blessed are the clean of heart,
for they will see God.
Blessed are the peacemakers,
for they will be called children of God.
Blessed are they who are persecuted for the sake of righteousness,
for theirs is the kingdom of heaven.
Blessed are you when they insult you and persecute you
and utter every kind of evil against you falsely because of me.
Rejoice and be glad,
for your reward will be great in heaven."

✤ Understanding the Word

John the seer relates two extraordinary apocalyptic visions that were granted
to him. Although they differ, the second adds a dimension to the first. The events
of the first vision seem to unfold on earth; those of the second take place in
heaven. Both visions depict vast assemblies of the righteous. There is no sug-
gestion that these people are martyrs. Instead they are those who have survived
the distress of the end-times because they were purified through the blood of
the sacrificial Lamb. This distinction certainly entitles them to participate in the
celebration held at the end of time.

The love of which the author of First John speaks is generative, transforming. It makes believers children of God. Everything that happens in their lives is a consequence of their having been recreated as God's children. They are a new reality; hence, they are not accepted by the world, the old reality. Certain similarities between Jesus and the believers are drawn. The world did not recognize the only begotten Son of God and it does not recognize these new children of God. The implications of this are clear. Believers should not be surprised if they encounter the very rejection—even persecution and death—that befell Jesus.

The teachings of Jesus are all in some way directed toward the establishment of the reign of God. The type of behavior he advocates is frequently the opposite of that espoused by society at large. This explains the challenges set before us in the Beatitudes. The first and the third Beatitudes claim that power is in the hands of the meek and the poor. The second and the fourth promise the alleviation of inner turmoil. The fifth, sixth, and seventh Beatitudes treat aspects of religious piety. The last Beatitude clearly warns that commitment to Jesus' cause can bring persecution. It is clear that each Beatitude invites us to turn the standards of our world and our way of life upside down and inside out.

❖ Reflecting on the Word

All Saints is the wonderful feast that reminds us how God rejoices in having a family of infinite variety, children who strive to trust in God, even in the midst of trials and difficulties, and who remain open to the working of the Holy Spirit in their lives so that Christ can be born again and again in our world.

The Beatitudes offer a profile of God's children. They should be heard first as good news, as gospel, proclaiming where God is to be found: with the poor in spirit, the mourners, the gentle, those who hunger and thirst for God's righteousness—that is, those concerned with living in right relationship with God, others, oneself, and all the earth. In Jesus' day these were not the usual crowd who were declared blessed, esteemed, and honored.

Only after hearing the Beatitudes as gospel should we hear them as a summons to action so our lives mirror the divine face revealed in Jesus: the face of mercy, of cleanliness of heart (a heart open to God), of peacemaking and reconciling, and of willingly suffering rejection in order to help bring about a world of righteous relationships.

God continues to work in us by sending the Holy Spirit, the gift of the Father and the Son, into our hearts to push and prod us, sometimes gently, sometimes forcefully, into a new birth, again and again, until we gradually grow up to become the divine offspring we are destined to be, God's holy ones, the saints.

- Who are some of the saints God has brought into your life within the last year? Ten years? Your lifetime?
- How do the Beatitudes speak a word of gospel to you? How do they summon you to action?

✛ Responding to the Word

Creator God, we thank you for the multitudes from every nation, race, people, and tongue who have heard your call to live in love, and to work for peace, reconciliation, and justice in our world. Draw us into deeper kinship with them so that we might one day join them in the kin-dom of heaven.

November 4, 2012

THIRTY-FIRST SUNDAY IN ORDINARY TIME

Today's Focus: Hear the Law of the Lord

As we draw close to the end of the church year and our reading of Mark's Gospel, we return to one of the basic lessons the Bible has to teach us: What is most important among the many commandments God has given to us for living a good life?

FIRST READING
Deuteronomy 6:2–6

Moses spoke to the people, saying: "Fear the LORD, your God, and keep, throughout the days of your lives, all his statutes and commandments which I enjoin on you, and thus have long life. Hear then, Israel, and be careful to observe them, that you may grow and prosper the more, in keeping with the promise of the LORD, the God of your fathers, to give you a land flowing with milk and honey.

"Hear, O Israel! The LORD is our God, the LORD alone! Therefore, you shall love the LORD, your God, with all your heart, and with all your soul, and with all your strength. Take to heart these words which I enjoin on you today."

PSALM RESPONSE
Psalm 18:2

I love you, Lord, my strength.

SECOND READING
Hebrews 7:23–28

Brothers and sisters: The levitical priests were many because they were prevented by death from remaining in office, but Jesus, because he remains forever, has a priesthood that does not pass away. Therefore, he is always able to save those who approach God through him, since he lives forever to make intercession for them.

It was fitting that we should have such a high priest: holy, innocent, undefiled, separated from sinners, higher than the heavens. He has no need, as did the high priests, to offer sacrifice day after day, first for his own sins and then for those of the people; he did that once for all when he offered himself. For the law appoints men subject to weakness to be high priests, but the word of the oath, which was taken after the law, appoints a son, who has been made perfect forever.

GOSPEL
Mark 12:28b–34

One of the scribes came to Jesus and asked him, "Which is the first of all the commandments?" Jesus replied, "The first is this:

Hear, O Israel!
The Lord our God is Lord alone!
You shall love the Lord your God with all your heart,
with all your soul,
with all your mind,
and with all your strength.

The second is this:

You shall love your neighbor as yourself.

There is no other commandment greater than these." The scribe said to him, "Well said, teacher. You are right in saying, 'He is One and there is no other than he.' And 'to love him with all your heart, with all your understanding, with all your strength, and to love your neighbor as yourself' is worth more than all burnt offerings and sacrifices." And when Jesus saw that he answered with understanding, he said to him, "You are not far from the kingdom of God." And no one dared ask him any more questions.

❖ Understanding the Word

The most significant prayer of Israel's religion is found in Deuteronomy. It is a profession of faith in the one God to whom Israel owes exclusive and undivided commitment and worship. This is the God who drew the people out of Egyptian bondage, led them through the perils of the wilderness, and brought them into the land of promise. This is also the God within whom all the attributes of deity can be found. It is not a divided deity whose various characteristics are worshiped at various shrines. This profession of faith is found within a summons to obedience.

The tradition that surrounded the enigmatic Melchizedek has been reinterpreted in order to typify particular aspects of Jesus' divine nature. First, his priesthood is permanent, enabling him to intercede without interruption, while the Levitical priests were all subject to death. Jesus' holiness is the second characteristic that distinguishes his priesthood from the other. He did not have to atone for his own sins, as the Levitical priests did. Finally, his priesthood is not traced back to the religious institution founded on Aaron. Rather, Jesus is identified with Melchizedek, whose priesthood was grounded in eternity and established by a divine oath.

By the time of Jesus, there were 613 commandments surrounding the official biblical law. Although all laws were considered binding, some were regarded more important than others. When questioned about the "first" law, Jesus endorses the summons that constitutes the *Shema*, the most significant prayer of Israel's faith. To the injunction to love God with all one's heart, soul, and strength (Deuteronomy 6:4–5), he adds the injunction to "love your neighbor as yourself" (cf. Leviticus 19:18). He insists that the second is like the first. The scribe, who is schooled in the religious tradition, recognizes Jesus' response as both accurate and profound. He calls him Teacher, a title that has special significance coming from one who was himself an official interpreter of the law.

As a boy I learned the Ten Commandments, the six precepts of the Church, the seven sacraments, the seven gifts and twelve fruits of the Holy Spirit. Having memorized these, I felt a sense of accomplishment. But can you imagine having to memorize the 613 laws found in the Torah? The Torah was the foundation of the covenant God made with the people of Israel.

If you go on line and do a search for "613 commandments," you will find them listed, along with a reference to the particular biblical book where each can be found. Some listings place the laws under various categories, such as God, Prayers and Blessings, Love and Brotherhood, the Poor and Unfortunate. The largest list relates to Sacrifices and Offerings—over one hundred of them.

When the scribe asked Jesus what was the first of all the commandments, he was asking a question most important to any devout Jew. Jesus looked within his own heart before giving his answer: Love the Lord your God with all your heart, all your soul, all your mind, all your strength (Deuteronomy 6:4–5) and love your neighbor as yourself (Leviticus 19:18).

His answer came from his heart, recognized in the Jewish tradition as the center of the human person, the seat of all thought, choice, value, and feeling. Moses' words to the people in today's first reading still stand: "Take to heart these words which I enjoin on you today" (Deuteronomy 6:1).

❖ Consider/Discuss

- What is the value of having a law to live by?
- Take time to read the 613 commandments, and consider how love is at the heart of the law of the first covenant. Then, read the Sermon on the Mount (Matthew 5–7) for the same lesson.

❖ Responding to the Word

Loving God, we thank you for the gift of your law that has been revealed in the teachings of Moses and of Jesus Christ. It offers us guidance and light for our lives. Your Holy Spirit continues to enlighten our way. May we be attentive to the direction that is offered.

November 11, 2012

THIRTY-SECOND SUNDAY
IN ORDINARY TIME

Today's Focus: A Window on Widows

The two widows in today's readings are women of great generosity, giving out of their need, not their surplus. For Elijah, the widow of Zarephath is a life-saver; for Jesus, the widow of Jerusalem is a motivator. Soon he will give all he has—for the redemption of the world.

FIRST READING
1 Kings 17:10–16

In those days, Elijah the prophet went to Zarephath. As he arrived at the entrance of the city, a widow was gathering sticks there; he called out to her, "Please bring me a small cupful of water to drink." She left to get it, and he called out after her, "Please bring along a bit of bread." She answered, "As the LORD, your God, lives, I have nothing baked; there is only a handful of flour in my jar and a little oil in my jug. Just now I was collecting a couple of sticks, to go in and prepare something for myself and my son; when we have eaten it, we shall die." Elijah said to her, "Do not be afraid. Go and do as you propose. But first make me a little cake and bring it to me. Then you can prepare something for yourself and your son. For the LORD, the God of Israel, says, 'The jar of flour shall not go empty, nor the jug of oil run dry, until the day when the LORD sends rain upon the earth.' " She left and did as Elijah had said. She was able to eat for a year, and he and her son as well; the jar of flour did not go empty, nor the jug of oil run dry, as the LORD had foretold through Elijah.

PSALM RESPONSE
Psalm 146:1b

Praise the Lord, my soul!

SECOND READING
Hebrews 9:24–28

Christ did not enter into a sanctuary made by hands, a copy of the true one, but heaven itself, that he might now appear before God on our behalf. Not that he might offer himself repeatedly, as the high priest enters each year into the sanctuary with blood that is not his own; if that were so, he would have had to suffer repeatedly from the foundation of the world. But now once for all he has appeared at the end of the ages to take away sin by his sacrifice. Just as it is appointed that human beings die once, and after this the judgment, so also Christ, offered once to take away the sins of many, will appear a second time, not to take away sin but to bring salvation to those who eagerly await him.

GOSPEL
Mark 12:38–44
or 12:41–44

[In the course of his teaching Jesus said to the crowds, "Beware of the scribes, who like to go around in long robes and accept greetings in the marketplaces, seats of honor in synagogues, and places of honor at banquets. They devour the houses of widows and, as a pretext, recite lengthy prayers. They will receive a severe condemnation."]

He sat down opposite the treasury and observed how the crowd put money into the treasury. Many rich people put in large sums. A poor widow also came and put in two small coins worth a few cents. Calling his disciples to himself, he said to them, "Amen, I say to you, this poor widow put in more than all the other contributors to the treasury. For they have all contributed from their surplus wealth, but she, from her poverty, has contributed all she had, her whole livelihood."

❖ Understanding the Word

The woman in the first reading is in a perilous situation. As a widow in a patriarchal society, she has no male protector and very few resources to call upon. She is in such dire straits because God withheld the rain, and her reserve of water and flour and oil is depleted. The prophet's request is not selfishly insensitive. Rather, it becomes the avenue through which God provides for the woman and her son. She follows the word of the prophet, and God's word spoken through the prophet comes to pass. Her miraculous supply of flour and oil lasts for a year.

The second reading contrasts the temple in Jerusalem with the heavenly temple. While the high priests performed their sacrificial duties in the earthly temple, the exalted Jesus entered the true sanctuary. The former cultic system enabled the people to participate in cosmic events by reenacting them. However, it was only able to actualize these events for a short period of time. This explains why the Day of Atonement ritual was reenacted year after year. In contrast to this, Jesus offered himself once for all. His sacrifice, like all cosmic acts, was unrepeatable. Earthly ritual may reenact his sacrifice, but there is no need for Jesus himself to repeat it.

Jesus condemned the ostentatious piety of the scribes. He further accused them of exploiting widows. This condemnation was called down on them because they had deprived the widows in the name of religion. Sitting in the temple, Jesus then contrasted donations of the wealthy with that of a poor woman. The wealthy loudly donated from their surplus; they gave what they did not need. The woman quietly donated the little that she had; she gave what she needed. Her wholehearted generosity demonstrated her absolute trust in God. The passage that opened with a condemnation of the false piety of the unscrupulous closes with praise of the genuine piety of the simple.

My earliest memory of a widow was Aunt Lizzie: white-haired, seemingly very old, but kindly. (I was four, so she was probably in her sixties then—how one's perspective on age changes with time!) She lived with my godmother and uncle, having contributed some of her savings to help them buy a house. My second memory was of Lana Turner playing *The Merry Widow* in the 1952 movie of the same name. Both were light years away, historically and culturally, from the widows in today's readings.

The widows in biblical times were imperiled. If they did not have sons who would care for them, their very lives could be endangered. The widow in the first reading has a young son; she is collecting sticks to build a fire to prepare the last of her flour so they can eat and die. When Elijah asks her to prepare a cake for him, she generously does so—which proves to be her salvation. Later he even restores her son to life.

Jesus watches a widow put in her last—literally—two cents in the temple's coffers. He has previously warned about the scribes who "devour the houses of widows" while reciting lengthy prayers. Some say Jesus is lamenting the foolishness of this widow, like the prophets of the past who railed against the neglect of widows and orphans. But most think he is praising her generosity in giving "all she had, her whole livelihood." Like her, Jesus will soon put all his trust in the Father.

✤ Consider/Discuss

- Do you see the widow in the Gospel as foolish, generous, or in another way?
- What would it cost you to put all your trust in the Lord?

✤ *Responding to the Word*

God of all, you have called to your people from the time of Moses and through your prophets past and present, but most especially through your Son, Jesus, to care for your little ones, for the poor, and the stranger. Help us today to be attentive and active doers of your word.

November 18, 2012

THIRTY-THIRD SUNDAY IN ORDINARY TIME

Today's Focus: All's Well That Ends Well

Every year at this time we hear what are called "apocalyptic readings," selections from the Old Testament and the Gospels that offered in veiled and imaginative language revelations about the future, picturing distress and tribulation, followed by a new age. They served then and now to call listeners to trust in the Lord.

FIRST
READING
Daniel 12:1–3

In those days, I, Daniel,
  heard this word of the Lord:
"At that time there shall arise
  Michael, the great prince,
  guardian of your people;
it shall be a time unsurpassed in distress
  since nations began until that time.
At that time your people shall escape,
  everyone who is found written in the book.

Many of those who sleep in the dust of the earth shall awake;
  some shall live forever,
  others shall be an everlasting horror and disgrace.

But the wise shall shine brightly
  like the splendor of the firmament,
and those who lead the many to justice
  shall be like the stars forever."

PSALM
RESPONSE
Psalm 16:1

You are my inheritance, O Lord!

SECOND
READING
Hebrews
10:11–14, 18

Brothers and sisters: Every priest stands daily at his ministry, offering frequently those same sacrifices that can never take away sins. But this one offered one sacrifice for sins, and took his seat forever at the right hand of God; now he waits until his enemies are made his footstool. For by one offering he has made perfect forever those who are being consecrated.

Where there is forgiveness of these, there is no longer offering for sin.

GOSPEL
Mark 13:24–32

Jesus said to his disciples:

"In those days after that tribulation
the sun will be darkened,
and the moon will not give its light,
and the stars will be falling from the sky,
and the powers in the heavens will be shaken.

"And then they will see 'the Son of Man coming in the clouds' with great power and glory, and then he will send out the angels and gather his elect from the four winds, from the end of the earth to the end of the sky.

"Learn a lesson from the fig tree. When its branch becomes tender and sprouts leaves, you know that summer is near. In the same way, when you see these things happening, know that he is near, at the gates. Amen, I say to you, this generation will not pass away until all these things have taken place. Heaven and earth will pass away, but my words will not pass away.

"But of that day or hour, no one knows, neither the angels in heaven, nor the Son, but only the Father."

❖❖❖ *Understanding the Word*

Today's apocalyptic scene is part of the revelation granted to the prophet Daniel. It depicts the final struggle at the end of time and the subsequent resurrection to a life of horror or one of glorification. The distress is probably that final tribulation that will come to pass before the appearance of the final reign of God. Known as the "birth pangs of the messiah," the agony preceded the birth of the reign of God. Daniel is told that those whose names appear in the book (the Book of the Righteous) will be spared. They may have to endure the agony of the endtime, but they will escape ultimate destruction.

This explanation of the unique sacrifice of Christ re-interprets an understanding of the Jewish practice of sin offering. The singular status of Jesus the priest and the inestimable value of Jesus the victim set his sacrifice apart from all others. Total and complete expiation has been accomplished through him. There is no need for Jesus to stand and offer another sacrifice. Therefore, he takes his seat next to God in glory. Jesus has decisively expiated all sin and conquered all evil. He has been able to accomplish what the sacrificial system of Israel, despite its preeminence, has been unable to achieve.

Mark describes the character and appearance of the end of time through allusions to earlier apocalyptic traditions. Chief among them are the reference to the tribulations that precede the advent of the new age and the coming of the Son of Man in the clouds. Cosmic occurrences will accompany the distress that will take hold of the world. The coming of the Son of Man in the clouds, an allusion to the mysterious figure found in the book of Daniel (7:13), heralds the advent of the new age. The exact time of the coming of the new age is shrouded in mystery. The lesson to be learned from all this: Be prepared!

✢ Reflecting on the Word

The end of the church year directs our attention to what scripture says about the end of time. Two of the words used to describe these texts are not part of our ordinary vocabulary: apocalyptic, which refers to receiving a "revelation" in a vision of something concealed up until now, and eschatological, which points to events of the endtime or final age (the *eschaton*), when the evil powers make their final struggle with God and are defeated.

These readings have one important point to make: that all will be well. God is in charge, even when it seems that everything is coming to a catastrophic end. As we hear in the first reading today, God has designated the angelic guardian Michael to watch over the people. Such a time will prove that how one lives life has consequences. The book of Daniel offers a word of consolation to the wise and those leaders who championed God's justice.

In the Gospel Mark's Jesus speaks of the coming of the Son of Man in great power and glory. While Jesus indicates in Mark's Gospel that this would happen soon, such was not the case. We continue to wait on the Lord.

When we pray the Our Father we always say, "Lead us not into temptation but deliver us from evil." Someone asked recently why we pray that God not lead us into temptation, finding it strange to think of God doing such a thing. What we pray for is that God not let us fail in the final testing that everyone has to undergo.

✢ Consider/Discuss

- Does the idea of an "endtime" have meaning for you?
- Do you find comfort in the message of these texts or do they evoke another response?

✢ Responding to the Word

Loving God, you created all that is in the heavens and on the earth; we know our future is in your hands. Help us to entrust ourselves to your mercy and care. Do not allow temptation to overwhelm us, but send your Spirit to lead us into your kingdom, where your Son reigns forever and ever.

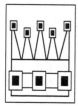

November 25, 2012

OUR LORD JESUS CHRIST, KING OF THE UNIVERSE

Today's Focus: The King of Hearts

Ending the church year with the celebration of the solemnity of Christ the King can seem a throwback to a time when kings used power for conquest and plunder, to subdue and subjugate their own and those weaker. Today's feast proclaims a different kind of power, a king who came to conquer hearts.

FIRST READING
Daniel 7:13–14

As the visions during the night continued, I saw
one like a Son of man coming,
on the clouds of heaven;
when he reached the Ancient One
and was presented before him,
the one like a Son of man received dominion, glory, and kingship;
all peoples, nations, and languages serve him.
His dominion is an everlasting dominion
that shall not be taken away,
his kingship shall not be destroyed.

PSALM RESPONSE
Psalm 93:1a

The Lord is king; he is robed in majesty.

SECOND READING
Revelation 1:5–8

Jesus Christ is the faithful witness, the firstborn of the dead and ruler of the kings of the earth. To him who loves us and has freed us from our sins by his blood, who has made us into a kingdom, priests for his God and Father, to him be glory and power forever and ever. Amen.

Behold, he is coming amid the clouds,
and every eye will see him,
even those who pierced him.
All the peoples of the earth will lament him.
Yes. Amen.

"I am the Alpha and the Omega," says the Lord God, "the one who is and who was and who is to come, the almighty."

GOSPEL
John 18:33b–37

Pilate said to Jesus, "Are you the King of the Jews?" Jesus answered, "Do you say this on your own or have others told you about me?" Pilate answered, "I am not a Jew, am I? Your own nation and the chief priests handed you over to me. What have you done?" Jesus answered, "My kingdom does not belong to this world. If my kingdom did belong to this world, my attendants would be fighting to keep me from being handed over to the Jews. But as it is, my kingdom is not here." So Pilate said to him, "Then you are a king?" Jesus answered, "You say I am a king. For this I was born and for this I came into the world, to testify to the truth. Everyone who belongs to the truth listens to my voice."

❖ Understanding the Word

The depiction of the coming and arrival of the Son of Man is colored with both mythic and royal tones. The figure comes with the clouds, which are the most frequent accompaniment of a theophany or revelation of God. He comes riding the clouds as one would ride a chariot. He is presented before God in the manner of courtly decorum. The one who sits on the throne is called the "Ancient One." This implies that God is the one who has endured and, presumably, will continue to endure. In other words, God is everlasting. The mysterious Son of Man is installed by God as ruler over the entire universe.

Jesus is first identified as the anointed one (the Christ) and then described as such. He is a witness who faithfully mediates to others the message that he has received from God. He is the firstborn, the one to whom belong both priority of place and sovereignty. He is the ruler of all the kings of the world. These epithets sketch a "high" Christology, one that emphasizes the more-than-human aspects of Jesus. The final statement reinforces this more-than-human character. Alpha and Omega connote totality, suggesting that Jesus comprises everything that is; he transcends the limits of time; he is the almighty, the ruler of all things.

For the Jewish people, King of the Jews was a messianic title. Pilate considered it a challenge to Roman political authority. The Roman asks about a political reality that may have a religious dimension, while Jesus speaks about a religious truth that certainly has political implications. By describing his kingdom through negative contrast, Jesus has indirectly admitted that he is a king. His answers show that both the Jewish leaders and the Roman officials had reason to be concerned about his claims. Though not of this world, his kingdom would indeed challenge both messianic expectations and the powers of this world.

Both the Jesus who stood before Pilate on his way to a brutal death and the Jesus who will come as the firstborn of the dead and ruler of all can seem too far away to make much of an impression on our lives. But holding these two images together can speak a profound truth, offering our lives meaning and value.

In John's Gospel Jesus is the revelation of the Father, the Word of God, communicating who God is and what God wants to do for us: to bring us eternal life. The image of Christ the king was one way of communicating that in Jesus, the Creator of all and everything began to reign in a way that "does not belong to this world."

The use of power in our world has been an endless story of one individual, family, group, or country using its strength, wealth, and talents to hold sway over as many as possible. To do so, any and all means of force and violence were often legitimate. But this is not the way of Christ or those who follow him.

"For this was I born and for this I came into the world, to testify to the truth" (John 18:37). What truth? That God so loved the world that the Father gave his only Son, "so that everyone who believes in him might not perish but might have eternal life" (3:16). That's the foundation of this kingdom and its use of power. That's the plan. Do you want in?

✦ Consider/Discuss

- Do you think of yourself as one who "belongs to the truth" to which Jesus testifies?
- What are some ways you try to listen to his voice?

✦ Responding to the Word

Father of our Lord Jesus Christ, you spoke and the world came into being. You spoke in the fullness of time and the Word became flesh. You continue to speak so all who listen may be born into your kin-dom through the power of your Holy Spirit. Help us to listen for and obey your voice.

Dianne Bergant, C.S.A., is Professor of Biblical Studies at Catholic Theological Union in Chicago. She holds master's and doctoral degrees in scripture studies from St. Louis University. She was president of the Catholic Biblical Association of America (2000–2001) and has been an active member of the Chicago Catholic/Jewish Scholars Dialogue for the past twenty years. For more than fifteen years, she was the Old Testament book reviewer of The Bible Today. Bergant was a member of the editorial board of that magazine for twenty-five years, five of those years as the magazine's general editor. She is now on the editorial board of Biblical Theology Bulletin and Chicago Studies. From 2002 through 2005, she wrote the weekly column "The Word" for America magazine.

James A. Wallace, C.Ss.R., is professor of homiletics at the Washington Theological Union, Washington, D.C. He is the author of Preaching to the Hungers of the Heart (Liturgical Press, 2002) and co-author of three books of homilies, Lift Up Your Hearts: Homilies for the A, B, and C Cycles (Paulist Press 2004, 2005, and 2006). He has served as president of the Academy of Homiletics, the Catholic Association of Teachers of Homiletics, and the Religious Speech Communication Association. His articles have appeared in various journals, and he has lectured on preaching in this country, Europe, and Asia.